"I have restored that which was in ruins; I have raised up that which was destroyed when the Aamu were in the midst of (Kemet), overthrowing that which had been made as they ruled in ignorance of Ra."

Queen Hatshepsut

KEMET

—— AND THE ——

AFRICAN WORLDVIEW

RESEARCH, RESCUE AND RESTORATION

SELECTED PAPERS OF THE PROCEEDINGS OF THE FIRST AND SECOND CONFERENCES OF THE ASSOCIATION FOR THE STUDY OF CLASSICAL AFRICAN CIVILIZATIONS, 24-26 FEBRUARY 1984 (6224 AFE), LOS ANGELES, AND 1-3 MARCH 1985 (6225 AFE), CHICAGO.

Edited by

MAULANA KARENGA • JACOB H. CARRUTHERS

UNIVERSITY OF SANKORE PRESS
LOS ANGELES

Artwork.   Kweli Kuumbisha

Cover Design: Limbiko Tembo

First Printing, 1986

ISBN 0-943412-07-2

To Cheikh Anta Diop

who, as he said of Alioune Diop, lived and died on the battlefield of African culture. "That which belongs to eternity knows no end." Therefore, his excellence will be remembered forever: his struggle is his name; his achievement is his memorial.

CONTENTS

CONTENTS

IV. CREATIVE PRODUCTION

PREFACE

"Come back to Kemet,
Come back to the place where you were born
Kiss the ground at the great gate
and mingle with the officials."

Sinuhe

Only the determined intellectual resistance waged by the 19th century Black Nationalists in the western hemisphere prevented the complete take over of the Nile Valley culture by the intellectual pirates who accompanied the Napoleonic invasion of Kemet (Egypt) in 1798. Those old African scrappers never left the high ground of the Nile Valley heritage and now their spirit like the Pharaoh Senwosret I of the 12th Dynasty (who lived about 4,000 years ago or 20th century B.C.E.) beckons us to come back to the Black land. Thus, it was in obedience to the summons of the most ancient and recent ancestors that Dr. Maulana Karenga and I convened the First Annual Ancient Egyptian Studies Conference in February, 1984 at Los Angeles.

The Conference was designed to go beyond the establishment of an annual intellectual homecoming celebration and the founding of another Black professional scholarly association. What was and is now needed is the organization of African people throughout the world toward the rescue of the African heritage and the restoration of African civilization. Such was the major objective of the Conference: the fruition of the dreams and visions of African people during the two thousands seasons of our distress.

In the struggle to liberate African people throughout the world, it is necessary that we mobilize the resources of the African heritage. It is also necessary that we advance the work and ideas of the brave Black people who have given their lives to keep this connection alive. What we are doing is not the result of a sudden flash of brilliance, but the culmination of the hard work of several generations of African Heroes and Heroines.

The enthusiastic response of Dr. Yosef ben-Jochannan and Dr. John Henrik Clarke placed the seal of authority on the project. The response from scholars in the field who answered the call for proposed papers at the Conference was also very encouraging. Most encouraging of all was the massive response of Black people from all walks of life who attended the Conference and for three days celebrated the ancestral connection. The elders were given great honors, the presenters were given standing ovations.

This renewal gave birth to the Association for the Study of Classical African Civilizations (ASCAC). It is through ASCAC that we will reestablish our spirit and cultural foundations. Such a restoration will in turn give African people the intellectual and theoretical framework for the development of institutions and movements that will enable us to "retake our fame."

The spirit that made the First Annual Conference an overwhelming success was maintained throughout 1984 and ushered in the Second Annual Conference in March 1985 at Chicago. In addition to the outstanding presentations and receptions, ASCAC was formally organized and began its operation with a slate of dedicated officers and members.

This volume presents the proceedings and some of the best presentations of the first and second ASCAC conferences. The papers were selected for their representativeness. Collectively the selections reflect the most recent thinking among those who work from an African worldview. The topical divisions group the papers by the dominant themes which they speak and are in some cases different from the topics of the panels from which they were presented. The papers, however, capture much of the spirit that inspired the call to the first conference and the ideas anticipate the vast potentialities inherent in our bold undertaking. Our stride is wide because we are walking in the footsteps of giants.

The presenters comprise both established scholars and those who are beginning. Thus, we have the African generational process at work. The methodological and theoretical trends which are being established by ASCAC as reflected in these papers will provide the model for the development of full fledged programs for the rescue and restoration of African civilization beginning with Ancient Kemet. For as my colleague, Dr. Maulana Karenga, who provided ASCAC with its name stated last year, "Ancient Egypt is currently our earliest known and greatest classical civilization and thus an excellent basis for beginning and expanding our understanding and appreciation of ancient African history in its rich diversity and unity."

Due to my involvement in other aspects of the ASCAC agenda, the major share of the work of editing this volume has fallen on the shoulders of Dr. Karenga, the first Vice-President of ASCAC. I am not only appreciative of his cheerful willingness to take on this awesome load, but I am so happy that we have such a committed and talented brother with broad shoulders and a brilliant mind.

Jacob H. Carruthers
Kemetic Institute, Chicago
February, 1986 (6226 A.F.E.)

INTRODUCTION

The historical project that Frantz Fanon posed of setting afoot a new man and woman has historically precoccupied Africans, in the diaspora and on the continent. Jacob Carruthers points out in his critical work, *Essays in Ancient Egyptian Studies,* that as early as the 19th century Black people in this country such as Hosea Easton, Henry Garnet and Martin Delaney had begun to ask themselves, "are we not different from the Europeans?" and what do we have to offer that makes us able to pose a human paradigm, morally richer and more humanly expansive than what the European has to offer? As Fanon observed, "we need a model", but "for many of us, the European model is most inspiring". However, he continues, "when I search for Man in the technique and style of Europe I see only the negation of Man". The need, then, he concludes is not to imitate Europe and its negations and become an obscene caricature of Europe but to join together in a new direction in a self-conscious attempt "to create a whole Man (and Woman) whom Europe has been incapable of bringing to triumphant birth".

The logic of the process which begins with rejection of the deformed and deforming paradigm of Europe and leads to bringing into being a new human and humanity, inevitably raises the question of where to begin. Cheikh Anta Diop in his work, *Civilization or Barbarism,* argues cogently that the unavoidable starting point for Africans to resue and reconstruct their history and humanity is in Kemet, i.e., ancient Egypt. "For us", he states, "the return to Egypt in all fields is a necessary condition to reconcile African civilization with history, to be able to build a body of human sciences and to renew African culture." In fact, "far from being a diversion in the past, a look toward ancient Egypt is the best way of conceiving and building our cultural future." It is, indeed, important for us to make a distinction between a diversion in the past and laying the basis for a new body of human sciences. Playing the same role as Greece and Rome in European culture, Diop contends, Kemet will offer fertile ground in the areas of philosophy, culture and science for a new African and a new paradigm for humanity which this implies.

The fundamental historical task becomes. then, one of rescuing and restoring the culture of Kemet and of exploring and expanding the human possibilities inherent in this process. It does not mean we minimize or neglect other African cultures, but that we have an authentic ancient classical culture as a point of departure, rich in primary sources and complex and inclusive enough to offer foundations in the various disciplines of human knowledge critical to the posing of an authentic African paradigm of human science, culture and society. Having established an authentic African frame-work for research and analysis, we cannot only reach out to explore other cultural centers in Africa, but identify and reject that which is intrusive and alien to the African human spirit and integrate that which is affirmative and expansive and contributive to human liberation and a higher level of human life.

It is this framework which my colleague, Dr. Carruthers, proposes when he states in his *Essays in Ancient Egyptian Studies,* that the fundamental requirement for this kind of research, the task of restoration and the posing of an African paradigm, is an *African worldview.* "The formulation of an African worldview is the essential beginning point for all research which is based upon the interest of African people," he asserts. For, "There can be no African history, no African social science without an African worldview." What is sought here then is not simply fitting within a research process which Europe has already begun, but the initiation of a process which self-consciously begins and becomes a clear rupture with the European paradigm. This, of necssity, requires a research process rooted in and at the same time contributive to the ongoing expansiveness of an African worldview. In a word, it is a creative challenge to reconstruct and construct, pose and put in place an African paradigm for both our liberation and ever higher levels of human life.

It is in this context that one realizes that when an authentic and inclusive intellectual history of Africans in America is written, the founding of the *Association for the Study of Classical African Civilizations* (ASCAC) in Los Angeles in 1984 will, of necessity, be recorded as a turning point in our struggle for both political and cultural liberation. For it is, first, a critical institutionalization of our various efforts and aspirations to rescue and reconstruct our history and humanity and shape them in our own image and interest. Secondly, it represents the centralization of and focus on pioneering individual efforts of George James, William Hansberry, Carter G. Woodson, John Jackson, Chancellor Williams and others as well as the current collective efforts of institutions like the Kemetic Institute in Chicago, directed by Jacob Carruthers, and the Institute of Pan-African Studies in Los Angeles, directed by this author, and also of others to rescue Kemetic culture from alien hands, restore it and place it in the hands of the descendants of the people who produced it. Finally, the founding of ASCAC is a self-conscious organized challenge and counter to one of the fundamental problems of humanity in our times – the progressive westernization of human consciousness. The work of restoration, then, goes beyond repairing the violation of our historical memory to the ongoing defense and practice of our right and responsibility to celebrate the glory and bear the burden of our own history and humanity and speak our special truth to the world. It means resisting the western homogenization of human culture, and as Diop taught us, living and dying on the battlefield of African culture. Moreover, it means cultivating and continuously expanding and enriching the African worldview and constantly making our own unique contribution to the forward flow of human history.

This volume seeks to explore and suggest the outlines of an African worldview in governance, history, spirituality and philosophy, and creative production as evidenced in Kemetic civilization. It is self-consciously a *restorative* project, an attempt to restore that which lay in ruins for centuries, a legacy unequalled in antiquity, and to explore the lessons it offers us today in conceiving and building our cultural future. Within this grand and awesome task, we realize the incipient character of our work, but we also understand the urgency of our engagement. For as King Kheti, father of Merikare taught, "Even one day is a donation to eternity and every hour is a contribution to the future."

Finally, let us pay homage to those who made this volume possible and real. First, I'm grateful to my colleague, Dr. Jacob Carruthers, for his leadership, companionship, scholarship and support. Secondly, I give honor to the contributors for their essential beginning efforts. And thirdly, I extend gratitude to the student *Seba* (moral teachers) of the Institute of Pan-African Studies who are studying to be worthy of the mission and mantle of the ancient Seba such as Ptahhotep, Ani, Amenomope, Kagemni and others and who read and proofread these essays as both a learning and corrective process, in a word, as part and parcel of their immersion in Kemetic Studies. They are: Jitahadi Imara; Tulivu Jadi; Tiamoyo Karenga; Subira Kifano; Chanzo Taalamu and Chimbuko Tembo. I encourage and praise them in the words of Seti I who said, "To do that which is of value is eternity. And (a person) called forth by his (or her) works does not die. . ."

Maulana Karenga
Institute of Pan-African Studies, Los Angeles
February, 1986 (6226 A.F.E.)

I. GOVERNANCE

THE WISDOM OF GOVERNANCE IN KEMET

JACOB H. CARRUTHERS

I. INTRODUCTION

The title of this paper could have been "The Political Philosophy of Ancient Egypt". Instead of Egypt I will use the name Kemet because that is a phonetic rendition of the name that the people called their country; the name Egypt derives from what the Greeks called the country which was based upon a gross linguistic misunderstanding.[1] Actually the formal name seems to have been Tawy (The Two Lands), but the commonly used name was Kemet which means the black settlement referring to the black land along the banks of the Nile River. The people called themselves Kemites, the Black ones.[2] It is thus appropriate that we honor the traditions of the ancestors by calling them by their name.

The concept of philosophy presents us with a different set of problems. George G.M. James has shown that what is called "Greek Philosophy" was a legacy stolen from the Ancient Kemetic Mystery System.[3] James goes on to show that this stolen wisdom was alien to the cultural values of the Greeks. Cheikh Anta Diop pointed out, "(t)he Greeks (by virtue of their materialistic tendencies) stripped (the wisdom texts) of the religious, idealistic shell in which the Egyptian had enveloped them."[4] "Once they had borrowed Egyptian values," continued Diop, "the worldly genius of the Greeks (and) their religious indifference, favored the existence of a secular worldly science."[5] The emergence of the European discipline called the "love of wisdom," or *philo* (love), *sophy* (wisdom) even though it attempted to incorporate what it stole from Kemet, was nonetheless "diametrically opposite of Egyptian moral values."[6] As one egyptologist put it, "(W)hat the Greeks borrowed, they transmuted."[7] This independence from the 'prescriptive sanctities of religion', makes Greek philosophy sufficiently different from Kemetic wisdom. Therefore in order to separate the two worldviews on this score, I will avoid as far as possible the use of the concept philosophy when referring to Kemetic wisdom.

As to the question of the existence of a consistent body of wisdom explaining the worldview of the ancient Kemites, I reject without comment the conclusions of the egyptologists as expressed by Henri Frankfort and his wife that "the ancients (including the Egyptian) were preoccupied with problems very similar to ours ... (and) ... their myths represent a charming but immature way of answering them."

Like philosophy, the concept politics and its derivatives are also diametrically opposed to the Kemetic worldview. In Kemet, there was governance without politics. Politics comes from the Greek root *polis* which means city or more appropriately, city-state. Therefore politics emerges as the act of governing the autonomous Greek city. The systematic theories concerning such governance are called collectively political philosophy or political science. The central problem of European political philosophy and political practice was how to reconcile the chronic conflicting interest groups within the polis. The polis was plagued by at least two mutually hostile groups, the haves and the have nots. The wisdom the Greeks used to analyze and respond to that problem is diametrically opposed to the wisdom which guided the governance of Kemet. Kemetic wisdom of governance (which developed in the context of a country rather than a city) did not admit the legitimacy of the division in the first place. Conflicts of interest were handled through litigation of private individuals and groups rather than through politics among constitutionally or philosophically based power groups. The combination of the territorial state and traditional wisdom about governance which denied the legitimacy of interest conflict over who governs produced a body of knowledge which was profound and comprehensive. It is with such wisdom that this paper is concerned.

The assumptions and conclusions discussed above lead directly to the acceptance of what may be called Diop's "Two Cradle Theory". In his major works Diop insists that "the history of humanity will remain confused as long as we fail to distinguish between the two early cradles (the African and Eurasian cultural matrixes) in which nature fashioned the instincts, temperament, habits, and ethical concepts of the two sub-divisions before they met each other after a long separation dating back to prehistoric times."[9] What Diop means is that there are two fundamental patterns of culture which developed independently of each other. Attempts to formulate a universal social science have for the most part denied the reality upon which Diop bases his theory. When we take an inventory of the basic cultural features of the two civilizations, Diop's conclusion is compelling.[10] For Diop, the Eurasian (Northern, Aryan) cradle is characterized by: a) hunting, b) nomadic land occupancy, c) patriarchal family, d) city-state as largest unit of governmental autonomy, e) xenophobia and provincialism, f) individualism, g) ideal of war, violence, crime and conquests, and h) pessimistic religious or metaphysical systems In contrast, the African (Southern, Meridional) cradle has these features: a) agricultural cultivation economy, b) sedentary land tenure, c) matrifocal family, d) countrywide governmental system, e) xenophilia and cosmopolitism, f) collectivism, g) ideal of peace, justice and goodness, h) optimism in religious and metaphysical institutions. It is from this viewpoint that the significance of a discussion of the Wisdom of Governance in Kemet goes beyond the Eurocentric fascination with the exotic.

A. Education for Governance in Kemet

What were the Kemites actually taught about governance? Pharaohs, prime ministers, other dignitaries and even commoners left written instructions for their "sons", who in some cases were expected to follow in the footsteps of their "fathers", what wisdom did these teachings convey concerning government? Whatever function such instruction may have served in the actual rearing of sons by their fathers, they comprised a part of a larger body of literary texts that constitute a major (go to next page) part of the curriculum material used in the schools for the education of future scribes. The lessons were studied and copied by the school boys as exercises not only in penmanship and literary form but also in decorum, ethics and social values. In the area of governance which Aristotle called the "master science" i.e., political science, the texts contained a great deal about the conduct and orientation of officials to their duties and functions. Indeed some of the literature can be labeled "speculative thought", to borrow a phrase from the egyptologists who did not believe the ancient Kemites had evolved to the point of philosophy which they believed started with the Greeks.[11]

Those who were educated in the scribal schools became the governmental officials, many apparently working their way up the bureaucracy from clerk to high office, even the highest offices such as that of prime minister. Since some of these texts were authored by kings, it is quite likely that the royal children including the heir designates were educated in a similar manner if not in the same classes with the other scribes-to-be. Undoubtedly, the precepts and values taught through the scribal wisdom literature were handed down to children and young people in all walks of life. Therefore, what was taught to the beginning scribes concerning official conduct, social values and how to govern had a great bearing on the governing process. This tradition of scribal education seems to have been in full effect during the Middle Kingdom when the instruction by Dau-Khety was apparently composed.[12] This text which is often dubbed "The Satire of the Trades", indicates that formal scribal education is the prerequisite for a career in government and that such careers are open to families from the ordinary ranks of life as well as the nobility and elite.

Education and governance were thus inseparable and the complex relations among the concepts of speech, knowledge and Maat (justice and truth) which constitute the form and substance of both were the foci of the curriculum materials. Two of the three known relatively complete instructional texts before the New Kingdom period will be used for analyses in this paper. One is the Instruction of Ptah Hotep, apparently written by a prime minister and the Instruction for Meryuka Re apparently written for a pharaoh for his son. A more complete study, of which this is the first completed part, will include analyses of several additional texts including Neferti and Khun-Anup, or The Eloquent Peasant.

B. The Wisdom of Kemetic Governance

Before turning to the curriculum texts, the traditional statement of governance wisdom needs to be explained. This statement appears in more or less formal and abbreviated form in many of the texts concerned directly with the pharaohs, especially the royal monumental formulas such as the royal titles. The pharaoh's titles include: Living Horus, the Lord of the Two Lands, The King of the Two Shores, The King of Upper and Lower Egypt and The Good God, among others. He is also the son of Re and the son of Osiris. According to the egyptologists, the meaning of these titles in short is that the pharaoh or king is the government and the country and its people belong to him. Furthermore, the king is a god and is thus aloof from the human world. Such reasoning misses the point and is at considerable variance with the wisdom that emerges from the texts examined here.

In order to better understand the traditional meaning of pharaohship, let us consider a text that apparently dates to the early dynastic period or the Old Kingdom.[13] The text is the "Shabaka Stone" commonly referred to as "The Memphite Theology". It is actually a text recopied during the reign of Shabaka in the 25th Dynasty and is concerned primarily with the divine basis for governance. The extant text is badly damaged and only a small part of the original is intelligible.[14]

The text begins with an explanation of the origin of Tawy (The Two United Lands). In the beginning there were two countries created by Atum, the land of the Su plant and the land of the Ha plant; these refer respectively to Upper Kemet and Lower Kemet. The original natural division was erased by the act of uniting the two lands through the establishment of Horus as the Nisut Bity, i.e., the pharaoh of Upper and Lower Egypt. This union is signified by the reconciliation of Horus and Seth who were, at first, each given lordship over one of the two countries as a compromise between the two who each originally claimed title over the entire land. It is significant that the two contenders had brought their claim before the Nine Netchers (Ennead, as the Europeans put it) who apparently served as a jury. The point seems to be that all partisan disputes are to be decided not by force but by legitimate decision. This anticipates the significance of the dispute and its outcome. According to the text, the division was judged wrong because Horus' claim to lordship was based upn legitimacy, i.e., the inheritance of the lordship from his father, Osiris, who in turn had received it from his father, Geb, (the personified earth). Seth's claim was based upon an unexplained source, but was evidently power or de facto rule. Thus it is in uniting the two countries and the two contenders that the principle of legitimacy subsumes the principle of might. Both are necessary to rule, but the priority of Right over might must never be doubted. Thus, Horus is the model for pharaohship and governance is itself divine. (This summary has omitted a consideration of much of the symbolism of the text).

The second part of the extant text explains the divine origin of the country and its institutions. According to this part of the statement, the Creator consciously fashioned the world and all its inhabitants including humanity. The Creator also created the social order and the institutions of the nation. Thus the whole worldly order is divinely ordered and ordained. Upholding and recreating this order is the duty and obligation of human beings. To ignore the divine pattern is to invite disaster. Pertinent to this idea is the relationship between Horus and Jehewty. Horus represents conceptualization and Jehewty represents articulation. Horus is the mind and Jehewty is the tongue. It is the mind which perceives, conceives and evaluates; this is the role of the pharaoh. It is the tongue, that is the civil servant, which "repeats what the mind thinks". The tongue then directs the movement of every limb, that is the people. The analogy thus divides the labor of governance between the pharaoh, Horus and the prime minister, Jehewty.

This traditional statement of the wisdom of governance was the assumption upon which the Old Kingdom Instructions were based. The wisdom of Ptah Hotep was designed to transmit that wisdom through the educational system to those who were to assume the offices of the government. This traditional statement also appears to have stood throughout the Old Kingdom period. During the First Intermediary Period, however, the weakness of the traditional order apparently caused the instructors to augment the traditional statement with one that incorporated the recent experiences which resulted from revolt and decentralization. Thus the establishment of the royal Instructions of which Meryuka Re is the most complete which will be analyzed in this paper.

C. A Research Note

Each text used in this paper was translated by me from official hieroglyphic transcripts. The lines quoted from the Instructions of Ptah Hotep and Meryuka Re are, unless otherwise noted, mine. I followed Erman and Lichtheim in general in developing different renditions that in some cases are significant.[15] In such cases my feeling is that the new renditions better capture the spirit of the original text. In any case, reading of the texts in the original language is invaluable in terms of developing understanding.

As indicated above, Kemet was a country made up of many

villages, towns, cities and cultivated settlements. Terms like citizen which apply to a different cultural tradition and a city-state governmental pattern are generally avoided here. Instead, folk is often used to categorize the general native population residing in the country.

The larger study, of which this is a part, will include a critical review of related literature and an analysis of other relevant texts especially the one called The Eloquent Peasant. I will also add comparisons of Kemetic governance with governance in other parts of Africa and with European governments.

II. THE INSTRUCTION OF PTAH HOTEP

The Instruction of Ptah Hotep is one of the three known Old Kingdom texts that are written in the form of instructions from fathers to their sons. This form symbolizes the traditional wisdom of education which is handed down from generation to generation by elders to their children. Evidently these texts were used from the time of composition during the Fifth and Sixth Dynasties until at least the 19th Dynasty. (The translation is from the Papyrus Prisse unless otherwise noted).[16] The Instruction of Ptah Hotep which is the only complete text of this type from the Old Kingdom must have been considered the epitome of form and content vis-a-vis scribal education. The text is concerned with manners and attitudes in various typical situations. In this context the several references to official conduct must be seen as the thrust of the Instruction. The clear implication of Ptah Hotep is that the quality of government is a function of the quality of the office holders. If good men hold office then government will be good. The quality of the office holders in turn is a function of the quality of education. Indeed the process of governing is education. Right acting, well-balanced and disciplined individuals result in a just and well-balanced government. Such wisdom can be ignored only to the detriment of the nation. This tradition denies the political wisdom of the modern West that justice is the interest of the stronger party.

The text falls into three major parts: The prologue, consisting of the title of the text and a petition to the king and the king's answer; the Instruction proper, consisting of a short introduction and 37 maxims; and a long epilogue, consisting of several verses admonishing the student to obey the Instruction. The format of the text is instructive in its own right. The significance of the Instruction is indicated by the fact that it is presented as a command of the king in response to a petition by the official, who is equivalent to the prime minister in modern governments. This, of course, demonstrates the proper relationship between the formal head of a country and the officials who are involved in the conduct of ordinary governmental business. The petition and answer are actually short preliminary statements of the philosophy of national education. The body of the Instruction consists of a code of conduct for an educated person, especially one who is likely to be a governmental official. The epilogue is a restatement of the philosophy of education. Viewed in this light, the prologue and epilogue are therefore just as significant in terms of substance as are the 37 maxims. The format is a model of good speech in writing, in form and content.

A. The Prologue

In the titularly of this particular text, not only are the name and titles of the official given but also the name of the pharaoh under whom he served. Peculiar to this text is the fact that the official Ptah Hotep, director of the (capital?) city and prime minister, seeks permission from the Pharaoh of Upper and Lower Egypt, Issi, to instruct his son. The petition is introduced by a qualifying statement that freely translated begins: "Whereas I am approaching old age and senility with their dangers and pains." Ptah Hotep, the aged official, then requests that the pharaoh "order" him to pass on to his son the words of those who listened to the ancestors, who in their turn listened to the divinities. Thus, the prime minister proposes to impart the collective wisdom of the country as a national duty. This then is the formula for education, i.e., the obligation of the elders to instruct their heirs in the ways of the ancestors who commune with the Creator. Such education, the official argues, is designed to "drive out" suffering from the country folk and inspire them to service. This is the true purpose of education, to educate the officers and country folk to their duties and proper conduct. Thus, education is the foundation of governance.

The pharaoh's answer is a further explication of the philosophy of education, emphasizing the point that the importance of the Instructions is that a son thusly educated will be a model for the "children of the officials". The pharaoh also stresses the other side of the educational formula which is that the son must listen to the teachings and inculcate his mind with the speech of his father. The pharaoh's response concludes with the summation of the philosophy of education, "no one is born wise"; thus, the necessity for education.

Considering the petition from another perspective, an inference concerning the division of responsibility for governance is warranted. Notice that even though the pharaoh is petitioned for permission to perform a parental duty, the initiative was taken by the prime minister who presented a proposal for the approval of the head of state. The protocol seems to support the idea that normally the chief civilian officer was responsible for the ordinary operation of the governing process and the role of the pharaoh was informal and ceremonial. Other texts imply that decision-making by the highest governmental officials are heavily influenced by an executive council made up of dignitaries or elders.

B. The Maxims

Now that the context and significance have been set forth, the text introduces the sayings concerning the conduct of educated persons. The preamble to the Instruction follows the formula for this genre and is the place where the other extant texts apparently begin. Here the emphasis is on the "good speaking" of Ptah Hotep, since good speech is the medium of education as well as an end product of education. Ptah Hotep's function is defined as teaching those who do not know knowledge "as well as the rules of good speech." Here we see the introduction of the formula for Maat or justice; the distribution of that which is needed. The ignorant need education, therefore, it is the duty of the educated to give them what they need. In other words, those who are good in speech, give good speech to the ignorant, thus displacing ignorance with wisdom; that is, to those who listen, i.e., obey. Those who transgress the good speech, i.e., those who do not obey, will reap only misery which again is an application of the formula for justice.

The omission of the name of the son of Ptah Hotep cannot be overlooked. The standard formula seems to be "Beginning of the Instruction made by N (with titles) for his son N." Such omission from this longer than usual "model" of "good speech" may indicate that the society at large is the object of this teaching rather than a particular son of the official. This focus thus dispels the notion that this Old Kingdom text was merely a "book of etiquette (continaining only) precepts for getting on with superiors."[17]

The first maxim contains the wisdom concerning knowledge and speech which are one and the same. The Instruction *warns* against the arrogance or pride of the educated and advises that the "ignorant" as well as the wise should be consulted. The student is informed that although good speech is rarer than precious stones, it may be found among the young women who pound grain. The suggestion is that true knowledge is no respector of rank or sex. Thus humility and respect for all persons regardless of rank is the appropriate orientation for the truly wise. This teaching therefore sets the context for the entire Instruction.

The next three maxims establish the basic categories into which most of the other 33 maxims may be arranged — relations with those of higher authority, peers and the general public. One group of sayings deal with situations in which one is relating to supervisors, persons of higher rank and the "great ones." Another group deals with the administrative leadership of those of lower rank and, in general, the folk of the country. A third group is concerned with relations among peers, friends and family. It may not be accidental that a plurality of about 15 of the maxims seem to deal with peer and family relations, i.e., relations among equals. The remaining 22 seem to be equally divided between relationships with superiors and subordinates. If the division was purposive, as I believe it was, then such division is the epitome of Maat or Justice which is based upon the principle of balance, a theme which will be dealt with later in the paper. Although maxims two, three and four deal respectively with the three basic types of relationships, the prescriptions are the same. When you are confronted with an argumentative person do not argue back. Treat him with the respect due his rank in relation to yours. Let him rant and rave; demonstrate reserve and self-control and you will win the argument.

1. Relations with Higher Authorities

I have placed maxims 2, 7, 8, 10, 13, 15, 23, 24, 26, 27, and the first part of 31 in the category of relations with those in positions of higher authority. The situations considered run the gamut from dining room etiquette, through efficiency in office to giving advice to your supervisor. The first maxim about relations with supervisors (2) instructs that vis-a-vis "a superior who is a trouble maker", be respectful; don't let his vituperative words upset you. The exercise of calmness and self-control will carry the day for you. Presumably those who witness the scene will discern how stupid the superior is in this case. The implication is that handling an argumentative superior is a good test of character. If you can pass such a test of adversity, then you should be able to handle less heated and intimidating situations. Subordinates are often tempted to seek to advance themselves by putting one great person against another, by agitating personality conflicts or by creating distrust through purposive distortions and innuendoes. Maxim (8) teaches "fight (against) slanderous words which embroil official against official . . . the Ka hates it." The consequences from getting caught in such negative behavior are obvious.

One should maintain a positive attitude toward status, success and wealth. This is especially crucial when one's superior is a man who once was lowly but has risen to a position of high rank with the accompanying wealth. The passage in part reads "respect him (for) his prosperity which he brought about, and which does not come through itself . . . the abundance he collected himself."

In view of the admonition to support and defer to one's superiors, what if the superior is a wrong doer? Here the instructions are a bit more subtle. We have already seen that if the superior is hotheaded he will be "called one who does not know" (Maxim 2). The coolness of the subordinate will be a match for the superior's reckless accusations. Since the subordinate is required to speak the truth about all matters, his boss may be tempted to punish the subordinate, if the truth is injurious to the boss. But Ptah Hotep teaches "concerning an official, his affairs will go wrong if he thinks of punishment for it" (Maxim 15). A final note on the subject is found in Maxim 26 where the subordinate is advised to indulge the whims of the superior because indulgence will pacify him and allow him to get his act together without losing face which will be a chip in favor of the subordinate.

The maxims concerning superiors also contain the formulas for "getting on with superiors" (as Wilson put it in *Before Philosophy*). The way to get ahead is to be honest, trustworthy, efficient, modest, respectful and supportive. One should avoid pushiness, belittling statements, and calumny. Above all, one should always avoid hot-headedness. Thus, advancement requires character efficiency and right doing. "All conduct . . . is measured," is the warning contained in one of the maxims. Measurement is the symbol of Justice or Maat. This concept of justice is also based upon the logic that your supervisors will return in kind what you give them. If you give them deference, resect, support, honesty and efficient service, they in turn will treat you with consideration, generosity, fairness and support. The principle of reciprocity is almost interchangeable with Maat, Justice or Truth, and this interest exchange is what makes governance work. Such wisdom distinguishes these practical rules from the conventional wisdom of the Greek sophists whom Plato attacked. Here, there is no way to get ahead but by right dealing.

2.   Relations with Peers

Maxims 3, 9, 11, 12, 18, 19, 20, 21, 22, 30, and the past part of 31, 32, 33, 34, 35 and 37 have been placed in this category. Maxim 3 is like maxim 2, concerned with meeting an argumentative person. However, the aggressor in this case is a peer. The instructions are virtually the same. Remain silent before his onslaught. Those who witness the demonstrations will talk about what happened and your even temper and self-control will be noted by the officials.

The other maxims concerning peer and personal relations deal with prosperity, generosity, loyalty, family devotion and friendship. These relationships while mostly private cannot be ignored during the education of public officials. The treatment of one's peers, neighbors, friends and family members while more informal than relations with superiors and subordinates is probably more indicative of ones true character than either of the latter. The implicit wisdom is that one must first be a good kinsman, friend and neighbor before one can be a good official. In African life it is not possible to make a clear distinction between private and public life just as it is not possible to make a clear distinction between sacred and and secular life. In general, these maxims teach kindness, consideration and generosity toward neighbors and friends. One should also be modest and calm in these relationships. One should not boast about success, wealth or children nor belittle those who are not so apparently prosperous and well-endowed in this regard. One should not compromise the wives, mothers and daughters of others. And one should eschew greed.

These do's and don't's are brought into clearer focus in the context of the values from which they spring. Tne enjoyment of life or "follow your heart" (Maxim 11) is a central value. The implication seems to be that one should not become so caught up in the pursuit of mundane things that one forgets one is not complete when one is depressed. Wealth exists to enhance the enjoyment of life. Another passage reads, "you should not trust in your accumulation which happened to you as a divine gift" (Maxim 30). The pursuit of property should not be so paramount that one loses focus on the true values. The main function of wealth is to enable one to be generous: "Please your friends with that which you brought forth, for that which happened is a divine favor" (Maxim 22). Generosity to friends and intimates is an often stated virtue. "Remembered is a man who is kind," asserts Maxim 34. Maxim 35 continues, "do not be mean, you should benefit your friends; they are greater than wealth . . . what belongs to one is the other's also." Although one earns one's wealth it is a "divine gift" and should be shared among friends. In terms of priority, friends are more valuable than property.

Generosity is also good policy because deprived people are dangerous to public officials and the public at large. Maxim 34 warns, "he whose stomach is empty is evil and becomes an opponent and grumbler." The perspective on the accumulation of wealth and generosity is naturally followed by an admonition against avarice: "If you desire that your conduct is good, fight against the fault of greed, a severe disease which is incurable. It alienates fathers, mothers as well as uncles and makes a dear friend bitter." Greed, then, is diametrically opposed to Maat (Order) because it creates disorder.

Family relations are also important. Individuals in order to be successful must treat their spouse with love and generosity and work toward harmonious relations in the home which of course is the domain of the *nbt pr* (the lady of the house). (Maxim 21). Children should be well-treated and loved. But if they are disobedient (after one has instructed them properly) punish them and warn them about the long-range consequences of disobedience (Maxim 12). Contained in these maxims that deal with peer relationships are standards of official conduct vis-a-vis friends and peers. "Do not rob a constituent's house," asserts Maxim 31. Public officials have opportunities to take advantage of their neighbors; however, such conduct is not only unjust but also imprudent. The maxim continues "a bully will be wretched in the district", presumably because his neighbors will "complain about you before you are heard." What about the situation where a public official has to investigate a friend? This is perhaps the most difficult situation facing a magistrate because it is the essence of "conflict of interests." The Kemetic official could not excuse himself and reassign the case to a more impartial official as is done in the modern Occidental ethic. He had to assume responsibility and face up to the inherent dilemmas. On this point, Ptah Hotep teaches: "as to your investigating the character of a friend, do not (immediately) litigate, (but first) approach him; spend time with him alone so as to not agonize over his conditions; argue with him after a while . . . test his heart about the fault of the matter. If what he has read has left him . . . do not respond with a hostile act . . . do not abandon him, do not humiliate him . . . his deed will not succeed (because) one does not escape that which is destined" (Maxim 33). The point seems to be that the wrongdoing of a friend will be properly punished so there is no need for private punishment in matters concerning friends.

Relations with peers, neighbors, friends and family were thus concerns of formal education. Since this education was primarily directed toward training governmental officials, we must infer that correct peer and intimate relations were vital to the functions of the office. These relationships are by their nature more self-directed than are relations with higher officials and the general clientele public which are regulated to a large extent by formal rules. Therefore, emphasis on this aspect of an officia's life implies that this is the area where character and ability are put to the acid test. Friends and family know more about the person than those who are related only in a formal manner. Thus, the judgment of one's peers is an acid test.

e. Relations with the General Public

The maxims dealing with subordinates or the people in general are more aproximate to the modern Occidental concept of justice. Maxim 1 which was discussed above established the essential equality of individuals: "Don't be high-minded about your nowledge. Confer with the unschooled as with the educated . . . Good speech is more hidden than green-stone, yet it is found among the women servants at the grindstone." Thus, regardless of social condition or sex, individuals were viewed as essentially equal in Kemetic society.

People are not equal, however, in societal relations. Higher public officials and individuals of wealth and distinction along with their families enjoy power and privileges not shared by the ordinary folk. Even the lower officials have power over the public in general.

Nowadays, the universal rhetoric of democracy tends to protect that fact of life from honest discussion and evaluation. The question is whether these relations are controlled through politics or through intra-governmental governance. The former is tne European way, the latter African.

Although there is evidence that children followed the professions of their parents, admission to scribal school seems to to have been open to children from all ranks of life. (See the "Instructions of Duauf"). Thus, the surest route to high status and power was open to most individuals, especially the males. In many of the Old Kingdom texts, we read of the public servant who started in a lowly position but through hard work was gradually promoted to high office and occasionally to the highest office of prime minister (see my *Essays*). The ascriptive aspects of society were therefore modified toward equal opportunity by the civil service system and the formal educational system which fed it.

The power that governmental officials have over the public is the real problem of governance, therefore, those entering public service must develop a commitment to right doing. It is in that sense that the instructions concerning leadership of "the people" are defined more in terms of Maat or Justice than are the other two categories of relationships.

"If you find a troublemaker (who is) a poor person, not your equal, you should not be oppressive against him because he is weak ... you will beat him through the reproval of the judges" (Maxim 4). Since an official has a power advantage against an ordinary country person, one need not be heavy-handed, the offender will be punished in the ordinary operation of the law enforcement system. This maxim sets the tone for the other teachings regarding these relationships.

Maxim 5 contains the classic statement of the relationship of governance to Maat:

"If you are a leader who commands the affairs of the masses, at all times seek out good deeds . . . Maat (Justice) is greater and enduring in its effectiveness . . . one repels the evader of law ... baseness does not land its affair (although) wrongdoing (often) seizes wealth . . . Maat (Justice) is the end — it endures. A man says it is my father's property."

The prospective leader is also warned "you should not do terror on the people (because) God avenges in like-kind" (Maxim 6). This is the crux of Maat: what one gives one receives in return. If one is able to escape the law, one still will meet the punishment of the Creator; for all must be balanced in the end. Thus, for every wrong there is a negative consequence (Maat). The irony of the text at this point is the epito'me of the connection between good speech and wisdom. In the instruction against wrongdoing, the scribe asserts:

> "When a man says, 'life is there!' He will lack bread for the mouth. When a man says, 'it is power!' He must then say, my (mis) perception trapped me. When a man says, 'satisfaction is there!' He will be lacking in bread for old age. When a man says he will rob another, he will end by being given to someone who does not know him because . . . The threats of people will not come to fruition; it is the command of God that comes about. (So) live peacefully at home" (Maxim 6).

How much better can one put the case for Maat, i.e., Right or Justice? The wrongdoer is miserable in this life as well as the next life by divine design. Thus Maat is the order of society as well as the cosmic order.

The official must maintain a certain image before the public. He should be known as one who makes the "constituents secure and satisfied" (Maxim 14). The instruction continues, "your body should be well-nourished, your face should be turned toward your kindred." A leader should not obey the voice of his gut because "he who obeys his gut belongs to the enemy." The latter refers both to the restraint of emotional behavior as well as the pursuit of greed. Prudence as well as justice dictates certain official conduct. One maxim begins, "If you are a leader you should do every good thing (because) no complaint comes in the midst of favors" (Maxim 16). Another advises about prudence in dealing with petitioners:

> "Listen patiently to the speech of the petitioner. Do not rebuff him for his gut accusations . . . One who feels the weight of injustice wants to pour out his heart (even) more than the results coming from it. (But) if a petition is rebuffed, one says why does he reject it? Not all requests can be granted but a good hearing calms the heart" (Maxim 17).

This teaching seems to anticipate a wisdom text apparently written during the First Intermediary Period and commonly referred to as the story of "The Eloquent Peasant." Continuing in that same view the scribe teaches, "If you are powerful you should demonstrate knowledge and facility of speech (and) stand guard against silence so that you may not offend a petitioner" (Maxim 25). Silence which is usually a prime virtue may be abused by an official who is trying to avoid dealing with a legitimate complaint. This is much of the problem in "The Eloquent Peasant". The same maxim warns against arrogance and advises a cooling off period when confronted by "words of flame."

Other maxims deal with corruption. Public officials should not take sides in a matter to be adjudicated not only because of the injustice but also because an offended petitioner may bring a charge against the crooked official (see Maxim 28). Maxim 29 asserts that an official should award favorable judgments only to those petitioners who are straightforward. Finally, the priority of the public official should be preventive justice. Ptah Hotep teaches, "instruct with virtue (because) the prevention of wrongdoing establishes character" (Maxim 36).

C. Epilogue

The epilogue consists of several verses which emphasize the wisdom of the educational process. The interest of the student is spoken to at the outset: "If you listen to or obey my sayings to you, all of your plans will be foremost" (ll. 507, 508). This is not only because they are Maat (true) but also because the people accept their wisdom. Therefore, if the student lives up to the maxims, he will enjoy life for many years and his memory will remain for many more. Furthermore, "sayings are good;" indeed they were "made for the Good." Thus, "when a man teaches, he speaks to the future" (l. 517). Teaching is the key to success because "if good direction occurs in the future leader, he will be well-formed for life and his wisdom will be eternal" (ll. 520-23). Education is thus nourishment for the Ba and wise people will so take heed by getting a "good foundation" (l. 525). Thus an educated person is known for his knowledge, his good service, his deliberate, articulate and forthright speech and his clear vision (ll. 526-530). "Hearing is useful to the attentive son" because listening (obedience) brings about good will and leads to a sound old age.

Obedience is thus commanded by God: "The listener (i.e., the obedient one) God loves; the non-listener (i.e., the disobedient) God hates" (ll. 545, 546). But the individual has a choice because it is one's "mind that causes its master to become a listener or non-listener" (ll. 550-51). Thus, the obedient person loves to listen and he in turn is beloved when he listens to his father (ll. 554-56). Indeed teaching (speaking) and learning (listening) are divinely ordained and are therefore the foundations of Maat. Given this, one who accepts the wisdom of the ancestors as passed down by the father, succeeds and one who chooses to disregard the teachings is miserable; "his character is there in the knowledge of the officials; every day gives him a living death" (ll. 584-85). A son who obeys is a "flower of Horus" (l. 588), that is to say, he is a good citizen. He will assure one aspect of immortality, because he passes what he learns through listening to his children who in turn "tell their children." Obedience thus is necessary for the well-being of future generations. The student is taught to "strengthen Maat (Truth) and your children will live" (I. 597).

The two verses that immediately precede the last verse of the epilogue review the general thrust of the 37 maxims, emphasizing in content and form the vital connection between Maat on the one hand and good speech and self-control on the other. This is in a sense a summary of the conduct expected of the students vis-a-vis their master (the teacher). The final verse begins "Behold the good son is a divine gift." He is one who does Maat (Right) because he was well-taught. The story comes to an end with the father advising the son to follow his example so that he will live according to the expectation of the king who makes the good-life possible. The son is told that the father enjoyed a good, loving life and accomplished a great deal, "honoring the ancestors and doing Maat (Right) for the pharaoh." In this context, the king is clearly seen not only as the symbol of the government but also of the nation.

D. Complementary Themes

Several themes seem to be repeated throughout the Instruction but for the most part they are complementary to the major emphasis. Since we must assume that all words, phrases, clauses and sentences were consciously constructed, these unemphasized concepts should also be considered as part of the Instruction. Five of these themes will be briefly reviewed here. Some of the themes have been touched in other contexts but still need another look.

1. Self-Control and Silence

Maxim 2 which advises that vis-a-vis a higher official who is a trouble-maker one should be respectful and reserved. "Your inner control will equal his spate." Thus self-discipline emerges as the cardinal virtue of the good man. Maxim 3 advises silence when confronted by an argumentative peer. The student is told that the man of silence is greatly respected. Certainly, as one passage puts it, "silence is better than chatter." Thus, it is better to remain silent when you have nothing to contribute to a discussion. This rather ordinary advice about discipline and silence becomes more significant when we consider the value of the speech. Needless to say, the hotheads and babblers are epitomes of the bad man.

2. Speech

The significance of speech, its relationship to education and wisdom, and the equality of its distribution among the national population have been indicated above. The concern with speech continues throughout the Instruction. One may say that the quantity and quality of speech indicates the worth of the person. For example, the "evil speech" of the superior man will expose him as ignorant (Maxim 2). And the "vile speech coming from the mouth" of the disobedient son should be met with punishment (Maxim 12). The abuse of speech is thus a liability for its perpetuator. It is better to remain silent vis-a-vis one who uses evil speech. Fluency in speech, on the other hand, is associated with good character (Maxim 15) The student is admonished that speech is the most difficult skill of all, but it is invaluable to those who master the art (Maxim 25). Gentleness in speaking is more preferred than commanding. Thus, good speech is the medium for social relations thorughout the society. This is why Jehewty, the deity of speech, was so popular throughout the history of Kemet.

3. Wealth

The discussion of wealth above needs to be re-emphasized since the concern with wealth continues throughout the teachings. Wealth is viewed as the reward of an individual's exemplary behavior and at the same time a "gift if God" (Maxims, 9, 10, 30 and 31). Thus, while the one who honestly acquires wealth deserves respect, those who "seize riches" through baseness will fail. However, the honest acquisition of wealth is not a sufficient moral claim for the good person. He must also continue to demonstratae his goodness by spending the wealth through generosity to the poor folk as well as to his friends and family. Thus wealth is viewed as only a means and not as an end in itself. In fact, according to Maxim 9, "the master of character is the master of property." This means that good character is a more valuable property than is material property, as the sage Ptah Hotep states (Maxim 9). Again, the Instruction asserts that friends are greater than "one's property" (Maxim 35). Therefore, wealth is inferior to good character and less significant than friendship.

4. Maat

Maat was emphasized in the maxims concerning relations with ordinary people. A man endures when he advances Maat (Justice and Truth) proclaims the teacher (Maxim 19). As indicated above, Maat is not only the essence of wisdom but also the measure of prudence. This principle guides the ambitious young scribe away from temptations which appear as opportunities. One could deceive one's superiors or even play them off against each other through false reporting. But however attractive this may appear, the young scribe is admonished "Hold on to Maat" (Truth). Maat is discipline because in most instances Maat is equated with balancing and measuring which in qualitative terms is reciprocity.

5. Divinity

The connection between earthly government and God has been the foci of most studies that deal with governance in ancient Kemet. (See Frankfort, *Kingship and the Gods;* Frankfort, et al, *Before Philosophy;* and Seligman, *Egypt and Negro Africa*). In view of the general impression given by these scholars, one is surprised at how secular the Instruction of Ptah Hotep is. One is almost unaware that divinity and divine concepts are dealt with at all. In fact, references to God permeate the text but in such a subtle manner that one feels that references are much like those which could be made by a contemporary man of equal status. God is viewed as the author of condign punishment against those who scheme to exploit people for material gain (Maxim 6). The text proclaims that "God's command prevails over the schemes of men." Thus God is the ultimate enforcer of Maat. If a wrongdoer succeeds in the short run, he will fail in the long run because of God's will.

God is presented as benevolent and concerned. He "fosters those who are alone" (Maxim 9). As indicated above, he rewards the Maat that men do on earth by status, wealth, friends and family (Maxims 10, 12, 13 and 30). In fact, God's observable attributes are the model for exemplary human conduct. Contrary to the myth created by the egyptologists, the ancient Kemites were not so obsessed with the divinity of pharaonic governance that they sacrificed practical wisdom to blind obedience to the god king. This conclusion will be supported in the section which deals with the Instruction for Meryuka Re. Let us simply conclude here that the divine nature of governance was very definitely a part of the wisdom of ancient Kemet, but the education of the civil servants and the conduct of government were based upon earthly concerns. A good man was a pious man, but he also had to operate by the rules of the world "living on top of the earth."

III. THE INSTRUCTIONS FOR MERYUKA RE

The first 25 lines of the text are so badly damaged that they are virtually unintelligible insofar as meaning is concerned. Fortunately, the name of the person for whom the *Instructions* were formally written is preserved. This information indicates that the recipient of the *Instructions* was Pharaoh Meryuka Re whose tenure occurred during the "First Intermediary Period" when the country was divided and apparently embroiled in civil war with two Great Houses contending for and claiming legitimate power over the whole country but each restricted to only a part of Tawy (The United Two Lands).

From the conditions which apparently inspired the text, or at least provided the context, either or both of two possible inferences may be drawn. I will first state the most likely reason. Conditions of turbulence such as civil war or revolt caused the master teachers (those responsible for the development and articulation of curriculum philosophy) to restate and explain the wisdom and principles upon which pharaonic governance was founded. The older statements of the wisdom of governance (such as on the Shabaka Stone) had perhaps either fallen into disuse or were considered archaic for instructional purposes under these less innocent times and circumstances. Supporting the argument is another type of literature that apparently emerged during and immediately following the First Intermediary Period, i.e., the "complaints". These texts are descriptions of the calamities that came about or may come about as a result of the breakdown of governance. The circumstances and thrust of the explanations are much like those of the royal instructions and reinforce the position taken here.

The other possible but less compelling inference is that because of the breakdown of governmental unity following the so-called Old Kingdom, the pharaoh found it expedient to publish a statement to "announce the direction of his policy and containing valid, rather than fictitious, historical information."[18] But this text is cased in the form of instruction following the model of several Old Kingdom texts, the most complete and well-known of which is the Instruction of Ptah Hotep for his son which is discussed above. Policy statements of newly installed pharaohs are usually found in the coronation decrees. Thus it may be inferred that "policy announcements" took a difference form and these instructional texts were designed for a more fundamental purpose. Furthermore, the older wisdom as articulated in the Shabaka Stone was by no means repudiated by these more recent teachings. In fact, the newer texts may not even have extended the wisdom, since only a minor portion of the Shabaka Stone is extant. The upshot of the contextual base of the Instruction is that the youth in the scribal schools were taught that the principles of governance can be best understood when government itself is in crisis.

I have divided the intelligible text into several sections which contain varying numbers of lines from the transcript of the text as published in W. Golenischeff, Les Papyrus Hieratiques.[19] These sections are sequential in relation to each other and build on several interrelated themes which will be dealt with in the concluding comment to this segment. The various sections along with the fragmented beginning fall into four major structural divisions. The first may be viewed as an explanation of the principles of governance and kingship as applied to several general situations or conditions. The second division is an explanation of certain recent aspects of the contemporary civil wars which demonstrates the principles of governance. The third division consists of a general statement of the divine nature of governance and kingship. And the brief final section contains a statement of admonition concerning the Instruction.

A. The General Principles of Governance

1. The Suppression of Politics

The first intelligible words seem to be a continuation of a discussion of the dangers and remedies for sedition, rebellion and what in general may be called factionalism. One fragment reads "police the disaffected person" (l. 4). Other fragments identify "partisans", "clansmen" and "associates" evidently being stirred up by a disaffected person. The fragments also indicate that these groups are "city folk." Still other passages aparently assert that these rabble rousers should be "subdued" and "destroyed." At the beginning of the Instruction one fragment suggests that this concern is "paramount" (hat) which may indicate that the effective prevention of the factionalism is the first principle of 'kingship'."[20] Such reading is certainly in accord with the first relatively intelligible passages: "The troublemaker is a confounder of the city folk. He creates partisans among the young folk . . . counsel him (or accuse him) before the counsellors and subdue (him); he is a rebel" (ll. 24-26).

The teaching here supports the general conclusion that division, partisanism, factionalism and politics, i.e., the attempt by a leadership group to take over governance by its power, are detrimental to the country and should be decisively and efficiently destroyed before damage is done. The accused, however, should be given due process, i.e., brought before the court. This wisdom is supported by the one explicit exception to the general advice against capital punishment. Execution should be avoided "except for the rebel whose scheme is discovered. God knows the rabble rouser. God wipes out his evil in blood" (ll. 49-50).

This interpretation is supported by the beginning section of the other royal Instruction, the Teachings of Amenemhat. In that text the student is first admonished, "listen to my sayings to you (so that) you may be King of the Land and Ruler of the Shores (or towns) and make an increase in happiness."[21] The text immediately continues, "Be united with the people and be on guard and wary of subjects who are either unknown or of whose plotting one is now aware" (This translation follows Lichtheim's). The discussion of factionalism as the first order of instruction indicates its general importance. The purpose of governance which is to increase happiness is jeopardized by what we call "politics" and thus politics should not be allowed to exist among the people.[22] After some more unintelligible fragments the text asserts, "May you be true of voice before God, then the people will say ... you punish in accordance ... a man's good nature is heaven but evilness is painful" (l. 31). Thus, the theory of condign punishment is a vital part of the wisdom of governance. In this regard, the governor (pharaoh) should demonstrate good nature rather than vindictiveness.

2. Speech and Knowledge

The next principle of wise governance taken up in the Instruction concerns speech and knowledge. "Be skilled in speech and you wil be victorious . . . the tongue is a weapon to (a pharaoh); words are more powerful than all fighting" (l. 32). A wise pharaoh educates his officials because "truth comes to him without corruption, like the wisdom in the sayings of the ancestors" (l. 34) Here, the relationship between speech, wisdom and prudence are given the same emphasis as they are in the earlier Instruction of Ptah Hotep. This advice is connected with the imperative, "Imitate your fathers who were first, their words are established in the writings" (l. 35). Governance should be established upon the legitimacy of the traditions through convincing speech rather than on brute force. Education and governance are thus synonymous from this aspect. Both are appropriately accomplished through speech. One could almost say that speech, education and governance are one and the same; all are gifts from the ancestors.

3. Governance Should be Benevolent

The character of government must be benevolent; as the text puts it "Benevolence is good" (l.36). Through benevolence the pharaoh achieves glory based on the love of the people. The pharaoh representing the government should show "respect" for the officials and bring "prosperity" to the people. The government should also stabilize the boundaries of the country and in general work for the future of the nation. The officials should be "made great and they will enforce the laws" (l. 42). Only by alleviating insecurity from official-dom does the government enable itself to rise above corruption and favoritism. The pharaoh is admonished to always "speak the truth so that the officials . . . will respect" the one to whom they are accountable, because "the front of the house puts respect in the rear" (ll. 45-46). In other words, the example set by the governors will be accepted by the people.

4. Justice is the Foundation

"Do Maat (Justice)" is the cornerstone for governance as attested by other texts which deal with the wisdom of governance. And this text is no exception. Here the fundamental rule is coupled with a part of the traditional formula for exemplary conduct, "comfort the weeper, do not oppress the widow, do not expel a man from the property of his father" (l. 47). The future pharaoh is admonished against unjust punishment and capital punishment with the exception noted above concerning the seditions. At this point it seems that the fundamental principles of governance have been set forth but the student is subsequently further admonished concerning the divine judgment so that these principles can be given proper weight. Justice is not only commanded by prudence but also by God. The section on generla principles ends with an emphasis on policies that were either stated or implicit in the foregoing lines. Policy should be geared toward the young generation so that they will be endowed with possessions which give them a stake in the country (ll. 57-61). This wise policy goes a long way toward preventing the basis for factionalism which often grows out of the alienation of the poor. The warning against favoritism is stressed in the statement, "do not promote the son of a man (of status) over a common man" (ll. 61-62). Finally, the king is advised to show respect to God by building sacred monuments and promoting the spiritual life of the people by setting a good example of spirituality (ll. 63-65).

B. Reflections on the Civil War

The second major section deals with an assessment of governance during the reign of Khety, the father of Meryuka Re. Beginning with the "prophecy of the ancestors" (l. 69) that civil war would break out, the Instruction warns against desecration of the tombs which occurred during the war. In terms of relations with the South, Khety suggests that the rules for civil war are different from those concerning warfare against foreigners. The conflict between the part of the country controlled by Khety and the "South" has evidently somewhat abated. So the young pharaoh-to-be is advised to not deal viciously with the South and in general to be lenient in dealing with the other part of the country. The old ruler claims to have acted in such a way that relations between the two sections are at a truce (ll. 71-81). Regarding the pacification of the North, Khety relates that he pacified the Northwestern Delta which evidently had posed severe problems for the government. He then turns to the campaign which he conducted in the Northeastern Delta which had been invaded and occupied by foreigners. Khety reports that these foreigners have been expelled; the provinces and cities have been restored and reorganized (ll. 83-91).

Kheti then turns to a commentary on the nature of the Aamu (Asiatics). He says:

"Lo! The vile Aamu; wretched is the place which he is from. Suffering from hidden water with barren trees and many dangerous paths because of the mountains. He is not from one place only. His legs walk about circling. He has been fighting since the time of Horus (yet) he does not conquer nor is he conquered. He does not announce the day of fighting like a robber who returns to the pack" (ll. 92-94).

This is perhaps the most "curious passage in the entire papyrus," as Gardiner observes.[23] Certainly Kemite negative criticism of other people is a rare occurrence in the texts. The passage does, however, enable us to get an insight into the way the ancient Kemites explained the culture of some of the peoples from the northern continent. The nomadic, bellicose, sneaky behavior is explained as environmentally determined which anticipates later so-called scientific explanations of cultural behavior. This theory of the origin of cultural behavior was not only borrowed by the Western philosophers and is still in use to this day, but it is also a position taken by Black scholars such as C.A. Diop and John Henrik Clarke.

Khety goes on to describe how he organized the Delta to rout the invading Asiatic horde. After the invasion, Kheti reorganized the Eastern Delta as far South as Menefer (Memphis), the old capital. He ends his appraisal by advising precautions against these perennial invaders and urges the development of the people to repel invaders. He advises his son to increase the urban population and "build buildings", because "an established city is not harmed" (l. 108). The appraisal of contemporary affairs ends with a reference to the wisdom of a Pharaoh Khety (either the author of the text or a predecessor). The crux of the teachings is that it is the duty of the government to oppose those who commit violence against sacred monuments. The ultimate sanction against such desecration is the retribution of God who will return pain for pain, in keeping with the principle of reciprocity which is at the core of Maat (Truth and Justice).

C. The Theory of Paraohship

The statement of the wisdom of pharaohship which begins the next section is the epitome of the Old Kingdom tradition. It reads, "The Pharaoh of the Two Shores knows all; not foolish is any pharaoh who has advisors. He is wise when he comes from inside the body . . . (ll. 115-116)." The passsage simply points out that pharaohship is a collective office because of the entourage of officers who actually participate in decision-making and governing.

But not only does the pharaoh have the council but also the traditions of pharaohship. Thus, contrary to the sobering wisdom of Ptah Hotep "that no one is born wise," the pharaoh *is* born wise. The text continues saying, "The functions of pharaohship are good. It has neither son nor brother to preserve its monument; yet one (pharaoh) endows the other. . . . His deeds are embellished by another who comes after him (ll. 116-118)." The wisdom continues by dealing with the continuity and impersonal nature of the institution. Although pharaohship has no son or brother as individual men do, it is, nevertheless, passed on from generation to generation by the tradition of pharaohship. Each new pharaoh continues the work of all of his predecessors. This is the significance of the Re-Horus and Osiris-Horus relationship. Whatever the actual biological connection, each pharaoh is the son of the preceding pharaoh and the direct descendant of all the pharaohs (nisut-bity). In theory, there is no change of direction because each pharaoh, upon the death of the old pharaoh, must become the son of the dead pharaoh and restore Maat (Truth) in place of falsehood after properly burying his "father" of whom the former is the "son of (his) body."

After the restatement of the principle of pharaohship, Khety confesses to a "vile deed that came about in my time" (l. 119). The pharaoh points out that he had responsibility for the evil activity, although he did not order it himself. This points to another aspect of pharaohship or governance, i.e., the government is responsible for the conduct of those acting on its authority whether such action was commanded or not. Again, the principle of reciprocity or Maat is invoked, "every blow is repayed by its kind" (l. 123). This judgment is reminiscent of the passage in the Khufu text that warns Pharaoh Khufu about the decline of his family lineage and the rise of another. Implicit in the warning was a prohecy about the rewards of corruption or irresponsibility in governance. The treatise on pharaohship concludes with a poetic statement on the divine nature of the nation and its institutions. Repeating the wisdom of the classic statement as per the Shabaka Stone, the text asserts not only did God create the heaven and earth and give mankind breath, he also created institutions and ways and means of governing and defending the nation and gave mankind the wisdom to use them wisely (ll. 123-138). Pharaohs are advised to "do Maat (Justice or Truth) upon which the heart relies" (l. 128). This is the only basis whereby one may die in peace — that is to say, if one wants his good name to endure and if he wants his soul to be integrated into the eternal cosmos.

D. Epilogue

The Instruction ends with a short admonition concerning the value of the Instruction; the crux of which is thusly stated: "My speech gives all the laws of pharaohship which instruct you that you may uplift the young" (ll. 138-139). Included in the closing words is a curious line which says "the followers of the king are divine" (ll. 140-141). This passage should be considered along with an earlier passage which reads, "he (the pharaoh) is singled out as foremost among the millions of the land" (l. 116). In the context of this teaching, those passages shed an interesting insight into the phenomenon called "divine kingship" by the egyptologists. The followers of the pharaoh can mean nothing but the people of the country. Thus, we learn here that not only is the pharaoh divine, as per the traditional formulas such as "The Good God" royal title, but the people are also divine. And since the pharaoh is one singled out from among the millions of the land, he evidently is human as well as divine. Let us recall that the aging prime minister Ptah Hotep, was also called divine in the model Instruction. The explanation is really simple; the entire nation in whole and part is divine. The myth of "divine kingship" thus disappears along with all other Eurocentric inventions.

IV. CONCLUSION

Let us now summarize the wisdom of the Kemites concerning governance. First of all, speaking and listening to speaking constitute the vehicles by which wisdom and truth are transmitted. The ancestors transmitted their doings through what they told the elders who in turn tell their children who repeat the sayings to their children as generation follows generation. This traditional wisdom and truth have withstood the test of time, because these sayings are sufficient guides for directing the deeds of all the people of the country, especially the officials. Education in this sense is synonymous with governance, both of which have as their objective the attainment and maintenance of Maat (Truth or Justice).

The Instruction of Ptah Hotep contained a collection of maxims which instructed the youth in the correct values, attitudes, and modes of behavior suited for those who would become the civil servants from the office of prime minister down. Indeed, in all probability, the future pharaoh also received this education along-side some of the children from various ranks including the poorest. These students were taught what was expected of a good official. A good official was wise and knowledgeable about the country and the people. He was wise enough to listen and learn from people in all walks of life, especially the so-called uneducated. He understood that listening was the major source of acquiring knowledge and wisdom. Above all, he understood that Maat (Truth and Justice) was the foundation of all existence and that it must be adhered to in all actions.

In relationship to his supervisors and persons of higher rank, the civil servant was always to show respect and trustworthiness. He was to carry out his orders with courtesy and discipline and give advice when asked, thus, gently teaching his supervisor. He was to avoid showing-off, pushiness and playing one superior off against another. He was also supposed to shun gossip and ridicule. In relationship to his peers and intimate associates, the official was to show friendship, loyalty and generosity. One was to respect wealth but not dote on it. Wealth primarily functioned to enable one to be generous. One should not boast of success, nor belittle those who are not so successful. The implicit wisdom was that one had to be a good kinsman, friend and neighbor before one could be a good official.

In relationship to the general population or the folk, the public servant was to always demonstrate a scrupulous attachment to justice and charity. One's speech should be gentle and encouraging. One was to listen patiently and indulgently even when folk are inarticulate and emotional in delivering their complaints. He should strive to make his constituents secure and satisfied. He should avoid corruption and in general, serve as a model for the masses and "instruct with virtue." As was indicated above, the general character of governance is educational. The good public official is a man of Maat in the sense of balance. He is cool in the face of the hotheaded, even vicious behavior. He is a self-disciplined person who speaks wisely because he speaks only when he has something worth saying. Otherwise, he is silent, thus listening, showing respect to others and demonstrating discipline at the same time. In other words, a good person makes a good official.

The Instruction of Ptah Hotep thus reinfoced the traditional concept of governance. In a well-ordered society, the function of governance was to maintain that order and embellish it. The Instruction of Meryuka Re was probably written to re-enforce the traditional wisdom of governance by extending the explanation to cover factual situations experienced during a time of trouble. The text asserts that it "has given all the laws of pharaohship so that the future pharaoh may instruct and raise up the young." The classical statement as expressed in the Shabaka Stone had begun with a mythical division of the country into two lands only to be reunited under the aegis of legitimate rule. Thus, the assumption of unity was unquestioned during the Old Kingdom. The restatement in Meryuka Re begins with a discussion of partisanism and rebellion which must be efficiently and awesomely destroyed. Such an act of force seems to contradict the wisdom that governance is education. But as we have seen, this concern with the suppression of partisanism is like the mythical division of the country between Horus and Seth which is rescinded prior to the primordial unity. This is the substitution of factual division for mythical division.

But once actual disunity occurs, wisdom itself is disunited. The wisdom that governance is education is challenged by the wisdom that governance requires might or force. But as expressed in the Shabaka Stone, the problem is to be brought before the council or as in the myth, before the Nine Netchers or the representatives of the people. Even when force must be used, it is used in the context of litigation and openness, thus giving the act of force legitimacy. This teaches the seditionist that he should have brought his complaint before the court as did Seth. The lesson anticipates the conclusion of the Horus-Seth conflict which is to subordinate might to Right. The negative situation produced by the threat of partisanism is brought to a just conclusion by putting forth a theory of condign punishment and admonishing the ruler to maintain good nature even in the face of adversity. Once the conflict in wisdom has been resolved and the unity of wisdom restored, the Instruction follows the pattern established in Ptah Hotep and begins again with a statement on the virtue of speech because "words are more powerful than fighting;" speech is the prime instrument of governance.

The Instruction goes on to confirm that wisdom which is received through speech is a gift of the ancestors just as governmental authority is the heritage from the ancestors of Horus. The text also teaches that government must be benevolent, ruling more by reward and promotion than punishment. This restatement is rounded out by a command to "Do Right" which is the cornerstone of governance. Maat is commanded by God. Meryuka Re then applies the wisdom to the actual contemporary civil war between two de facto regimes, each ruling over one division of the country. The laws of civil war are different from the rules governing foreign wars because of historical national relations and because of the bonds of kinship and the common sacred sites throughout the country. The Instruction concludes with a very lengthy but poetical restatement of the divine creation of the cosmic and social order which reconfirms and renews the traditional statement found on the Shabaka Stone.

What is the relevance of this research for African people today? This essay has produced a partial restoration of the African world-view as it applies to the vital function of governance. This worldview should be the wisdom that leads African people as we attempt to rebuild our societies based on the restoration of Maat to replace the disorder that pervades our lands and people as our leaders still seek the "political kingdom" in vain!

NOTES

1. John G. Jackson, *Introduction to African Civilization,* Secaucus, NY: The Citadel Press, 1980, p. 1 53.
2. Jacob H. Carruthers, *Essays in Ancient Egyptian Studies,* Los Angeles: Kawaida Publications, 1984.
3. George G.M. James, *Stolen Legacy,* San Francisco: Julian Richardson Associates, 1976.
4. Cheikh Anta Diop, *The African Origin of Civilization,* Westport, CT: Lawrence Hill & Co., 1974, p. 230.
5. Ibid, p. 231.
6. Ibid, p. 230.
7. Henri and H.A. Frankfort, *"The Emancipation of Thought From Myth,"* in Henri and H.A. Frankfort, *Before Philosophy,* London: Harmondsworth, 1949.
8   Ibid, preface.
9   Cheikh Anta Diop, *Cultural Unity of Black Africa,* Chicago: Third World Press, 1978, p. 11ff.
10. Ibid.
11. Frankfort and Frankfort, op. cit., passim.
12. Miriam Lichtheim, *Ancient Egyptian Literature,* Volume I, Berkeley: University of California Press, 1980, pp. 184-18 5.
13. Ibid., p. 51.
14. Carruthers, op. cit., pp. 81-84.
1 5. Adolf Erman, *The Literature of the Ancient Egyptians,* London: Methuen & Co., 1927; Lichtheim, op. cit.
16. Z. Zaba, *Les Maximes de Ptahhotep,* Prague, 19 56.
17. John Wilson in Frankfort and Frankfort, op. cit., p. 109.
18. A.H. Gardiner, *Journal of Egyptian Archaeology,* I (1914), pp. 20-36.
19. Lichtheim, op. cit., p. 97; W. Golenischeff, *Les Papyrus Hieratiques,* St. Petersburg, 1916, pp. 3-82, plates 1-4).
20. Gardiner, op. cit., p. 23.
21. F.Ll. Griffith, "The Mulligan Papyrus," *ZAS,* 34 (1896), p. 39.
22. Carruthers, op. cit., pp. 78ff.
23. Gardiner, op. cit., p. 30.

THE ROLE OF ROYAL WOMEN IN ANCIENT EGYPT

IFE JOGUNOSIMI

INTRODUCTION

One of the most interesting aspects of kingship in ancient Egypt is the phenomenon of the female monarchy. During ancient Egypt's long history, from the pre-dynastic era to the end of the thirtieth dynasty, a period spanning over 3,000 years, several women at various times assumed the throne and ruled over the entire nation. In spite of the rare and unorthodox occurrence of female monarchs, four apparently assumed this role: Nitocris, Sebeck-Neferu-ra, Hatshepsut and Tawsret. Although Hatshepsut's ascendency to the throne during the 18th Dynasty caused bitter reaction, it had occurred before! At least two other females had ruled legitimately as kings before her. The evidence is vague as to whether their reigns received the same reaction.

This paper will attempt to explore the data concerning the female monarchs but in order to sharpen our focus, it is first of all necessary to look at the wider role of royal women in the institution of Egyptian monarchy, i.e., Queen Mother, legitimizer of all heirs; Royal Wife, Royal Mother, Great Wife of the king, Great Heiress, High Priestess, and perhaps most important, Queen regent. The role of royal women seems to have no parallel in the contemporary Middle Eastern civilization, such as Mesopotamia, et al but does seem to be related to the role of royal women in other traditional African national cultures; i.e. Axum (Ethiopia), Meroe (Nubia), West African Kingdoms and Southern Africa.[1] Thus, the examination of monarchy and the role of royal women in Africa may shed light on this phenomenon.

In the remainder of the paper, I will address the following: Monarchy and Royal Women in Africa, Monarchy and Royal Women in Egypt, and Four Cases of Women Monarchs.

MONARCHY AND ROYAL WOMEN IN AFRICA

Unlike her counterpart in the Ancient Near East and Classical Greece and Rome, the woman in Africa occupied a position of equality and respect. She inherited as well as sold property; signed legal documents and played a very important part in the daily life of the state. In addition to these powers, the natural line of inheritance was through the woman. Dr. Chiekh Anta Diop said that African societies were matrilineal with descent traced from the woman's side of the family or through the female line. He further states, "the line of descent is matrilineal and it is the man who brings the dowry to the woman. The latter does not leave her family group and can turn out her husband (who necessarily belongs to a different gens) if he fails to provide enough food for the common provender. Whatever may be the reason for any separation, the children remain entirely in the mother's gens".[2] Thus, we are able to see the source of the African woman's power.

The creation of the family unit by the African man and woman laid the foundation for the organization of all subsequent institutions in the society. The important position of the woman in that unit is further attested to by the fact that in many parts of Africa, it is thought that a child owes more to his mother than to his father. "Heredity on the mother's side is more important than the father's side. In Africa, the woman, after marriage retains all her individuality. Her name does not change. She continues to bear the name of her family. The African child calls his mother's sister mother and his father's brother father".[3] The same was true in ancient Egypt, as Dr. Breasted relates in his *History of Egypt:* "The closest ties of blood were through the mother, and a man's natural protector, even in preference to his own father, was the father of his mother."[4] Concerning ancient Ghana, Ibn Batouta stated: "they (the Blacks) are named after their maternal uncles and not after their fathers; it is not the sons who inherit from their father, but the nephews, the sons of the father's sister".[5]

In ancient Africa, the woman not only had a special place within the context of the family but often ruled nations wielding much power. One only has to look at the ancient nation states of Egypt, Kush, and Ethiopia to see women in positions of leadership and power (Royal women in Egypt will be addressed later in the paper).

It is evident from the many royal inscriptions and reliefs found in Meroe, Napata, and other parts of Nubia, that women enjoyed an unusually high place in society. Queens served as consorts and as dowagers and often acted as counselor and regents for their sons.[6] The 25th Dynasty pharaoh, Taharqa, recorded in one of his inscriptions that he summoned his mother all the way from Napata to be present at his coronation in Egypt.[7] The wealth and prominence of Queens' tombs excavated from the Nubian cemetary also speaks to their high status.

Many of the ancient writers, including Herodotus, Diordorus Siculus, Strabo, and Pliny knew of and wrote about Meroe.[8] Strabo in his account of a war between Meroe and the Romans between 25 and 21 B.C. states that the Commander of the Meroitic army was a general of Candace. Pliny in giving an account of the same battle tells us that Meroe was ruled by a queen whose name was Candace.[9] According to Roman tradition, Kush was governed by a hereditary line of female rulers, all named Candace.[10] Long thought to be a proper name, it is now known to be a Meroitic title (Kdke) perhaps meaning Queen Mother, or Queen.[11]

Further references to Meroe and the lines of queens named Candace can be found in the New Testament of the Holy Bible. In the book of Acts, chapter 8, 26-29, the story is told of Philip baptizing "a man of Ethiopia, a eunuch of great authority under Candace, Queen of the Ethiopians."[12] This is but one more indication of how well known Meroe was.

When we look at the chronology of Napatan and Meroitic rulers (Shinnie, *Meroe*, pp. 58-61) we find at least five queens regnant during the later centuries of the Kushite dynasty. It is important to bear in mind that no two of them ruled in succession and the circumstances by which they ascended the throne, in preference to males is not known. Two of the most often mentioned queens are Amanirenas and Amanishakhete. Their names have been left in inscriptions in the temples of Meroe and Napata. Another familiar name is that of Queen Amanitere. Her name is always seen with that of King Netekamani, which seems to suggest that they ruled jointly. From the various inscriptions found on temple walls, stelae and burial tombs, it appears that they were involved in great restoration projects as well as building projects.[13]

Great similarities can be seen between Meroitic and Egyptian culture. It has been said that from the beginning of the XXV Dynasty onwards, the culture of Napata was almost wholly imitative of pharaonic Egypt (Adams, et al). John Wilson as cited by Adams, remarks of Piankhi, the first Nubain ruler in Egypt that "his culture was a provincial imitation of earlier Egypt."[14] However, in view of the Ta-Setti findings reported in 1980 by Professor Bruce Williams of the Oriental Institute, University of Chicago, we can be fairly certain that pharaonic culture originated in Nubia.[15]

Let us now turn to female monarchy in another ancient African nation, that of Axum. The story of the Queen of Sheba is one of the most famous legends in history. It has been written about by ancient and modern scholars alike. Accounts of the story are derived from Ethiopian and non-Ethiopian sources, the latter including the Bible and the Koran. The Ethiopian account of the legend is taken from the Kebra Nagast and Fatha Nagast (royal Ethiopian Chronicles), Axumite inscriptions and oral traditions.[16] According to Ethiopian tradition, the Queen of Sheba was an Ethiopian queen named Makeda. Many Western authors including the famous Jewish historian Flavius Josephus and Father of the Church, Saint Augustine, support the Ethiopian tradition.[17]

Makeda, in the absence of male heirs is said to have ascended the throne about the year 1005 B.C. and reigned until the year 955 B.C. The story of this "Queen of the South", her wealth and beauty, her famous visit to King Solomon, and the birth of her son Ebna Hakim, meaning "son of the wise man" who took the throne name Menelik I, is so well known that it is not necessary to detail here. However, it is of utmost importance to note that while based upon legend, the story of Makeda, known as the Queen of Sheba or Queen of the South is none the less evidence of the compatibility of female monarchy with the African cultures.

The great queens of Kush and Africa are by no means the only ones in African history. From ancient times to relatively recent times, there is evidence of female rule. The chronicles of Queen Dahia al Kahina of Mauritania who led the African resistance against Muslim invaders in the late 690's; Queen Ann Nzinga of Angola who protected her country against the Portugese in the sixteenth century and Yaa Asantewaa, the Queen of Ejisu who led a rebellion against the British in 1900, when they demanded the Ashanti surrender their Golden Stool, all attest to the long line of African female queens.[18] While it was not the rule but rather the exception to have female monarchs, the relative widespread occurrence in space and time of the phenonemon is further evidence of the cultural unity of pharaonic Egypt and the rest of Africa.

MONARCHY AND ROYAL WOMEN IN EGYPT

Before beginning an examination of royal women in Egypt, it is necessary to take a brief look at the function of kingship in ancient Egypt. According to the national myth, kingship came into being when being itself came into being. The Egyptian social order was conceived as a preordained portion of the cosmic order. The Memphite Theology, a text written in an early phase of the Egyptian history gives a theory of kingship. The text describes the order of creation and the Egyptian nation's inseparable place in that order.[19]

In the concept of Divine Kingship, the office of the king is endowed with divine power and acts as an intermediary between man and the cosmic forces.[20] Central to this idea are the concepts of HRW (Horus, the symbol of legitmacy and authority) and Maat (order, truth and justice).[21] The king is the embodiment of the nation and as such, he is the source of right action. Therefore the nation could not be complete without a pharaoh at the head. In the Memphite Theology, Horus is Sma Tawi (Uniter of the two lands). Thus, the king is the descendant of the original father of the nation. The principle of unity is the fundamental concept of order both cosmic and social.[22] Unity is again implicit in the title "ity" (which some egyptologists translate as sovereign but probably is derived from "it" which means father). The theme of unity is further attested in the king's titulary by Nbty (The Two Ladies) and Niwst Bity (The one of the Swt Plant and the Bee), both of which symbolize the union of the two lands. It is in this context, unity, that one can understand the very vital role of royal women.

While the Pharaoh, a male sovereign, was the personification of divine authority, it was the queen, a female who was the recognized transmitter of sovereignty. As indicated above, descent in the royal family was reckoned through the maternal line. There was only one legal wife, the queen; who was of royal or high noble birth. Sometimes referred to as "the daughter of god" meaning the daughter of the late king, she was often times the sister of her husband, as consanguineous marriages were common among royalty. Breasted tells us that "a man possessed but one legal wife who was the mother of his heirs" and who "was in every respect his equal".[23] The titles held by the queen attest to her rank and power in the society. The queens of the Early Period bore the titles: Royal Wife, Royal Mother, Great Wife of the King, Great Heiress, Ruler of All Women, Divine Wife, Great Royal Wife joined to the Beautiful White Crown. The Late Period titles are: Royal sister, Divine Wife of Amun, Lady of the Two Lands, Divine Chantress, Divine Adorer of Amen and Chief Prophetess of Amen.[24] Erman gives additional titles for both periods; the queen of the Old Empire is called: "She who sees the Gods Horus and Set" (i.e. the possessor of both halves of the kingdom), "the most pleasant, the highly praised, the friend of Horus, the beloved of him who wears the two diadems". The queen under the New Empire is called: "The Consort of the god, the Mother of the god, the great consort of the King".[25] Erman further states that the queen was of equal birth with her husband and had a share in all honors. The queen's power was not diminished upon the death of her husband as she continued to play a part at court. Also as "royal mother", she maintained her own property and was paid honors long after her death.[26]

The most prevalent expression of the significance of the role of the royal woman is that of queen mother. A symbolic expression of the role of queen mother can be inferred from the Osirian myth. Isis is "the embodiment of marital devotion and motherly love" and her principal function in conjunction with Hathor is that of motherhood. The king as a divinity is Horus, son of Hathor and when viewed as the heir and successor in the royal line, he is the son of Osiris and Isis is called his mother.[27] A further indication of the role of the queen mother can be seen in the belief that the queen mother was impregnated by the Ntr in order that she produce a divine heir to the throne. An Old Kingdom tale describes how he begot the first three kings of the Fifth Dynasty on the wife of the high priest of the Sun Temple at Heliopolis. The same tale has the queen mother being delivered by the goddesses Isis, Nephthys, Hequet and Meskhent.[28] We are very familiar with the New Kingdom reliefs showing the birth of Hatshepsut. Amon-Ra embodies himself in the king and visits Queen Ahmose to begat a successor.[29] A final instance of right to rule emanating from the queen mother is found in the Prophesy of Neferti. In the narrative, the prophet predicts that order will be restored by a future Pharaoh Amenemhat who will be born to a woman from Nubia.[30] Thus, we have examples of legitimacy bestowed by a queen mother for each of the major historical periods.

More factual instances of mother-right vis-a-vis legitimate rule are the existence of the mother's name in the King's tombs and in certain royal proclamations even when the name of the father of the pharaoh is not mentioned. Another instance is the inclusion of queen mothers' names on the Palermo Stone.

Marriage to the right woman (royal wife, mother or daughter) is another base of legitimate rule. According to Gardiner, Snofru, the first king of Dynasty IV, attained the right to rule by marrying the "daughter of the God" i.e., the pharaoh Huny's daughter.[31] Thutmose I, although not of royal blood became pharaoh when he married the princess Ahmose, who according to Gardiner was "a lady evidently of very exalted parentage".[32]

Another important role of royal women in Egypt was that of queen regent. When the pharaoh died and left no male heir, the queen served until a new dynasty was begun or in cases where the only heir was too young to hold the office, the queen reigned until the child reached maturity.

During Dynasty I we find the name of Mer (it) Neith listed on the Palermo Stone as the mother of Den. According to Edwards, as a woman she "attained a position seldom if ever equalled by a member of her sex in early dynastic times."[33] It is believed that she served as regent while her son Den was still a minor. Edwards further states that such a high position could only have been occupied by a woman who was queen. From this he implies that she was "the wife of Djet and the mother of Den."[34] Two royal tombs, one at Saqqara in the north, and one at Abydos in the south have been identified as belonging to Mer Neith. An inscription referring to her treasury is evidence of her sovereign status. The fact that her tombs were constructed in the same manner as those of the kings is further evidence of the power, prestige, and status she held.

Mer Neith was not the only woman during this period to hold such a prominent position. Her predecessor, Neith-Hotep, whose name was enclosed in a serekh and found at the Nagada tomb of Aha/Memes may have been the first queen-regent.[35] Kaplong, as cited by Wimby, suggested that she may have been queen-regent for Djer, her uncle, who was too young to assume the kingship.[36] The evidence is so scanty, that we can only speculate about her position; although the fact that her name was found in a serekh implies that she had an extraordinary role.

Queen Iput, the wife of King Teti, the first king of Dynasty VI, and the mother of Pepi I was a highly esteemed royal woman. According to Smith, her titles indicate that "like certain other great ladies, she carried the royal blood over into the new dynasty". When King Teti died, Usekare reigned briefly while Queen Iput served as regent for her young son Pepi I.[37]

Pepi I married two sisters who bore the same name Enekhnes-

Merire; and they became the mothers of the two kings who followed him; Kings Merenre and Pepi II.

Pepi II's reign of 99 years closed out Dynasty VI and brought to a temporary end the absolute power of the pharaohs.

During what is known as the First Intermediate period, authority was held by the Monarchs. It appears that the Monarchs followed the same rules of succession, as did the Old Kingdom pharaohs. Several tombs dating from the period of the Ninth and Tenth Dynasties inform us of three monarchs in Siut: Tefibi, Kheti I and Kheti II. Of the latter, we know from inscriptions that upon the death of his maternal grandfather, Kheti's mother ruled until he grew up to succeed to his maternal heritage.

> "The son of his daughter made his name to live and glorified him. His daughter ruled in Siut, the worthy stock of her father doing good to her city . . . beloved of Upwawet, rejoicing in beloved of the king, his favorite. The city was satisfied with that which she said. She acted as lord until her son became strong armed . . ."[38]

During the Second Intermediate period, Egypt was invaded by foreigners from Asia known as the Hyksos. After almost 200 years of foreign rule, Kamose, the last king of the Seventeenth Dynasty is credited with initiating the movement to liberate Egypt from foreign rule. His reign was very short and his burial suggests that he died suddenly and was succeeded by his brother Amosis.[39]

Kamose being only a child when his father died, assumed the throne with his mother Queen Ahotep ruling as regent. The daughter of Queen Tetisheri and King Seqenere, Ahotep occupied a prominent position in Egypt. She is praised in Kamose's stela as "one who cares for Egypt." "She has looked after her soldiers, she has guarded her deserters, she has brought back her fugitives and collected together her deserters; she has pacified Upper Egypt and expelled her rebels."[40] This seems to indicate that she played an important role in helping to restore order and unity in Egypt at the time of the Hyksos invasion. James suggests that this may have occurred on the death of Seqenenre or Kamose and that she also may have served as co-regent with Amosis during the early part of his reign.[41]

Perhaps the most famous queen regent was Hatshepsut of the Eighteenth Dynasty who ruled as regent with her stepson and nephew King Thutmose III. Since Hatshepsut actually ruled as a Horus, further discussion of her reign will be treated later.

Hatshepsut was by no means the last queen to serve as regent. During the latter part of the Eighteenth Dynasty, Queen Mutemwia acted as regent for her son Amenophis III and in the Nineteenth Dynasty Tausert served as regent.

In conjunction with the role of royal women as queen regents, it appears that some of them had active roles as co-rulers with their pharaonic husbands. This seems to be the case with Tetisheri and Ahotep of the Seventeenth Dynasty and Ahmose Nefetari, Tiy and Nefertetti of the Eighteenth Dynasty.

It must also be mentioned that in addition to these roles of the royal women, another was that of high priestess. In the interest of brevity, this role has not been explored in the paper.

FOUR CASES OF FEMALE MONARCHS

In the ancient Egyptian theory of kingship (as discussed earlier in the paper), the king was endowed with divine power and had the responsibility for maintaining Maat; order, truth, and justice in the nation. This concept of kingship appears to have denied the right to rule as women, yet we find that in each of the major historical periods, there is evidence of female rule. At least four women actually occupied the office of king in their own names.

Tombs in Nagada and Abydos dating to the Early Dynastic Period have revealed the names of two queens of Dynasty I, (already mentioned) whose names were enclosed in a serekh. In the Nagada tomb of Aha Menes, the name of Queen Neit Hetepu appears. Hetepu is enclosed in a serekh surmounted by the crossed arrows. In a tomb in Abydos a stela with the name Mer Neith inscribed serekh was also discovered.[42] These unusual instances may indicate that an honorary title of monarch was bestowed on these woman. Such bestowal, perhaps inadvertently anticipated the occurrence of female monarchs.

The first attested female king is Nitocris, the last ruler of the Sixth Dynasty. Unfortunately, there is very little historical evidence for her reign. However, she is listed in the Turin Canon as a Nsw Bity.[43] "She was the noblest and loveliest of the women of her time, of fair complexion", is the description Manetho gives to this queen. Herodotus also mentions this queen. Many legends have been written about her, two of which include the building of the Third Pyramid and the avenging of the murder of her brother followed by her committing suicide.[44] (Both have been found to be untrue.) However, there seems to be agreement that the last ruler of Dynasty Six was a woman. Since she is listed in the Turin Canon as Nsw Bity Nt-jgrty, we will take this as evidence of her sovereignty.

The next instance of a female monarch, is in the Twelfth Dynasty. The last ruler of this dynasty was "the Female Horus, Meryetre, the King of Upper and Lower Egypt, Sobkkare, the Daughter of Ra".[45] Her reign is evidenced by the inclusion of her name on the Karnak, Saqqara and Turin lists. The Turin Canon gives her a reign of three years and ten months and a cylinder in the British Museum gives her an almost full titulary.[46] Further evidence of her reign can be found inscribed on monuments. These include a Nile Mark at the Second Cataract, dated to Regnae Year 3, a sphinx and three statues of the female Horus found at Khata'na in the Delta, and a fragmentary architrave from Kom el-'Aqarib, near Heracleopolis, bears her praenomen as "king" and her personal name.[47] With this amount of historical evidence, we can feel comfortable about the role of this Female Horus.

The best known of all the female monarchs is Hatshepsut of Dynasty Eighteen. She was the daughter of King Thutmose I and his chief royal wife Queen Ahmose. Her father was succeeded to the throne by Thutmose II, a son by a secondary wife. To legitimize himself on the throne he married his half sister, Hatshepsut. Thutmose II reigned only a short while and died, leaving no legitimate male heirs, for Hatshepsut had given birth to only girls. A son by a palace concubine was wed to Hatshepsut's daughter, his half sister, and became Thutmose III. He being a minor, his aunt and step mother, was well qualified to serve as regent, since she bore the titles "Great Royal Wife, Wife of the God, Daughter of the King and his Great Wife."[48]

After serving as regent for Thutmose III for two years, Hatshepsut proclaimed herself King.

"Came forth the king of the gods, Amon-Ra, from his temple, saying: "welcome my sweet daughter, my favorite, the King of Upper and Lower Egypt, Maatkare, Hatshepsut. Thou art the king taking possession of the Two Lands."[49]

Hatshepsut, truly became the personification of a male Horus. She donned male attire and wore the king's crown and an artificial beard. The scribes were instructed to substitute the pronoun "he" instead of "she" when referring to her.

Hatshepsut's reign is noted for the peace and prosperity that was evident during her reign. Trade flourished and building works gave employment to the people. She added to the Temple of Amon at Karnak and built several Obelisks. Her temple at Deir el Bahri is considered the most beautiful temple in Egypt and the finest of all ancient buildings. On the temple walls, is an account for her famous expedition to Punt. The ships are seen returning with gold, ivory, and myrrh trees, among other things.

Thus, we have a female who not only succeeded in gaining the throne but in holding it for twenty years.

The last female monarch to call herself pharaoh was Ta-wsret. Evidence about this queen is rather scanty but it is believed that she may have been married to two kings in the Nineteenth dynasty. Jewelry discovered in a cache of the Biban el Maluk shows her to have been Setho II's principal wife.[50] She is known to have married Sitptah a son of Setho II by an unknown woman, at a later time to legitimize his rule. After Sitptah's rule, Ta-wsret, according to Manetho reigned for a period of eight years. She is the only woman other than Hatshepsut to have a tomb in the Valley of the Kings. Further evidence of her rule includes a funerary sanctuary to the south of the Ramesseum with a cartouche bearing her name and according to Gardiner there are traces of her reign in the Delta and at the turquoise mines of Sanai.

Nictocris, Sebek-Neferu-ra, Hatshepsut and Ta-wsret were females who assumed the role of kings. While female monarchy was the exception rather than the rule, they never the less served their nation admirably in that capacity.

CONCLUSIONS

"The functions of royalty in ancient Egypt were regarded as being transmitted in the female line. While every Egyptian princess of the Royal House was born a queen and bore the title and dignities of the office from the day of her birth, a man only acquired them at his coronation, and could do so only by becoming the consort of the royal princess . . . Those features of the constitution of Egyptian royalty are not singular. They are substantially identical with those obtaining in all other African kingdoms."[51]

The conclusions of Dr. Briffault aptly summarizes the institutional foundation from which the Women Pharaohs of ancient Egypt arose. While only four women actually ruled as monarchs in their own names, such occurrences are not at odds with the more orthodox roles of the Royal women. Indeed the traditional sexual division of labor in ancient Egypt as well as the rest of precolonial Africa bestowed on the royal woman not only honor and prestige but the exercise of considerable power, formal as well as informal.

Three major roles of the "Great Wife of the Nesu-Bity" were explored in this paper; Queen Mother, Queen Regent and Female Pharaoh. Queen Motherhood, the real base for the other two functions, determined who would occupy the office of King — whether through the birth of her children or marriage to an otherwise non-royal aspirant. The Royal Wife who is also the Queen mother seems to be the normal choice for ruling regent when the Pharaoh dies before the heir has reached the age of maturity. This certainly seems to be the case for which we have considerable documentation. Thus we may conclude that Queen Regent was a normally expected function of the Royal Wife should the occasion arise.

The bestowal (or assumption) of Kingship on Royal Women seems to have occurred during the regency of the four women who "appeared as Horus". In other African societies such bestowal seems to be at least an approved role for some Royal Women. The circumstances of the transition in Egypt are not clear but practice might well have been due to crises of succession of Kingship and thus conformed with the general patterns in Africa.

The unique roles of the Royal Women in Egyptian governance supports the generally accepted conclusion that the roots of Egyptian Monarchy are in the African tradition.

NOTES

1. Chiekh Anta, Diop *The Cultural Unity of Africa.* Chicago: Third World Press, 1978.
2. Ibid., p. 17.
3. G.K. Osei, *The African: His Antecedents, His Genius and His Destiny.* New Hyde Park: University Books, Inc., 1971, p. 22.
4. James Henry Breasted, *A History of Egypt.* New York: Charles Scribner's Sons, 1937, p. 86.
5. Batouta as cited by Osei.
6. William Y. Adams, *Nubia Corridor to Africa.* London· Penguin Books Ltd., 1977, p. 260.
7. Ibid.
8. P.L. Shinnie, *Meroe,* New York: Frederick A. Praeger, 1967.
9. Ibid., pp. 19-20.
10. Adams, op. cit., p. 260.
11. Ibid.
12. The term was used by ancient writers to mean Kush, Nubian, African or Black.
13. Adams, op. cit., p. 312.
14. Ibid., p.252.
15. Bruce, Williams, "The Last Pharaohs of Nubia", *Archaeology, 33,* (1980).
16. William Leo Hansberry, *Pillars in Ethiopian History,* Vol. I, Washington, D.C.: Howard University Press, 1974, p. 33.
17. Ibid., p. 35.
18. See introduction by John Clarke to Diop's *Cultural Unity of Black Africa.*
19. *Henri Frankfort, Kingship and the Gods,* Chicago: The University of Chicago Press, 1978, p. 24.
20. Ibid.
21. Jacob H. Carruthers, *Essays in Ancient Egyptian Studies,* Los Angeles: University of Sankore Press, 1984, p. 81.
22. _____, "Governance in Ancient Kemet", Paper presented at the First Annual Ancient Egyptian Studies Conference, Los Angeles, California, February, 1984.
23. Breasted, op. cit., p. 85.
24. Diedre Wimby, "The Female Horuses and Great Wives of Kemet", Journal of African Civilizations, 6, 1 (April, 1984), 36-48.
25. Adolf Erman, *Life in Ancient Egypt.* New York: Dover Publications, Inc., 1971, p. 74.
26. Ibid.
27. Frankfort, op. cit., p. 44.
28. Ibid., p. 45.
29. See Frankfort, Breasted, et al.
30. Miriam Lichtheim, "The Prophecies of Neferti", *Ancient Egyptian Literature,* Vol. I, Berkeley: University of California Press, 1975.

31. Alan, Gardiner, *Egypt of the Pharaohs.* London: Oxford University Press, 1980.p. 77.
32. Ibid., p. 177.
33. I.E.S. Edwards, *The Early Dynastic Period in Egypt,* Vol. I, Cambridge: University Press, 1964, p. 20.
34. Ibid., p. 21.
35. Gardiner, op. cit., p. 411.
36. Wimby, op. cit., p. 38.
37. W. Stevenson Smith, *The Old Kingdom in Egypt and the Beginning of the First Intermediate Period,* Vol. I, Cambridge: University Press, 1962, p. 6.
38. James H. Breasted, *Ancient Records of Egypt,* Vol. I, New York: Russell and Russell 1962, p. 191.
39. T.G.H. James, *Egypt From the Expulsion of the Hyksos to Amenophis I, Vol. II,* Cambridge: University Press, 1965, p. 6.
40. Ibid., p. 20.
41. Ibid., p.21
42. Gardiner, op. cit., p. 412.
43. Smith, op. cit., p. 55.
44. Barbara Mertz, *Temples, Tombs and Hieroglyphs.* New York: Dodd, Mead, and Company, 1978, p. 91.
45. William C. Hayes, *Egypt From the Death of Ammenemes III to Seqenenre II, VOL. II,* Cambridge: University Press, 1962, p. 4.
46. Gardiner, op. cit., p. 141.
47. Hayes, op. cit., p. 4.
48. Mertz, op. cit., p. 151.
49. Ibid.
50. Gardiner, op. cit., p. 279.
51. Robert Briffault, *The Mothers,* cited by John G. Jackson, *Man, God and Civilization.*

II. HISTORY

AFRICA IN THE ANCIENT WORLD

JOHN HENRIK CLARKE

There is a flutter of excitment in some parts of the African World Community over some new revelations by white writers, especially the article,"The Lost Pharaoh of Nubia," by Professor Bruce Williams of the University of Chicago. I am pleased about the attention that Professor Bruce is getting. He is a fellow worker in another Academic factory and I know that when he applies for promotion and tenure, the publication of this article will help his case, inspite of the fact that there is nothing in this article that was not said, better, by other writers over a hundred years ago. Now, just what did Professor Bruce Williams tell us. He says in essence:

> "that the people in Nubia (sometimes called Kush) had an advanced political organization hundreds of years before the first dynasty of Egypt, and what we think of as Egyptian civilization may have moved from South to North a concept which is contrary to current thinking on the subject."[1]

This is more than a twice told story. Chancellor Williams said this more extensively in his book, *The Destruction of Black Civilization,* in the chapter called, "Ethiopia's Oldest Daughter: Egypt."[2] The same information is in John G. Jackson's book, *Introduction to African Civilization.*[3]

From ancient times to the present,Africa has been an attraction for the scholars of the world. Our own great historian W.E.B. DuBois[4] tells us:

> "Always Africa is giving us something new.... On its Black bosom arose one of the earliest, if not the earliest, of self-protecting civilizations, and grew so mighty that it still furnishes superlatives to thinking and speaking men. Out of its darker and more remote forest fastnesses came, if we may credit many recent scientists, the first welding of iron, and we know that agriculture and trade flourished there when Europe was a wilderness."
>
> Dr. DuBois tells us further that, "Nearly every human empire that has risen in the world, material and spiritual, has found some of its greatest crises on the continent of Africa. It was through Africa that Christianity became the religion of the world. In Africa the last flood of Germanic invasions spent itself within hearing of the last gasp of Byzantium, and it was

again through Africa that Islam came to play its great role
of conqueror and civilizer."

Carter G. Woodson in his book, *The African Background Outlined,*
makes the first attempt to write a survey of the history of the African
world.[5] At Howard University, William Leo Hansberry, laid the foundation for the systematic study of African history, culture and politics.[6] He
taught at Howard University for thirty-seven years and is considered to
be Black America's greatest scholar on African subjects. The search for
the proper place of African people in world history was his mission and
his journey. It was his priesthood and he was always faithful to it.

I have named only a few of the committed African scholars who have
helped me shape my mission and put me on my journey into this field.
My journey to this conference has taken most of the years of my life. It
started with me as a young Baptist Sunday School teacher searching
for the image of my people in the Bible at a time when I thought that the
Bible was the supreme book of history and everything in it was the Truth
and that Truth was beyond dispute. There is where I encountered the
dilemma of Egypt and Africa, in general. I had to deal with the white images in the Sunday School lessons, and the fact that nobody in these
lessons looked like my people.

I looked for the name "Negro," and could not find it. I did not know,
at that time, that there is no such thing as a "Negro", ethnically speaking. My curiosity was intensified when I read an essay called, "The Negro
Digs Up His Past," by a Puerto Rican writer of African descent with a
German sounding name, Arthur A. Schomburg.[7] I met Arthur Schomburg toward the end of my first year in New York City. He taught me how
to understand African history, by understanding world history. I was a
young depression radical trying to decide between Socialism and Nationalism. Today I consider myself to be an African World Nationalist,
a Pan-Africanist and a Socialist, and I see no contradiction in being all
three, simultaneously.

Now back to history: I became active in the History Club of the Harlem
branch of the Y.M.C.A. that later became the Blyden Society. The teacher
was Willis N. Huggins, a teacher of history in the High School System of
New York City. His outstanding prodigy was John G. Jackson, who had
already written a number of pamphlets on little known aspects of African
history and had collaborated with Willis N. Huggins in the writing of two
books whose contents came out of the lectures delivered before the
Harlem History Club and the Blyden Society. The two books were: *A Guide
to Studies in African History* and *An Introduction To African Civilization.*

These books opened a door to the broader dimensions of African
history and had introduced me to a body of literature I had not previously known.

The Italian-Ethiopian War reinforced our interest in African history and
made us reconsider the teachings of Marcus Garvey.[8] The untimely

death of Willis N. Huggins and the atmosphere on the eve of the World War II brought an end to the African History Clubs. My personal interest continued in my relationships with John G. Jackson, J.A. Rogers, and occasionally with William Leo Hansberry, when he came to New York City in lectures. The men that I have mentioned here were my intellectual fathers and teachers. In my journey to this conference, a journey that started over fifty years ago, these teachers have been with me as I search for the true meaning of the role of African people in World History.

Because this search has been a mission, the mission my existence, I have a tendency to gravitate towards other people who have a similar mission. In the early sixties, when I was Director of the Heritage teaching Program of an Anti-Poverty Program in Harlem, where we both still live, I invited Dr. Yosef ben-Jochannan to give a lecture to one of the young groups that I supervised. We have been friends, colleagues, and supporters of each other in this mission for more than twenty years.

In the field of Ancient African History, I lean very heavily on his works, especially his books, *Black Man of The Nile, African Origins of Major Western Religions, Africa: Mother of Western Civilizations,* and his latest book, *We The Black Jews.* The contents of this book alone could be the basis of a conference.

I would like to begin my conclusion with a reference to the works of Cheikh Anta Diop, for he is one of the most able of present day scholars writing about Africa. He is also one of the greatest living Black Historians. His first major work, *"Nations Negres et Culture"* is still disturbing the white historians who have made quick reputations as authorities on African history and culture.[9] In this book Dr. Diop shows the interrelationships between African nations, north and south, and proves, because in this case proof is needed again and again, that ancient Egypt was a distinct African nation and was not historically or culturally a part of Asia or Europe. More myths about Africa are put to rest in another one of his books, *The Cultural Unity of Negro Africa.*[10] The publication of his first book in the United States, *The African Origin of Civilization, Myth Or Reality,* is a cause for celebration.[11] This book and others of recent years, all by Black writers, have called for a total reconsideration of the role that African people have played in history and their impact on the development of early societies and institutions.

Cheikh Anta Diop was born in the town of Diourbel, in Senegal, on the west coast of Africa in 1923. His birthplace has a long tradition of producing Muslim scholars and oral historians. This is where his inspiration and interest in history, the humanities and social sciences from an African point of view began. After the publication of his first book *Nations Negres et Culture,* that had been rejected as a Ph.D. thesis at the Sorbonne in Paris, he became one of the most controversial of present day African historians. *Nations Negres et Culture* is both a reassessment of the African past and a challenge to Western scholarship on Africa. He refutes the myth of Egypt as a white nation and shows its southern

African origins. It is his intention to prove that, through Egyptian civilization, Africa has made the oldest and one of the most significant contributions to world culture. This is not a new argument that started with Cheikh
Anta Diop's generation of Africans. The Ghanaian historian, Joseph B.
Danquah, in his introduction to the book, *United West Africa At The Bar
of the Family Of Nations,* by Ladipo Solanke, published in 1927, three years
after Cheikh anta Diop was born, said exactly the same thing. His statement reads:

> "By the time Alexander the Great was sweeping the civiliz-
> ed world with conquest after conquest from Chaeronia to
> Gaza, from Babylon to Cabul; by the time the first Aryan con-
> querors were learning the rudiments of war and government
> at the feet of the philosopher Aristotle; and by the time Athens
> was laying down the foundations of European civilization, the
> earliest and greatest Ethiopian culture had already flourish-
> ed and dominated the civilized world for over four centuries
> and a half. Imperial Ethiopia had conquered Egypt and found-
> ed the XXVth Dynasty, and for a century and a half the cen-
> tral seat of civilization in the known world was held by the
> ancestors of the modern Negro, maintaining and defending
> it against the Assyrian and Persian Empires of the East."
> "This at the time when Ethiopia was leading the civilized world
> in culture and conquest. East was East, but West was not,
> and the first European (Grecian) Olympiad was yet to be held.
> Rome was nowhere to be seen on the map, and sixteen cen-
> turies were to pass before Charlemagne would rule in Europe
> and Egbert become first king of England. Even the, history
> was to drag on for another seven hundred weary years, before
> Roman Catholic Europe could see fit to end the Great Schism,
> soon to be followed by the disturbing news of the discovery
> of America and the fateful rebirth of the youngest of world
> civlizations."[12]

Here Dr. Danquah is showing that African history is the foundation
of world history. In the present book by Cheikh Anta Diop, and in most
of his other works, his objective is the same, in his first major work on
history, Dr. Diop has said:

> "The greatest problem confronting African history is this: how
> to reorganize effectively, through meaningful research, all of
> the fragments of the past into a single ancient epoch, a com-
> mon orign which will re-establish African continuity . . . if the
> ancients were not victims of the mirage, it should be easy
> enough to draw upon another series of arguments and pro-
> ofs for the union of the history of Ethiopia and Egyptian

societies with the rest of Africa. Thus combined, these histories would lend to a properly patterned past in which it would be seen that (ancient) Ghana rose in the interior (West Africa) of the continent at the moment of Egyptian decline, just as the Western European empires were born with the decline of Rome."

While using Africa as the vantage point and the basis for his thesis Dr. Diop does not neglect the broader dimensions of history. He shows that history cannot be restricted by the limits of ethnic group, nation, or culture. Roman history is Greek as well as Roman, and both the Greek and the Roman history are Egyptian because the entire Mediterranean was civilized by Egypt; and Egypt in turn borrowed from other parts of Africa, especially Ethiopia.

Africa came into the Mediterranean world, mainly, through Greece, which had been under African influence. The first Greek invasion of Africa was peaceful and scholarly. This invasion brought in Herodotus. Egypt had lost its independence over a century before his visit. This was the beginning of the period of foreign domination over Egypt that would last, in different form, for two thousand years.

The African Origin Of Civilization, Myth Or Reality is a one-volume translation of the major sections of the first and last of the books by Cheikh Anta Diop, i.e., Nations, Negres et Culture and Anteriorite Des Civilizations Negres. These two works have challenged and changed the direction of attitudes about the place of African people in history in scholarly circles around the world. It was largely due to these works that Cheikh Anta Diop, with W.E.B. DuBois, was honored as "the writer who had exerted the greatest influence on African People in the 20th Century," at the World Festival of Arts held in Dakar, Senegal, in 1966.

The main thesis of the present work is a redefinition of the place of Egypt in African history in particular and in world history in general. Dr. Diop calls attention to the historical, archeological, and anthropological evidence that supports his thesis. The civilization of Egypt, he maintains is African in origin and in early development. In his book Dr. Diop says:

"the history of Africa will remain suspended in air and cannot be written correctly until African historians connect it with the history of Egypt."

Dr. Diop approaches the history of Africa frontally, head on with explanations, but no apologies. In locating Egypt on the map of human geography he asks and answers the questions: who were the Egyptians of the ancient World?

The Ethiopians say that the Egyptians were one of their colonies which was brought into Egypt by the deity Osiris. The Greek writer Herodotus repeatedly referred to the Egyptians as being dard-skinned people with woolly hair. "They" he says, "have the same tint of skin which approaches that of the Ethiopians." The opinion of the ancient writers on the Egyptians is more or less summed up by Gaston Maspero (1846-1916), when he says, "By the almost unanimous testimony of ancient historians, they, (the Egyptians), belong to an African race which first settled in Ethiopia on the Middle Nile following the course of the river they gradually reached the seas."

"The Greek writer, Herodotus, may be mistaken," Cheikh Anta Diop tells us "when he reports the customs of a people, but one must grant that he was at least capable of recognizing the skin color of the inhabitants of countries he visited." His descriptions of the Egyptians were the descriptions of a Black people. At this point the reader needs to be reminded of the fact that at the time of Herodotus's visit to Egypt and other parts of Africa (between 480 and 425 B.C.) Egypt's Golden Age was over. Egypt has suffered from several invasions, mainly the Kushite invasions, coming from within Africa and starting in 751 B.C., and the Assyrians' invasions from Western Asia, (called the Middle East), starting in 671 B.C. If Egypt, after years of invasions by other people and nations was a distinct Black African nation at the time of Hereodotus, shouldn't we at least assume that it was more so before these invasions occurred?

If Egypt is a dilemma in Western historiography, it is a created dilemma. The Western historians, in most cases, have rested the foundation of what is called "Western Civilization" on the false assumptions, or claim, that the ancient Egyptians were white people. To do this they had to ignore great masterpieces on Egyptian history written by other white historians who did not support this point of view, such as Gerald Massey's great classic, *Ancient Egypt, The Light of the World* (1907), and his other works, *A Book Of The Beginnings*, and *The Natural Genesis*. Other neglected works by white writers are *Politics, Intercourse, And Trade Of The Carthaginians, Ethiopians, and Egyptians*, by A.H.L. Heeren (1833), and *Ruins Of Empires*, by Count Volney (1787).

In the first chapter of his book, Dr. Diop refers to the Southern African origins of the people later known as Egyptians. Here he is on sound ground with a lot of support coming from another group of neglected white writers. In his book, *Egypt*, sir E.A. Wallis Budge says: "The prehistoric native of Egypt, both in the old and in the new Stone Ages, was African and there is every reason for saying that the earliest settlers came from the South." He further states: "There are many things in the manners and customs and religions of the historic Egyptians that suggests that the original home of their prehistoric ancestors was in a country in the neighbourhood of Uganda and Punt." (Some historians believe that the Biblical land of Punt was in the area known on modern maps as Somalia.)

European interest in Ethiopia and the Origin of civilization dates from the early part of the 19th century and is best reflected in a little known, though important paper, i.e.'Karl Richard Lepsius.' "Incomparable Survey

of The Momumental Ruins in The Ethiopian Nile Valley in 1843-1844."
The records found by Lepsius tend to show how Ethiopia was once
able to sustain an ancient population that was numerous and powerful
enough not only to challenge, but on a number of occasions to conquer
completely the populous land of Egypt. Further, these records showed
that the antiquity of Ethiopian civilization had a direct link with civilization of ancient Egypt.

Many of the leading antiquarians of the time, based largely on the
strength of what the classical author, particularly Diodorus Siculus and
Stephanus of Byzantium had to say on the matter were exponents of the
view that the ancient Ethiopians or at any rate, the Black people of remote
antiquity were the earliest of all civilized peoples and that the first civilized inhabitants of ancient Egypt were members of what is referred to as
the Black race who entered the country as emigrants from Ethiopia. A
number of Europe's leading writers are Bruce, Count Volney, Fabre,
d'Olivet, and Heeren. In spite of the fact that these writers defended this
thesis with all the learning at their command, and documented their
defense, most of the present-day writers of African history continue to
ignore their findings.

In 1825, German backwardness in this respect came definitely to an
end. In that year, Arnold Hermann Heeren (1760-1842). Professor of
History and Politics in the University of Gottingen and one of the ablest
of the early exponents of the economic interpretation of history, published, in the fourth and revised edition of his great work *Ideen Uber Die Politik,
Den Verkehr Und Den Handel Der Vornehmsten Volker Der Alten Weld,*
a lengthy essay on the history, culture, and commerce of the ancient Ethiopians, which had profound influence on contemporary writers in the conclusion that it was among these ancient Black people of Africa and Asia
that international trade was first developed, and he thinks that as a by-
product of these international contacts there was an exchange of ideas
and cultural practices that laid the foundation of the earliest civilizations
of the ancient world.

The French writer Count C.F. Volney, in his important work, The *Ruins
of Empires,* extends this point of view by saying that, the Egyptians were
the first people to "attain the physical and moral sciences necessary to
civilized life."[13] In referring to the basis of this achievement he states
further that, "it was, then, on the borders of the Upper Nile, among a
Black race of men, that was organized the complicated system of worship of the stars, considered in relation to the productions of the earth
and the labors of agriculture under their own forms and national attributes,
was a simple proceeding of the human mind."

Over a generation ago African-American historians such as: Carter
G. Woodson, W.E.B. DuBois, Willis N. Huggins, J.A. Rogers, and Charles
C. Seifort read the works of these radical writer historians and began to
expand on their findings. This tradition continued and is reflected in the
works of present-day Black historians such as: John G. Jackson' *Introduc-*

*tion to African Civilizations,*1970, Yosef ben-Jochannans' *Black Man of The Nile,* 1972, and Chancellor Williams' *The Destruction of Black Civilizations: Great Issues Of A Race from 4500 B.C. to 2000 A.D.,* 1971.

Until the publication of James G. Spadys' article "Negritude, Pan-Benegritude And The Diopian Philosophy of African History," in *A Current Bibliography on African Affairs,* volume 5, number I, January, 1972, and the recent interview by Harun Kofi Wangara, published in Black World Magazine, February, 1974, Dr. Cheikh anta Diop was known to only a small group of Black writers and teachers in the United States. For over seven years his books were offered to American Publishers with no show of interest. Now, two of his books will be published in the United States within one year. The Third World Press, in Chicago, is preparing to publish his book *The Cultural Unity of Negro Africa.* All of his books were originally published by Presence Africaine, the Paris based publication arm of The International Society of African Culture.

Egyptology develped in concurrence with the development of the slave trade and the colonial system. It was during this period that Egypt was literally taken out of Africa, academically, and made an extension of Europe. In many ways Egypt is the key to ancient African history. African history is out of kilter until ancient Egypt is looked upon as a distinct African nation.

The Nile river played a major role in the relationship of Egypt to the nations of Southeast Africa. During the early history of Africa, the Nile was a great cultural highway on which elements of civilization came into and out inner Africa. Egypt's relationship with the people in the south was both good and bad, depending on the period and the dynasty in power.

In his chapter called, "What were the Egyptians?", Dr. Diop explains the rise and fall of Egypt's Golden Age and the beginnings of the invasions, first from Western Asia, that turned this nation's first age of greatness into a nightmare. This was the period of the Hyksos, or Shepherd Kings. During this time seventy Jews, grouped into twelve patriarchal families, nomads without industry or culture, entered Egypt. These Jews left Egypt four hundred years later, 600,000 strong, after acquiring from African people all of the elements of their future religion, tradition, and culture, including monotheism. Whosoever the Jews were when they entered Africa, when they left, four hundred years later, they were ethnically, culturally, and religiously an African people. In this part of his book, Cheikh Anta Diop leaves no room for argument.

In the chapter called, "Birth of the Negro Myth," Dr. Diop shows how African people, whose civilizations were old before Europe was born, were systematically read out of the respectful commentary of human history. This examination is continued in the chapter called, "Modern Falsification of History," Here, Cheikh anta Diop deals with how Western historians, for the last five hundred years, wrote or rewrote history glorifying the people of European extraction and distorted the history of the rest of the world. Those who read this book seriously are in for a shock and a rewarding experience in learning.

CONCLUSION

It is our responsibility to redefine African History and to restore it to its proper place in World History. To start this task , we should begin by redefining it to ourselves.

I would like to conclude with my most often quoted belief:

"History is the Clock that people use to tell their time of Day;
It is the compass they can use to find themselves On the map of Human Geography."

It is the role of history to tell a people where they have been, What they have been, where they are and what they are, but most importantly it is the role of history to tell a people *where* they still must go and *what* they still must be.

NOTES

1. Bruce Williams, "The Lost Pharaohs of Nubia", *Archaeology* (September-October, 1980); Henri Labaret, *Africa Before the WhiteMan* New York: Walker & Co., pp. 3-43.
2. Chancellor Williams, *The Destruction of Black Civilization,* Chicago: Third World Press, 1976, pp.64-100.
3. John G. Jackson, *Introduction to African Civilizations,* Secaucus, NJ· Citadel Press, 1980, pp. 60-92.
4. Dr. W.E.B. DuBois wrote three books with the main focus on Africa: *The Negro,* New York: Harry Holt & Co., 1915, reprinted by Oxford University Press, 1970; *Black Folks Then and Now,* New York: Harry Holt & Co., 1939; *The World and Africa,* New York: Viking Press, 1968.
5. Carter G. Woodson, *The African Backgound Outlined,* Washington, D.C.: Association for the Study of Negro Life and History, 1936.
6. While Professor Hansberry's articles and conference papers appeared in journals throughout the world, his only two books that were published were: *Africa & Africans As Seen by Classical Writers,* Washington, D.C.: Howard University press, 1977 and *Pillars in Ethiopian History,* Washington, D.C.: Howard University Press, 1974.
7. Arthur Schomberg, "The Negro Digs Up His Past."
8. Marcus Garvey, *Philosophy and Opinions,* New York: Atheneum, 1977. Also see J.A. Rogers, *The Real Facts About Ethiopia,* London: The African publication Society.
9. Cheikh Anta Diop, *Nations Negres et Culture,* Paris: Editions Africaines, 1954
10. _____. *The Cultural Unity of Black Africa,* Chicago: Third World Press, 1978.

11. _____. *African Origin of Civilization: Myth or Reality,* Westport, CN: Lawrence Hill & co., 1974.
12. Ladipa Solanke, *United West Africa (or Africa) at the Bar of the Family Nations,* London: African Publications Society, 1969.
13. C.F. Volney, *The Ruins of Meditation on Revolutions of Empires and the Law of Nature,* New York: Peter Eckler, 1890.

THE FIRST AND SECOND INTERMEDIATE PERIODS IN KEMETIC HISTORY

A. JOSEPH BEN-LEVI

INTRODUCTION

The First and Second Intermediate Periods in Kemetic history are the most baffling equations confronting the African historian whose primary interest is Kemet. Of the two periods it is the first which provides the least information and which is the least understood. If African historians are to reclaim the glory of ancient Kemet and restore its prominence, the perplexing issues surrounding the First and Second Intermediate periods need to be given careful examination.

Consequently, I have taken up the challenge to explore those areas of interest in order to contribute to the deluge of truth which must ultimately lead to the liberation of the African past. It is my intention to share with you data on the conditions around which the First and Second Intermediate Periods developed, the ethnic composition of the populations whom disrupted the continuity of Kemet at those times, and look at the Habiru, Hebrew, Apiru, SA. GAZ issue as it relates to the Second Intermediate Period.

I. The First Intermediate Period (2300-2065 B.C.)

The First Intermediate Period was called such by European egyptologists because it stands intermediate between the Old and Middle Kingdoms. In order to appraise the significance of the First Intermediate Period it will be necessary to touch upon some of the historical circumstances which led to the collapse of the Old Kingdom which preceded it. As a point of departure I will commence with some of the events in the Fifth Dynasty (2563-2423 B.C.) or the Late Old Kingdom.

II. The Late Old Kingdom

During this period nomarchs, rulers of various districts or nomes, began to assert themselves against the throne to such an extent that a Prime Minister from Upper Kemet had to be appointed in the second half of the dynasty. His major function seems to have been the reestablishment of Maat or right order and justice[1]. But the throne further seems to have contributed to its own downfall by making generous grants of land and money to the priesthood and nobility.

The Fifth Dynasty rulers also increased their foreign campaigns on a

55

larger scale at this time, seeds of which shall appear later. In particular, Sahurah conducted major operations against the Asiatics in the form of sieges and pitched battles[2]. During the Sixth Dynasty (2423-2300 B.C.) the military campaigns became even more extensive. Lengthy concentrations of troops in Upper Kemet for the purpose of assaults in Nubia rendered Lower Kemet, her defenses neglected, a tempting prey for the tribesmen of the Eastern desert who eventually overran the Delta[3]. With the King spending much of his time in Memphis, the balance of power shifted more in favor of the rulers of Upper Kemet. While they preoccupied themselves with their own affairs, Lower Kemet fell victim to the Asiatics[4].

However, there were some bright spots in the Sixth Dynasty under Pepi I and Pepi II. Pepi I ruled for over half a century. His troops not only made the customary forays to mines and quarries but penetrated as far as Palestine. The general on this occasion was Weni. Weni was sent on five campaigns against the various desert tribesmen in Palestine. Pepi I also was a builder of temples at Bubastis, Tanis, Dendera, Koptos, and Abydos. He married the two daughters of a leading citizen of Abydos, the birthplace of Osiris. The elder bore him Mer-n-Ra and the younger Pepi II[5].

Pepi II's reign was the longest in Kemetic history, stretching over one hundred years. The first half of his reign was prosperous and uneventful, but once he began to grow old and senile the final wings of conflict began hovering over the Old Kingdom. The populus began to take advantage of his senility and the nomarchs pushed for control by demanding social reforms which were easily granted. This decrepit King gave way to the priesthood and the nomarchs who were demanding additional land and privileges. The priests were also demanding tax-free gifts of land which was practically given away by Pepi II[6].

It is also possible that the economic structure of the Old Kingdom had been undermined by excessive architectural activity from the Fourth Dynasty onward. Only the nomarchs of Upper Kemet showed steadfast restraint in dealing with one another in the face of growing popular agitation. They were able to hold firm when the invaders flooded into Lower Kemet at about the time the populus was breaking out in open rebellion. The Delta and Middle Kemet were plunged into chaos. Their nobles were dispossessed, a reign of terror commenced, palaces and temples were destroyed. For nearly 300 years, from the closing years of Pepi II to the foundation of the Middle Kingdom, anarchy ruled in Kemet[7].

It's difficult to understand the tumultuous times facing Kemet at this period without the account of an eyewitness. We are provided with such a witness in the text called *the Admonition of Ipuwer* who provides a vivid account of these circumstances when he wrote:

> "A man regards his son as his enemy . . . the tribes of the desert
> have become Kemites everywhere . . . what the ancestors foretold
> has arrived at fruition . . . the land is full of confederates, and a man

goes out to plough with his shield . . . Indeed, hearts are violent, pestilence is everywhere, blood is throughout the land, death is not lacking, and the mummy-cloth speaks even before one comes near it. Indeed, the land turns round like a potter's-wheel; the robber is a possessor of riches and the rich man has become a plunderer . . . barbarians from abroad have come to Kemet. Those who were Kemites have become foreigners and are thrust aside . . . and the man of rank can no longer be distinguished from him who is nobody . . . All is ruined."[8]

This is just a glimpse at the horror which befell the Old Kingdom. However, we have yet to diagnose the forces behind the Delta invasion who established themselves as a viable entity during the First Intermediate Period. In order to solve this equation we must look at the forces in Asia which could serve as a link in this fractured chain of events.

III. The Storm Over Asia

During the same period in which the Old Kingdom was at its lowest ebb, similar events were taking place or had taken place in other parts of the ancient east such as Mesopotamia, Syria and Palestine. These are the areas Dr. Diop describes as the *"Zone of Confluence"* in his *"Two Cradles Theory"*[9]. Interestingly enough, these centers of high culture were also going through what may be called their First Intermediate Period.

During this period, about 2300 B.C., there was a widespread decline in the level of civilization. Mesopotamia had fallen into anarchy and general decadence. The Akkadians under Shar-Kali-Sharri, son of Naram-Sin (2270-2233 B.C.), third ruler of the Sargonid Dynasty, were overcome by divine retribution, according to the literature, because of a sacrilege against the holy city of Nippur and its god Enlil (god of wind and rain). As a result Enlil, it is written:

"Would not allow the herald to proceed on his journey, the sea-rider could not sail his boat . . . Robbers dwelt on the road; the doors of the gates of the land turned into clay . . . the great fields and meadows produced no grain; the fisheries no fish; the water garden neither honey nor wine, because his beloved house had been attacked. What destruction wrought, and brought down upon Akkad a people which brokes no control."[10]

These "people which brokes no control" were an Aryan horde called the Guti or Gutians. The Gutians were Caucasian tribesmen from the Zargos Mountains and related to another group of Zargos tribesmen known as the Kassites. These mountain folks overran the Kingdom of Akkad and extended their foreign rule over Mesopotamia from about 2190-2100 B.C.[11]

The Guttians were finally expelled from Mesopotamia by a resurgence of the Black Sumerians in 2100 B.C. The Sumerian ruler Ur-Nammu

(2070-1960 B.C.) reestablished the third Ur Dynasty and wrote the final chapter of Sumerian history[12]. This Ur Dynasty lasted all of the twenty-first century B.C. and was finally overrun by the Amorites.

In Palestine and Syria about 2200 B.C. there was also an abrupt halt in the development of civilization among the Black Canaanites. The cause of this disruption can be linked to the Amorites[13] This name first appears during the latter half of the 3rd millennium B.C. Sumerian and Akkadian inscriptions refer to the Amorites (Sumerian-Mar-tu, Akkadian-Amurru) as a desert people unacquainted with civilized life, grain, houses, cities or government. This name first appears in the Old Testament in Genesis 15:16 and even then it just pops up out of nowhere. About 2000 B.C. these people, who had been infiltrating for centuries, moved into Babylon in force. The general unrest of the years 2100-1800 B.C. was closely connected with increased Amorite movement. The break in occupation of several cities in Palestine between the Early and Middle Bronze Age was caused by an influx of nomadic folk who left many graves behind them, but little traces of buildings. It is in all probability they who destroyed the ancient Kingdom of Ebla in Syria while on their way toward Palestine and eventually Kemet[14]. It is this horde of barbarians who serve as the primer candidates for those invaders which profited from the destruction of the Old Kingdom.

These contentions add support to Dr. Diop's position that there exists nothing comparable to a Semitic type. The Semitic world was born in proto-historic times, not of a biological mutation but of a crossbred issue from the confluence of Blacks and whites in Western Asia[15]. Dr. Diop further points out that archaeological facts confirmed by abundant testimonies in the so-called Semitic literature (Biblical Hebrew, Arabic, Aramaic, etc.) attest to the fact that all the actual habitats of the Semites were occupied originally, from pre-historic to the threshold of the historic epoch by Blacks who were not transients, but mixed with a white element that came from elsewhere[16].

Therefore, the invasion of the Gutians and Amorites provide us with a possible answer for what appears to have been the first white invasions upon indigenous Black civilizations of the so-called Ancient Near East and particularly Black civilizations of the so-called Ancient Near East and particularly upon Kemet to institute the First Intermediate Period. This period included the Seventh through the Eleventh Dynasties (2242-2065 B.C.). According to Manetho during the Seventh Dynasty seventy (70) kings supposedly ruled in seventy days. The Memphite succession was maintained down to about 2422 B.C. or the Eighth Dynasty, which had nominal control over Lower Kemet. Later Kheti I acquired the throne of Lower Kemet and founded the Ninth Dynasty (2242-2150 B.C.)[17].

It was almost a century before the Upper Kemites found a deliverer in Intef I, founder of the Eleventh Dynasty. At the same time there was a dynasty in Lower Kemet, the Tenth (2150-2060 B.C.) which was really an extension of the Ninth with the accession of Kheti II. Intef I and his two namesakes following him were the first to adopt the title King of Upper and Lower Kemet. After a century of run-ins the fifth ruler of the Thebans, Menthuhotep (2065-2062 B.C.) began to set the affairs of state in order. He reunited Kemet ending an era of internal strife through the establishment of the Middle Kingdom (2065-1785 B.C.)[18].

IV. The Second Intermediate Period (1785-1580 B.C.)

The cursory look at the Old Kingdom and its decline only served as a vehicle for shedding light on the First Intermediate Period. The accomplishments of the Middle Kingdom and its rulers is well documented. However, the Second Intermediate Period has provoked as many if not more questions than the First Intermediate Period. The one phenomena which stands firm is the Hyksos invasion. The problem is that very little is known about the origin of the Hyksos and how it was possible for them to control Kemet without a struggle.

Therefore, in this section it is my intention to 1) take a fresh look at the Apiru, Habiru, Hebrew , SA. GAZ. issue as it relates to the Hyksos presence in Kemet, 2) whether the Hyksos were the ancient Israelites of the Old Testament, 3) the ethnic origin of the Hyksos and 4) shed light on evidence that elements of the Hyksos exited in Kemet as early as the Twelfth Dynasty.

V. A Call for Clarification

Much has been written by European sages about the Hebrews though less about the Habiru, Apiru and SA. GAZ. But before addressing the issues surrounding the Hyksos invasion these terms must be clarified.

The word Hebrew has been associated with words like "Habiru", "Apiru" and "SA. GAZ". These are terms first found by egyptologists in the *Tell-El-Amarna Correspondence* between the pharaohs of the so-called Eighteenth Dynasty and the rulers of Asia [19]. Tell-El-Amarna is about 200 miles up the Nile from Cairo. It was the capital of Akenaton which he called Akhet-Aton (the Horizon of Aton). The term Habiru has been used by some scholars to explain the Hebrew presence in Kemet written in the Book of Exodus (Shemot) in the Old Testament. It is further believed possible, if not probable, that the Hebrews were the Hyksos invaders of Kemet during the Second Intermediate Period. However, I want to shed some light of my own upon this subject.

The terms Habiru and Apiru are found in two types of inscriptions, those from the Mesopotamian region of the Tigris and Euphrates River and those from the Nile Valley. The Mesopotamian inscriptions are nine (9) in total: 1) Records from Ur and Larsa at the end of the 20th century B.C., 2) From Alisar in Turkey, 3) The letters of Hammurapi of the late 18th century B.C., 4) Letters of Hammurapi from the Kingdom of Mari on the Upper Euphrates, 5) Akkadian texts of the Hurrian city of Nuzi (15th century B.C.), 6) Hittite texts from Boghaz-Koi in Turkey (14th and 15th century B.C.), 7) Hittite texts of the romance of Naram-Sin, 8) Text from the time of Ninurta-Tukul-Assur, King of Assyria (12th century B.C.), and Babylonian text of the 11th century B.C.[20].

In some of these documents SA. GAZ. seems to interchange with Habiru but it does not necessarily follow that SA. GAZ. in every instance is to be interpreted as Habiru. The term Habiru appears in the Kemetic text as Apiru. These occurrences are seven in all: 1) The Memphite Stela of Amenophis II (15th century B.C.), 2) The stela of Seti (14th century B.C.), 3) The so-called "Harris Papyrus" from the time of Seti I, 4) The Leyden Papyrus from the time of Ramesses I, (13th century B.C.), 5) The Leyden Papyrus from the time of Ramesses II (12th century B.C.), 6) The Great Harris Papyrus from the time of Ramesses III (12th century B.C.), and 7) The Wadi Hammamat inscriptions of the time of Ramesses IV.[21].

The words "Apiru" and "Habiru" weren't originally terms which identified any particular nation or race. They represented a confluence of nationalities both African and Aryan with the Aryans having a tendency to dominate at certain periods.[22]. At no time is there any indication from these texts that the Habiru and Apiru and Hebrews are one and the same term linguistically. For the sake of clarity I would like to illuminate this discussion based on my knowledge of the so-called Hebrew language.

The term "Hebrew" is supposed to have derived from the mythical name Eber, one of the sons of Shem in Genesis 10:21, the so-called father of the Shemitic peoples. But in reality, Hebrew comes from a three letter root I-B-R (ﻉﻭﻕ) in the ancient Canaanite language. It is a verb which means "to pass" or "to crossover", as in pass by a window or cross a street and synonymous phrases. The term Hebrew (H-E-B-R-E-W) is a Greco-Roman misrepresentation. The Old Testament first records this word in Genesis 14:13, as a slang term used by the ancient Black Canaanites of Palestine to identify Abraham calling him "Ha-Ibri" or "The one who crossed over", that is, the one who crossed over the Euphrates River to journey in the Land of the Canaanites or Canaan. At no time, in the Old Testament literature, does it mean anything else.

In fact there is no mention of a Hebrew King or Kingdom of the Hebrews in the Old Testament. Such terms come from a much later period.[23]. The term Habiru means something like "plunderers" and "nomads" of which the so-called Hebrews were neither contrary to popular opinion. It is therefore grammatically impossible, except figuratively, to represent the term Hebrew. It appears to have been used in an attempt by European theologians, Biblical scholars and egyptologists to find something, anything that would support the notion of a white Hebrew migration into a white Kemet.

VI. The Hyksos Question and the Israelites in Kemet

An overwhelming number of western scholars seek to link the ancient Israelites with the Hyksos who invaded Kemet and ruled for about 200 years during the Second Intermediate Period. Agreement among western scholars on the supposed white or Asian origin of the Hyksos does not mean that the ancient Israelites were so. The presence of the infamous Hyksos in ancient Kemetic history has proven to be a most convenient tool in the hands of Eurocentrics who were and still are bent on white-washing the true history of the African people.

There are basically two ethnological hypotheses upon which the Hyksos-Israelite assumptions are made. The first comes from Flavius Josephus, which was, and still is, defended up to the present day by egyptologists and historians. The second hypothesis is suggested by the ancient Greek geographer Strabo and supported by the so-called father of psycho-analysis Sigmund Freud.[24].

Josephus was a scribe of the Pharisees who led a revolt against the Romans in Galilee. Rather than be put to death by the Roman general Titus Flavius Vespasian for his actions, he found favour in Vespasian's eyes. Josephus had predicted that Vespasian would soon become Emperor of Rome. Just as he predicted, Nero committed suicide and Vespasian became Emperor of Rome about 68 A.D.[25] When this happened, Josephus was granted Roman citizenship and his name was changed from Josef Ben Mattitiyahu to Flavius Josephus. It was at that time he began writing his *Complete Works* which was a history of the Hebrew peoples, and his dissertation against the Roman philosopher Apion who questioned the antiquity of the Hebrews.[26]. Josephus, with the support of the egyptologists, suggested strongly that the Hebrew presence in the Old Testament story of Josef are to be identified with the Hyksos. Hence, according to the European sages, the Exodus of the Children of Israel from Kemet would be contemporary with the driving out of the Hyksos under Kamose the Theban.[27].

This is illustrated by Josephus in his "*Contra Apion*" or Against Apion. After explaining how the Hyksos supposedly came into Kemet, he goes on to say:

> "But that Thummosis the son of Alisphragmothosis, made an attempt to take them by force and by siege, with four hundred and eighty thousand men to lie round about them; but that, upon his despair in taking the city by that siege, they came to a composition with them, that they should leave Kemet, and go without any harm to be done to them, whithersoever they would; and that they went away with their whole families and effects, not fewer than two hundred and forty thousand, and took their journey from Kemet, through the wilderness of Syria; but that as they were in fear of the Assyrians, who had then the dominion over Asia, they built a city in that country which is now called Judea, and that large enough to contain this great number of

men, and called it Jerusalem."[28]

In the second instance according to Strabo, Moses and the leaders of the Hebrews were not Hebrews at all but high ranking Kemite priests who broke away from the belief system of that time. This concept would in turn lend support to the notion that the ancient Israelites were Kemites and consequently an African people.

Anyway, Moses was supposed to have been a governor of the Osirian nomes or districts who became dissatisfied with the beliefs of the time and departed Kemet taking those who supported his views along with him. He was alleged to have taught against the concept of depicting animals as deities. For him there was only one Divine Power and he wanted to go somewhere and build a temple where no image of a Divinity could be seen. *Sherabit-Al-Kadem* in the Sinai desert may have been an early attempt at one of these temples.

In Josephus' case his assumptions are a gross error and if he is quoting from the second book of Manetho's history, as he claims he is, then Manetho too is to be questioned. For example, he says, according to Manetho, there were 240,000 people who left Kemet during the exodus. The Old Testament records 603,550 men, not counting women and children.[28] He further says that they journeyed in the wilderness of Syria. This too is an error. The journey of the Children of Israel took place in the Sinai peninsula which belonged to Kemet about 200 miles south of Syria. He also mentions the Assyrians didn't become a nation until the time of Nabu-Mukin-Zeri (731-729 B.C.) and his son Tiglath-Pileser III (728-727 B.C.), in other words, about 1,000 years after the Hyksos.[29] He then says that these same people built the city of Jerusalem. Again he is in error. The original inhabitants of Jerusalem were a Black Canaanite people called the Jebusites. They built the city and corresponded with the Pharaohs of the so-called 18th Dynasty as is attested in the *Tell-El-Amarna letters* from this period. Hence, Jerusalem was the name of that city long before the Israelites came to live in it.[30] Perhaps Josephus' motives and frame of reference must be questioned in this instance, seeing that he was a priest and scribe of the Pharisees and had access to the proper information.

In the case of Strabo and Freud who supports his views the issue is different. Freud argues that not only the priestly clan of the Levites but also their belief in monotheism were of direct Kemite origin. Supposedly this derives from the Sun Divinity Aton of the time of Akhenaton. After leaving Kemet, Moses was to have blessed his followers with the Kemite rite of circumcision, already an ancient custom in Kemet, giving them laws such as the Ten Sayings or Commandments, and giving them the Aton belief system of Akhenaton which was rejected by the priest of Amon at Thebes.[31] Freud's argument, though refutable in some aspects, has many strong qualities to it. Suffice to say, however, that what is good about his position is that he, as a European Jew, is admitting that the ancient Israelites were not whites related to Europeans but Blacks related to Kemet.

There are some sidelights to this Hyksos-Israelite issue. One of the most obvious is the fact that the name Apophis, ruler of the Hyksos cannot be found in the annals of the Israelite kings. Even more intriguing is the fact that there is virtually no trace of the Israelites presence in ancient Kemetic records outside the so-called "*Israel Stela*" of Pharaoh Meruptah, son of Ramesses II (19th Dynasty).[32] In it Israel is mentioned as one of the conquered nations of Kemet and at no time is Israel connected with residence in Kemet. The name Israel as reflected in the "Israel Stela" does not make them appear to be a fleeing nation. It does, however, imply that Kemet was aware of their presence in the ancient world.

Furthermore, if we calculate the time that the Hyksos ruled Kemet, about 200 years, according to the egyptologists, and subtract the time of their expulsion in about 1580 B.C. from the time of Meruptah's death about 1214 B.C. there is about a 400 year difference. The Old Testament scribes wrote that work on the temple which Solomon had built in Jerusalem began in the 480th year after the Children of Israel had come out of Kemet, in the fourth year of Solomon's reign right after the Spring equinox which opens the Hebrew year. If Solomon began to reign about 968 B.C. by adding 480 years to that figure we arrive at 1448 B.C. which would put the so-called exodus in the reign of Thutmose III or Amenhotep II of the Eighteenth Dynasty or about 220 years before Meruptah and 130 years after the Hyksos.[33]

Consequently, if the Hyksos were not the so-called Hebrews, who were they?

VII. The Ethnic Origin of the Hyksos

The ethnic origin of the Hyksos remains the most controversial aspect of the Hyksos problem. The choices have narrowed down to 1) a group of Aryans from Southern Russia who later became the Hurrians of Asia Minor, 2) a so-called Semitic people such as the Hebrews or Israelites of the Bible, and 3) some combination of the two. A clear choice among these possibilities is most essential for an understanding of the so-called Middle Bronze Age in Syria and Palestine, the rise of the Hyksos power in Kemet, and the contributions of this period of foreign invasion upon subsequent Kemetic civilizations.

In order to provide a panorama of the events surrounding the Hyksos invasion of Kemet, it is important that we regress for a moment and see these people as they step on the pages of history. If you recall in Mesopotamia two invasions from the Northern Caucasus had already taken place. The Gutians had overran the Akkadians and after a brief interval, in which the third ancient Kushite dynasty of Ur in Sumer was reestablished, there was a wave of Amorites from the Kingdom of Mari on the Upper Euphrates River who invaded Palestine. In the meantime, sitting off in what is now called Georgia, Southern Russia, a people called the Hurrians had already begun to make their presence felt.[34]

Just about 2200 B.C., or roughly the First Intermediate Period, the Hurrians from the Caucasian north between Lake Van and The Zargos Mountains were invading the area east of the Tigris River. They seem to have been running from the Hittites who had made considerable migrations southward during this time.[35] The Hurrians were of Old Teutonic (Germanic) stock, though the proto-Hittites were probably Black. At this same time period Aryan invasions were taking place upon the Kushite cultures of Harappa and Mohenjo-Daro in the Indus Valley, devastating that civilization. Thus, there were white Aryans in the Indus Valley, white Kassite-Iranians in Central Mesopotamia, Amorites in Palestine and Hurrians in Syria. With this worldview we can begin to look at the Hurrians who provide the most vivid picture of the Aryans who invaded Kemet. They seem to have been the final upheaval in a series of invasions initiated by the Gutians.

The Hurrians were a branch of the Aryans from the Caucasian Mountains who migrated into and invaded areas of North and Northeastern Mesopotamia in the 2nd millennium B.C. Later they spread into the fertile lowlands of Syria and Mesopotamia, eventually reaching Palestine and the border of Kemet in the seventeenth century B.C.[37] It is through these Aryans that ancient Europeans began their first real stranglehold on the ancient Kushite Kingdoms of the Mediterranean Sea areas. Factions of this group founded the Mitannian Empire in ancient Turkey. Still others crossed the Balkan Passes to overthrow the Mycenean Empire in ancient Greece. Under the names Yuei-Chi and Hsing-Nu they invaded China and Southeast Asia.[37]

These Hurrians began to rule from northern Mesopotamia. They overthrew the Babylonian ruler Hammurapi and established a settler colony. They were the culmination of an Aryan wave of conquest carrying away with it tribes and races and mingling their blood with its own.[38] Descendants of these Aryans formed a small aristocracy in the Hurrian nation called the Maryannu (chariot-warriors).[39] They brought with them their crude sitting images, their still undecipherable language, their faith in a father-god and most significantly their two-wheeled, horse-drawn war chariots.[40] In fact, though it is true that the ass was rode in Kemet for some time, it is not until the time of Ahmose I that the earliest reference to horses (htrw) is found in the *Carnarvon Tablet I* from the Eighteenth Dynasty.

But what relationship do the Hurrians have with the Hyksos? In order to bring this point closer to home, it is essential that we look at the terminology used in Mdw Ntr or the "Divine Language" of ancient Kemet to describe these foreigners. Manetho calls these foreigners "Hyksos" according to Flavius Josephus, which he explains to mean "Shepherd Kings."[41] This term, however, is to be more correctly explained as made up of the Kemetic words "Heka", (?), - ruler over, govern;

and "Khaswt", (𓈎𓏏 𓉐𓉐), - foreigner, desert-dweller, or "Rulers over the Desert-dwellers". The latter phrase is found on a few scarabs of the Second Intermediate Period bearing the names of foreign rulers and exclusively in literature for the Hyksos. Examples of this are the *Speos Artemidos Inscriptions* from the time of Hatshepsut,[42] *Tell-el-Yahudiyyah* in the Delta, *Tell-el-Mishrife* or ancient Qatna in Syria, *Tel-Beit-Mirsim* in Palestine, the *Tombs of Beni Hasan* in Kemet and the *Turin Papyrus* where it says, dmd hka Khaswt 6 ir.n.sn rnp.t 108, "Total six Hyksos, they ruled 108 years." Moreover, when the term "Heka Khaswt" is used in the Middle Kingdom, in the *Story of Sinuhe*, it refers to the rulers of Syria and Palestine. In the New Kingdom, the term occurs in the *Amada Stela of Amenhotep II* alongside the "Princes of Retjenu". Apophis, in the *Second Stela of Kamose*, is called a "Chief of Retjenu", and Retjenu is often spoken of as made up of foreign countries or "Khaswt".[43]

The term used in Kemetic literature to designate the foreign population in Kemet during Hyksos period is Aamu (𓏏𓄿𓀀). To define this term as "Asiatic" is misleading. That translation should be reserved for "Setchetyw" (𓏏𓄿𓈖𓀀), the generic of Setchet, "Asia", or "Moncheyw", (𓈖𓈖 𓃀𓏏𓀀), i.e., "Bedouin". Nor is Aamu simply an occupational term, it is restricted to the population of Palestine and refers to both the sedentary and nomadic peoples.[44] The term Aamu makes its first appearance in the Sixth Dynasty, where it refers to a group of sedentary Asiatics. In the First Intermediate Period, Aamu are described in the *Instructions of Merikare* as the semi-nomadic population of Palestine. In the Middle Kingdom the term is again used to designate the ethnic population of Syria and Palestine, and the Aamu are also linked with the Heka Khaswt. The conclusion can hardly be avoided that Aamu designates the Amorite populations of Syria and Palestine.

Furthermore, the fact that the foreign population of Kemet and its leaders in the Hyksos period are called by the same terminology strongly suggest that the Kemites recognized a direct ethnic and cultural continuity in these foreigners with those of Syria and Palestine in the Middle Kingdom. Toward the end of the Eighteenth Dynasty, Aamu is largely replaced by Khurru (Hurrians) as the most important ethnic component in Syria and Palestine.

To this evidence of terminology may be added the indications from the New Kingdom of a strong Amorite-Canaanite, i.e. white-Black, cultural element in the Delta as a result of the Hyksos period. The archeaological remains of the Hyksos period in Kemet and in Syria-Palestine indicate that the Amorites were the foundation of Hyksos culture to which was later added a large dose of the Hurrians. It had strong ties to Kemet throughout the Hyksos period and there is every indication that the foreign culture in Kemet in the Second Intermediate Period was in continuity with the Amorite culture of Syria and Palestine. The long acculturation of coastal Syria and Palestine to Kemetic ways seems to have fully prepared the "Rulers of the Desert-dwellers" and their supporters for the taking of

Kemet. This was achieved, not by a sudden invasion from without, but in cooperation with a fifth column Amorite group already settled in the Delta during the Middle Kingdom. The strong Amorite princes of Syria and Palestine became heirs to the Kemetic throne in a time of the latter's dynastic decline. It should be of interest that materials uncovered stratigraphically in Palestine have been used as a yardstick for measuring the Hyksos period in Kemet.[45]

VIII. The Hyksos Element in the Middle Kingdom

After the rise of Menthuhotep in the late Eleventh Dynasty, the reestablishment of Black Theban control and the supposed expulsion of the Asiatics, Kemet's problems had only begun. These Asians had only retreated long enough to regroup and prepare for a more decisive onslaught. The attitude of goodwill shown in the royal gifts of Amenemhat III and IV to Asiatic princes is reciprocated in the cooperation of Asiatics in the Sinai expeditions. On the other hand, the increasing number of Asiatic slaves in Kemet during the Thirteenth Dynasty may suggest the end of good relations and a period of hostility leading to the rise of the Hyksos.[46]

An important source of information on the status of Asiatics in the Middle Kingdom are the *Inscriptions of Sinai*. From these it is clear that in the time of Amenemhat III, in particular, Asiatics were regularly used to conduct overland caravans from the eastern Delta into the Sinai mines for the purpose of transporting valuable turquoise and perhaps also copper. Some of these Asiatics or Aamu, are spoken of as coming from "Hami", a place in southern Palestine. Most of the Aamu, however, were probably residents in Kemet employed as cheap labor for trade and mining expeditions.[47]

The cultural contract between Asiatics and Kemites must have been more than occassional since it was also in this period that these Asiatics attempted to write their language in the Kemetic script Mdw Ntr, thereby, creating the so-called "*Proto-Sinatic Script*" found near *Sherabit al-Kadem*, the Kemetic temple to Hathor in the Sinai.[48] Kemet's relations with Asia in the Middle Kingdom must also be considered in the light of the large Asiatic slave population there. The chief source of information on these Asiatic slaves is *A Papyrus of the Late Middle Kingdom* in the Brooklyn Museum and the *Hieratic Papyri from Kahum, Gurob and Hawara*. The references to Asiatic slaves seems to date from the time of Amenemhat III to the middle of the Thirteenth Dynasty, and they are more numerous in the Thirteenth Dynasty than in the Twelfth. Most of these Asiatics were assimilated into the culture of Kemet in every respect, except for their ethnic designation as Aamu.[49]

Nevertheless, in the Thirteenth Dynasty, around the time of Neferhotep, there is evidence to suggest serious hostilities in Palestine.[50] Consequently, it is likely that Asiatic slaves in Kemet, after the time of Amenemhat III, represent prisoners taken in Asia itself. During

Amenemhat III's reign there were many Aamu who settled in the eastern Delta, in the so-called Arabian nome, as part of the labor force of the "Priest of the Crop of Soped, Lord of the East," and were used as caravaneers for expeditions in to the Sinai peninsula. It is from the eastern Delta that Amenemhat III drew large bands of laborers for his projects in the Fayyum area. As an important political and economic entity, the eastern Delta constituted the stronghold for the Hyksos domination of Kemet.[51]

CONCLUSION

The First and Second Intermediate periods raise myriads of questions and though the answers appear to be limited are available nonetheless. The Gutians who assisted in the initiation of the First Intermediate period were part of a much larger migration of ancient Europeans into the Meridonial or Southern world. An analysis of Mesopotamian text (Akkadian, Babylonian, Sumerian) will be essential to grasping a primary understanding of events leading to Kemet's first demise.

The Second Intermediate period is more squarely determined but the Hyksos question is still perplexing though it doesn't have to be so. The Hurrians and their various consanguine kinsmen were part of a scheme of ancient European expansion that had them occupying considerable territory in eastern and southeastern Europe by 2500 B.C.[52] They didn't bring any practical innovations to Kemet or areas of Mesopotamia except the use of the horse. They brought along the concept of a tribal society in which the leader was always a war-chief. This trend is found from the Hittites of the sixteenth century B.C. to the present day Germans and Americans. Their impact upon the Hyksos invasion of Kemet should not be overlooked.

As for the Israelite question as it relates to the Hyksos, there is no practical evidence outside of the Old Testament of the Israelites being in Kemet nor should it be used as a guide in any attempt to answer the complex questions posed by the biblical account.[53] The records of Kemet are clear on this. The Habiru must be viewed in the context of the surroundings outlined in the Amarna Correspondence of Rib-Adda versus the soldiers of Abdi-Ashirta and his call for assistance against the Amorites (Amurru) among whom were the habiru or "refugees".[54] That the only mention of "Israel" in Kemetic literature is not consistent with the view of the Old Testament raises serious questions about biblical perceptions and biblical studies as a whole.

As African people attempt to reclaim their ancient past it is important to "retool" or "tool-up" research and technical skills. It will require learning languages such as Arabic, Hebrew, Mdw Ntr, Coptic, Akkadian, Ugaritic, Canaanite, etc. in order to expand our perceptions of the ancient world as the people themselves saw it. Only then can we dismiss Eurocentrisms and develop an Afrocentric worldview that will remain as a legacy for action. Only then can those great wonders of our past be extrapolated in order to shed light on paths to the future. A future that will demand movement from the realm of ideas to the realm of action. It is this action that will lead to victory in the struggle for the African mind, so long as its quest is for truth.

NOTES

1. J. E. White, *Ancient Egypt*, N.Y.: Dover Pub. Co., 1970, p. 149.
2. James Breasted, *A History of Egypt*, N.Y.: Chas. Scribner's Sons, 1909, p. 127.
3. White, op. cit., p. 150.
4. Rosalie A. David, *The Ancient Egyptians*, London: Routledge & Kegan Paul, 1982, p. 90.
5. Alan Gardiner, *Egypt of the Pharaohs*, Oxford U. Press, 1961, p.93
6. John Wilson, *The Culture of Ancient Egypt*, Chgo: U. of Chgo. Press, 1951, p. 100.
7. White, op. cit., p. 152.
8. Miriam Lichtheim, *Ancient Egyptian Literature*, Berkeley: U. of California Press, 1975, Vol. I, p. 149.
9. Vulinedela Wobogo, "Diop's Two Cradle Theory and the Origin of White Racism", *Black Books Bulletin*, Vol. 4, No. 4, Winter, 1976, p. 20.
10. George Roux, *Ancient Iraq*, London: Penquin Books, 1966, p. 146.
11. Leonard C. Wooley, *The Sumerians*, N.Y.: W. W. Norton & Co., 1965, p. 83.
12. Leonard C. Wooley, *Ur of the Chaldees*, N.Y.: W. W. Norton & Co., 1965, p. 112.
13. Roux, op. cit., p. 165.
14. Paola Matthiae, *Ebla*, N.Y.: Doubleday & Co., 1981, p. 212.
15. Cheikh Anta Diop, *The African Origin of Civilization*, Westport: Lawrence HIll & Co., 1974, p. 113.
16. Cheikh Anta Diop, *Parente Genetique de L'Egyptien de L'Egyptien Pharaonique et des Langues Negro-Africaines*, Dakar: Fontamental Institute de Afriqu Noire, 1977, p. XXLX.
17. Breasted, op. cit., p. 149.
18. White, op. cit., p. 155.
19. James Breasted, *Ancient Records of Egypt*, N.Y.: Russell & Russell, 1906, Vol. 2, p. 977.
20. Theophile J. Meeks, *Hebrew Origins*, N.Y.: Harper & Row, 1956, p. 9.
21. Ibid., p. 12.
22. Ibid., p. 13.
23. Alan Godbey, *Lost Tribes-A Myth*, Durham: Duke U. Press, 1930, p. 34.
24. Amaziyah Levi, "The Hebrew Presence in Kemetic History", *History, The Bible, and the Black Man*, Vol. 2, No. 2, 1980, p. 17.
25. Flavius Josephus, "The Fall of Gamla", *Biblical Archaeology Review*, Vol. 5, No. 1, Jan. - Feb. 1979, p. 20.
26. William Whiston, *Josephus Complete works*, Chgo: Thompson & Thomas, 1901.
27. George Mendenhall, *The Tenth Generation*, Baltimore: Johns Hopkins U. Press, 1973, p. 20.
28. Whiston, op. cit., p. 713.
29. Roux, op. cit., p. 274.
30. Kelly O. Ingram, *Jerusalem*, Durham: Triangle Friends of the Middle East, 1978, p. 2.

31. Sigmund Freud, *Moses and Monotheism,* N.Y.: Vantage Books, 1939, p. 45.
32. James B. Pritchard, *The Ancient Near East,* Princeton: Princeton U. Press, 1958, p. 231.
33. I Kings 6:1.
34. Ignace J. Gelb, *Hurrians and Subarians,* Chgo: U. of Chgo. Press, 1944, p. 231.
35. Aaron Kempinski, "Hittites in the Bible: What Does Archaelolgy Say", *Biblical Archaeology Review,* Vol. 5, No. 4, Sept.-Oct., 1979, p. 26.
36. Roux, op. cit., p. 211.
37. E. D. Phillips, *The Royal Hordes: Nomad People of the Steppes,* London: Thames & Hudson, 1965, p. 111.
38. Herbert Wendt, *It Began in Babel,* N.Y.: Delta Books, 1964, p. 70.
39. Gelb, op. cit., p. 231.
40. Wendt, op. cit., p. 90.
41. Whiston, op. cit., p. 712.
42. Eliezer D. Oren, "How not to Create a History of the Exodus — A Critique of Professor Goedlicke's Theories", *Biblical Archaeology Review,* Vol. 7, No. 6, Nov.-Dec., 1981, p. 49.
43. Labib Habachi, *The Second Stela of Kamose,* Gluckstadt: verlag J. J. Augustin, 1972.
44. Pierre Montet, *Eternal Egypt,* N.Y.: Mentor Books, 1964, p. 45.
45. Robert M. Engberg, *The Hyksos Reconsidered,* Chgo: U. of Chgo. Press, 1939, p. 29.
46. Ibid, p. 28.
47. Breasted, op. cit., p. 713.
48. Breasted, op. cit., p. 724.
49. Engberg, op. cit., p. 27.
50. Breasted, op. cit., p. 753.
51. Engberg, op. cit., p. 30.
52. R. A. Crossland, "Immigrants From the North", *The Cambridge Ancient History,* Vol. 1, Chap. 27, Cambridge: Univ. Press, 1967, p. 48.
53. O. Eissfeldt, "Palestine in the Time of the Nineteenth Dynasty", *The Cambridge Ancient History,* Vol. 1, Chap. 26, Cambridge: Univ. Press, 1965, p. 3.
54. Mario Liverani, *Three Amarna Essays,* Malibu: Undena Pub., 1979, p. 16.

THE POWER OF SPIRITUAL DETERMINISM IN ANCIENT EGYPTIAN CITY LIFE

EARL WALTER FARUQ

INTRODUCTION

A popular view among historians is that civilization takes place in the 'city'. That is, people develop a refined cultural and political unit after enough food is grown to free a portion of them from the land and place them in a permanent man-made territory. Babylon, Rome and Athens are cited as early bastions of civilization. These were 'city states' with legal jurisdiction, vast acreage and complex political and military bureaucracy. Each had a distinct 'physical' presence which generated an illusion of power and culture. Such power could transform peasants into civilized men and women, so they believed.

Africans in ancient Egypt, however, provide an opposite example of civilization as a creation of the city. Instead, the city in Egypt evolved from a flourishing civilization in rural areas. Unlike the Western models, the Egyptian city was an extension of spiritual development in people who kept their roots in the agricultural village. The city was a place where people could demonstrate their spiritual determination to live a pure life; a life worthy of the gods.

This desire for perfection we shall call, spiritual determinism. It was a unique quality in city life.

The purpose of the paper is to explore spiritual determinism in ancient cities, Memphis, Thebes and Tell el'Amarna. We shall discuss:
- Geographic and cultural factors shaping Egyptian city life
- Social and physical accomplishments stimulated by spiritualism
- Some lessons in the ancient past for present cities in the Pan African world.

THE EFFECTS OF EGYPT'S GEOGRAPHY ON HUMAN INTERCOURSE

The geography of ancient Egypt is distinguished from other areas in the world. Egypt is essentially a red desert, without rainfall. The land would be completely inhabitable, if not for the rushing waters of the Nile River. The Nile generates life through Egypt and makes possible an oasis of fertile black soil along it's banks. This unique stroke of nature makes possible a rich agricultural capability when properly cultivated.[1]

The Nile floods annually and turns surrounding delta land into jungles of reeds and brush. Observing this raw vegetation, the people sensed the keys to their survival in transforming these swamps into usable farmland. The tedious and never ending challenge of clearing the marsh, cultivating the land and controlling flood waters became the economic basis for Egyptian civilization.[2]

Working the floodlands required a continuous watchfulness and discipline among the people. Cultivation meant the construction of canals and dikes to channel and preserve flood waters. It meant the division of the country into carefully laid farm plots, bounded by walls to hold back the flooding water. It meant the development of a complex irrigation system to allow for the expansion of farmable land into the desert. It meant a large supply of competent energetic workers and a highly perfected administration.[3]

It is believed the technical precision required for pyramid building, began with the engineering and construction of irrigation projects along the Nile. While the masses worked the land, a civil service class emerged to coordinate the collective affairs of the community or 'nome'. Civil servants managed irrigation, collected taxes, managed royal property and administered justice. They knew how to write and keep detailed records in the very first Dynasty (3100 BC). They fulfilled intellectual, scientific and religious functions for the nation.[4]

The Nile, then, was like a giant snake whose deception required close and consistent monitoring. It became a fundamental life force around which people constantly organized and directed their skills. An effective hierarchy of workers transformed raging waters into an orderly sprinkling system. The harsh landscape was tamed to produce agricultural abundance for thousands of years.

Secondly, Egypt's geography isolated its people from frequent contact or instrusion by foreigners for 1,000 years. Surrounding desert corridors, mountains and sea sheltered Egyptians from foreign armies and mass population movements. There was a sense of permanence in Egyptian culture made possible by remote geographical conditions. This relative freedom from foreign attack had a calming effect on Egytian life and allowed the people to concentrate almost exclusively on internal development.[5]

CULTURAL FACTORS SHAPING EGYPTIAN CITY LIFE

On top of high level organization and technical skill among ancient Egyptians was a religious devotion which consumed daily life. Activities of life had a spiritual purpose for the 'after life.' The key to a prosperous life after death was a natural life which was honorable, productive and free from sin.[6] Gods of worship took many forms in village nomes. As dynasties evolved, Gods became personifications of kings or pharoahs. By the Third Dynasty (2700 BC), the Egyptians had documented a clear intellectual concept of the origin of God and the destiny of humans.

Memphite Theology, taken from the city of Memphis, shows the existence of intelligence which interprets nature and provides a framework for judging right and wrong.

> "It is the heart (mind) which causes every completed concept to come forth, and it is the tongue (voice) which announces what the heart thinks. Thus all the gods were formed. . . . Indeed, all the divine order came into being through what the heart thought and the tongue commanded. . . . (Thus justice was given to) him who does what is desired. Thus life was given to him who has peace, and death was given to him who has sin. Thus were made all work and all crafts, the action of the arms, the movement of the legs, and the activity of every member of the body, in conformance with the command which the heart thought, which came forth through the tongue and which gives the value of everthing."

In addition to religious philosophy, documents from the Third Dynasty show advanced thinking in science. Medical surgeons classified broken bones, explained technical terms, prescribed medication and treatment and observed the progress of patients. Already in use was a 365 day calendar linking the annual rise of the Nile and the visibility of the Dog Star on the eastern horizon with specified days.[8]

Work for the Egyptian people, took on an atmosphere of ritual. There was a pervasive desire in the individual to enter the realm of the divine through good deeds. The Egyptian psychology of life gave animation to everything in the universe and made no sharp distinction among living and dead, human and divine. Such thinking allowed one to blend the human with god so each could enter into the category of the other. The person sought godliness through a devotion to labor. The result was a culture unsurpassed in its power to master the elements of survival and artistic expression.[9]

CITY LIFE IN ANCIENT EGYPT

There are two specific periods chosen to discuss three cities in Ancient Egypt. One period is the Third Dynasty (2700 BC) where the city of Memphis is reviewed. The other is the Eighteenth Dynasty (1570-1300 BC) where the cities of Thebes and Tell el'Amarna are profiled. Memphis is chosen in the Third Dynasty for this is the place and time many feel the Egyptians achieved their greatest accomplishments in art and architecture. Twenty major pyramids were built during this period, the largest of which were located at Giza and Saqquarah in the 'greater' Memphis area.[10]

The Eighteenth Dynasty was chosen to observe life when the Empire aggressively interacted with foreign cultures and achieved it's greatest territorial power. Thebes became the political and cultural center of the world. Amarna housed a religious and cultural revolution against the powers of Thebes, altering the Egyptian empire for a generation and setting forth religious principles which have endured throughout history.

MEMPHIS

Memphis was founded in 3100 BC by King Menes. It was built on a river bed after engineers redirected the flow of the Nile to create a 'protected' site. Memphis was the first capitol of Egypt and remained an important religious and political center for 2800 years. By 2700 BC, it was the focus of some of the great architectural and engineering innovations the world has known. Memphis was an administrative center for the excavation of the first copper mines and stone quarries. It headquartered the engineering of Nile irrigation projects. It housed the great minds who engineered the pyramids at Giza and Saqquarah. Yet, to describe Memphis is to shed a new outlook on the concept of city. (World Book)

Unlike other cities in the ancient world, there were no surrounding walls at Memphis. In Babylon, for example, people entered and left the city through bronze gates erected for containment and defense purposes. In Memphis, natural security barriers were provided by the desert and mountains. Memphis, therefore, included nearby villages as 'suburbs'. The city centers housed the tombs of the gods, pharaohs and people.[12]

Around the pyramids at Giza, there is an 'urban' settlement of tombs laid in orderly rows, complete with streets and cross streets. These tombs, called 'mastabas' had the appearance of houses and were permanent stone structures. There was a lot of attention given to the dead and the city had a religious and sacred atmosphere. Considering there was no sharp distinction between the living and dead in Egyptian thinking, Memphis must be classified a city instead of a giant cemetary serving a number of surrounding villages.[13]

The residents of central Memphis appear to have been the civil servants who administered the affairs of government and commerce. The masses maintained residence in the village and small market areas. Memphis was relatively free of psychological tension and personal anxieties associated with masses of people living in a limited space. The primary work in Memphis was the construction of pyramids, temples and tombs. The common laborer must have had a unique sophistication in his work. Talent plus a strong spiritual frame of reference resulted in almost superhuman offerings.[14]

Pyramids of the Third and Fourth Dyanasties represent a precision and magnitude of proportions unparallelled in history. I.E.S. Edwards notes the cold precision in the Great pyramid of the Fourth Dynasty:

"Here were six and a quarter million tons of stone, with case blocks averaging as much as two and a half tons each;

yet these casing blocks were dressed and fitted with a joint
of one-fiftieth of an inch - a scrupulous nicety worthy of the
jeweler's craft. Here the margin of error in the squareness
of the north and south sides was .09% and of the east and
west sides, .03%. This mighty mass of stone was set upon
a dressed rock pavement which, from opposite corners, had
a deviation from a true plane of only .004%.''[15]

The intellectual honesty of the Memphite is revealed in his precision
and detail with architecture and artistry. The walls of the tombs and
temples are everywhere filled with artwork laying out Egyptian culture
in meticulous detail. The understanding and communication among Mem-
phites must have been remarkable for their energy was so well organized and channelled.[16]

In summary, a spiritual force settled in the city of Memphis around
the tombs of the gods, pharoahs, priests, officers and servants. Entering the city of Memphis may have been synonomous with entering church
on Sunday morning. There was an unquestioned expectation to
demonstrate Maat which was a created and inherited good or truth which
brings about divinity. No walls were needed to keep persons on or out
of this sacred territory. People were attracted to the city
for motivation and strength to accomplish their daily tasks with divine
precision and devotion.[17]

THEBES

The 'Hyksos' were wanderers of apparently Caucasian persuasion
who infiltrated Egypt around the Eighth Dynasty (1800 BC). Their origin
is undocumented, though it is thought that they came from across the
Caucasus, through Mesopotamia and the Near East. By the time the
Hyksos reached Egypt, they were a group of mixed ethnicity (Caucasian,
Asiatic, Semitic).[18] Soon after the arrival of Hyksos, the first walls were
seen around Egyptian cities for defense purposes. They brought an aggressive mentality and new mechanisms of force including the horse,
chariot,body armor, sword and dagger.The Hyksos had a distinct military
advantage over the Egyptians. The Hyksos dominated Egypt for 200
years. Finally, around 1600 BC, Egyptians were able to liberate
themselves from foreign domination. The war started from Thebes and
when it was over, Thebes emerged as the political and religious capitol
of Egypt.

Thebes at the Eighteenth Dynasty (1570 BC) was similar to Third
Dynasty Memphis in its pursuit of Maat as the religious goal.A major difference, however, was style. Atmosphere in Thebes was more
cosmopolitan and aggressive as a result of evolution ad the influence
of the Hyksos. International affairs were a new dimension to Egyptian city life. Much more emphasis was placed on the secular affairs of state.

Queen Hatshepsut restored the traditional Egyptian culture back to the nation. Magnificent temples at Luxor and Karnak were constructed. Pyramids, obelisks and majestic processional ways, collonades and granite sculptures at Thebes, created the most awesome monuments anywhere in the ancient world.[19]

Monumental art signified the existence of organized city life in Thebes. Other signs of urban activity were captured in miniature models found in tombs. Butcher shops, embalmers' establishments, bakehouses and palaces were carved out of wood and buried with the kings and queens in the Nile Valley.[20]

A greater indicator of city life in Thebes is the remains of the heavy construction industry. The exploitation of stone quarries, construction of religious buildings, transport of stone and erection of columns required intensive labor and effective management.[21]

Thutmose III followed Hatshepsut's internal development program with military campaigns into foreign nations (1470 BC). Egypt conquered numerous states in Mesopotamia, the Mediteranean Sea, Nubia and surrounding African territory. One list found in Palestine, numbers Egyptian 'objects' at close to 500.[22] The Egyptian empire, with Thebes as the capitol, was the greatest of empires in its day.[23]

Evidence shows spiritual determinism in the people directed the domestic and foreign activities of the nationa. Amon Ra, the invisible god of air, was the King of the Gods. The Pharoah communicated directly with God and held authority over high priests, viziers, civil officials and army heads. The direction of the city and the Empire was in the hands of the gods via the Pharoah. The people did not question the Pharoah's ability to communciate with and represent God. Instead, they would present thousands of objects to the Gods buried in the valleys around Thebes, in demonstration of their faith. The Empire, with Thebes as the capitol, prevailed without interruption for 200 years.[24]

TELL EL'AMARNA

Around 1350 BC, Amenophis IV (also called Amenhotep IV) inherited the mightiest army and richest empire of the then civilized world. Thebes was a booming metropolis where merchants, ambassadors and artisans from various countries met. No other city compared to Thebes in physical magnificence and luxury.[25]

Rulers of the known world would journey to Thebes to bow before Amenophis IV. However, he was indifferent to the magificence of Thebes and the submission by foreign rulers. Amenophis IV was at odds with the concept of the hidden God, Amon and he resisted the spoils Amon had secured for the Egyptian empire. He began to worship a new god, Aton (The Sun). He abandoned Thebes, changed his name to Akhenaton (he who is serviceable to the Aton) and moved his court to the new city Akhetaton (now Tell el'Amarna).[26]

Great importance was attached to cleanliness in Amarna, as in other Egyptian cities. Toilets and sewers were in use to dispose waste. Soap was made for washing the body. Perfumes and essences were popular against body odor. A solution of natron was used to keep insects from houses. Even under revolutionary conditions, there seems to have been an 'all-embracing' order and cleanliness dominating the organization of state and family life.[27]

Amarna was landscaped with flowers and beautiful gardens as part of Akhenaton's land use scheme. Amarna may have been the first planned "garden city" (a concept in urban planning referring to a deliberate breakup of strictly man made functions with patches of nature in the city).[28]

The temples and personal chapels built throughtout the city were open to the air. This allowed for the worship of the sun which was contrasted to the closed tmples in Thebes. Officials laid out great estates, attractively incorporating nature into their plans. Workman houses were erected on well ordered streets in grid iron fashion.[29]

The unusual openness and freedom of artistic expression in Amarna is considered a major cause for its fall. Under Akhenaton, the royal lineage was stripped of its hidden and sacred mystique. Emphasis was placed on making the ruling class one with the people. As a result, Akhenaton became vulnerablke to the aggressive descendants of the traditional order, and also to leaders of foreign nations.[30]

It appears that Akhenaton's commitment to peace kept him from seriously defending his empire when moved upon. Akhenaton remained determined in his principles, however. He is credited with pioneering 'monotheism', one of the great spiritual ideas in all history. The rest of Egypt and her subjects never internalized Akhenaton's beliefs in the One God. Akhenaton was considered a heretic and unworthy of respect. A city born of a spiritual missionary, also died almost immediately upon his death.[31]

SUMMARY

There was high level organization, technical skill and religious devotion among ancient Africans in Egypt before the advent of city life in 3100 BC. Impressive human capabilities were established in a desert agricultural setting,around a deceptive water source: the Nile river. After mastering the Nile floodwaters and turning its deltas into fertile farmland, Africans were able to pursue higher religious and political activity in the city.

A spiritual motivation and determinism founded the city of Memphis and caused construciton of great pyramids and temples in tribute to the gods and kings. A spiritual motivation and determinism elevated the city of Thebes into a booming international metropolis, uncontested in physical magnificence and luxury. This same motivation and determinism founded Akhetaton or Tell el'Amarna which staged the great cultural revolution from which the concept of monotheism was born.

The African in Ancient Egypt shows clearly that spiritualism combined with intellectual honesty and physical labor, can create a human energy of cold precision and almost superhuman magnitude. A major revelation of city life in ancient Egypt is that human expression, as far back as 3100 BC, was as organized and often better implemented than similar expressions in city living today.

LESSONS FOR TODAY'S PAN AFRICAN CITY

There are at least three instructive statements on the urban experience in ancient Egypt which have meaning for Africian citylife at present:
1. Migration into the city from rural area seems to have been relatively controlled, rather than spontaneous.
2. People migrating to the ancient city for the first time seem to have had the intellectual and technical capacity to make a smooth transition.
3. Values and work functions within the city seem to have been well coordinated to achieve society's cultural objectives.

(1) Spontaneous migration into many contemporary cities has often meant social imbalance in both the city and surrounding rural areas. Cities have a tendency to attract more men than women, particularly in developing stages. Rarely are there sufficient jobs for the amount of people available to work. There may be lacking administrative and natural resources to secure food, water, sanitation, transportation and recreation for a random influx of people. The results tend toward decreased social control, higher unemployment, more blight and disease, greater psychological tension and reduced productivity in rural areas.[32]

The ancient African policy of controlled in-migration might scale down and clarify what amounts to social chaos in cities due to population overload. In all three cities, reference to the residents are always related to specific work functions they perfomred in service of the Gods. The masses maintained their village residence and seemed to travel to the city for purposes of assignment rather than escape from their traditional habitat.

(2) Individual reasons for migrating into today's city are often selfish rather thatn collective. There is a common search for personal gain: employment, excitement, education, freedom from family controls, entertainment .. The quest for personal advancement often conflicts with group needs. The commitment to 'community' remains in the village while citylife is reserved for the rugged pursuit of individualism. The result is often a group of people vying to get more from the city than they are willing to give to its overall welfare.[33]

On the other hand, the ancient African brought a more collective and 'giving' spirit. The city was an extension of community life. Personal needs were defined within a collective goal which was Maat, an inherited goodness or truth which brought divinity. The result was a people who literally gave their lives to work on behalf of the whole, at least in the earlier dynasties (I-IV).

The ancient African appears to have kept his identity and spiritual frame of reference during the transition from rural to city life. There was consistency in rules and regulations in both environments. A person felt accountable for his actions wherever he journeyed. The spiritual nature of the city made the people even more accountable for their actions.

(3) colonialism represents a process of disruption in African life today, just as the 'Hyksos' represented in ancient Egypt. The city in both cases, is a place where Africans sought a remedy to maladjustments caused by foreign intrusion.[34] The influence of former oppressors remains in the values and technology of many African cities. In fact, significant numbers of non-Africans continue to live in present African cities as merchants and educators.[35] The result is disjointed city life which, in many ways, conflicts with goals of self-determination and economic independence.

The work of Queen Hatshepsut in Thebes illustrates the successful restoration of traditional culture back to the city after expulsion of foreign oppressors. It was female leadership which restored the sacred and tradtional back into the people's life. Her successor, Thutmose III appears more interested in conquering the world than solidifying the internal fabric of Egypt. Likewise, present Aftrican leaders seem more interested in international statesmanship and imported progress than tough local development at the village level. Is it possible Hatshepsut's leadership could restore a greater sense of economic self-sufficiency in the Pan African world?

Certainly, the success of any culture requires a wide variety of strengths from all levels of the population. The African model in ancient Egypt shows how a well rounded people moved with spiritual determination and developed a world empire. At the top of the model was 'effective' participation of masses of people in meaningful work. At the bottom was a clear and functional concept of life, which revealed itself in positive reality.

NOTES

1. Stanley Beaver *A Regional Georgraphy - Africa*, Part II, London: Longmans, Green and Company, 1964, p.212.
2. John A. Wilson *The Culture of Ancient Egypt*, Chicago: University of Chicago Press, 1951, p. 10.
3. Jean Louis De Ceneval *Living Architecture, Egyptian*, New York: Grosset and Dunlap, 1964, p.9.
4. Ibid., p.79.

5. Lewis Mumford *The City in History,* New York: Harcourt, Brace and World, 1961, p.88.
6. Ibid., p.79.
7. Wilson, op. cit., p.60.
8. Ibid., p.59.
9. Henri Frankfort *The Intellectual Adventure of Ancient Man* Chicago: The University of Chicago Press, 1946, p.62; De Ceneval, op. cit., p.3.
10. George Posener *The Encyclopedia of Egyptian Civilization,* New York: Tudor Publishing Company, 1959.
11. Josef Ben Jochannan *Black Man of the Nile and His Family,* New York: Alkebu-lan Books, 1981, p.495.
12. Mumford, op. cit., p.81.
13. Ibid.
14. De Ceneval, op. cit., p.4.
15. Wilson, op. cit., p.88.
16. Mumfor, op. cit., p.88.
17. Wilson, op. cit., p.17.
18. Ibid., p.155.
19. J.A. Rogers *World's Great Man of Color,* Vol. I New York: Collier Books. 1946, p.43.
20. Mumford, op. cit., p.80.
21. Posener, op. cit., p. 282
22. Wilson, op. cit., p.184.
23. John G. Jackson *Introduction to African Civilizations,* Secaucus, NJ: Citadel Press, 1970, p. 109.
24. Wilson, op. cit., p.171
25. Arthur Weigall *The Life and Times of Akhenaton,* London: Thornton Butterworth Ltd., 1923.
26. Rogers, op. cit., p.59
27. Waley-el-dine Sameh *Daily Life in Ancient Egypt,* New York: McGraw Hill, 1964, pp.10, 77.
28. Rogers, op. cit., p.60
29. Mumford, op. cit., p.86; Wilson, op. cit., p.215.
30. Posener, op.cit., p.7
31. Wilson, op. cit., p.31.
32. Akin Mabogunje *Urbanization in Nigeria* New York: Africana Publishing Company, 1969, p.270.
33. William and Judith Hanna *Urban Dynamics in Black Africa,* New York: Aldine Atherton Bookds, 1971, p.42
34. Ibid., p.29
35. John Hutton *Urban Challenge in East Africa,* Kenya: East African Publishing House, 1970, p.6

III. SPIRITUALITY AND PHILOSOPHY

RESTORATION OF THE HUSIA:
REVIVING A SACRED LEGACY

MAULANA KARENGA

I. INTRODUCTION

Of all the efforts being made to rescue and restore the rich and varied legacy of Kemet, none is more important than those to restore its sacred legacy, i.e., its moral and spiritual contribution to the dawn and development of human conscience. Although for years western scholarship assigned Kemet's legacy to Judaism and later Christianity, James Breasted, America's pioneer egyptologist, was honest enough to eventually admit that "the ripe social and moral development of mankind in the Nile Valley which is three thousand years older than that of the Hebrews, contributed essentially to the formation of the Hebrew literature which we call the Old Testament".[1] He continues saying, "Our moral heritage therefore derives from a wider human past enormously older than the Hebrews, and it has come to us rather *through* the Hebrews than *from* them." Less accommodating to the racial ego of the Europeans proper, he reminds them that Kemet had produced this "profound moral vision" and "wrought monumental wonders along the Nile at a time when all Europe was still living in Stone Age barbarism and there was none to teach a civilization of the past ."[2]

The primary purpose of the above citation is not to embarrass Europe about its late development or even to impose on it a much-needed racial modesty. It is above all to reaffirm the admitted great debt Europe owes to Kemet in particular and Africa in general and to emphasize the recognized richness of the moral and spiritual legacy of Kemet. The first thrust is to set right the historical record or as Cheikh Anta Diop says "to reconcile African civilizations with history" which Europe distorted in order to deny both the accomplishments of African history and the reality of our humanity.[3] The second thrust is to reinforce the historical and human value of the Kemetic moral and spiritual legacy and thereby reaffirm the need to appreciate, preserve and promote it.

The quest to restore Kemet's moral and spiritual legacy is a direct outgrowth of the struggle to develop a Black Theology and to produce an authentic Black sacred text. The quest, however, evolved in four fundamental phases. The first phase did not directly involve Kemet, but involved a process of attempting to Africanize the Jewish, Christian and Muslim faiths and build a more responsive Black tradition in them.[4] This was essentially part of the general thrust of re-Africanization in the 60's.

But it involved no serious discussion of or thrust for an original African theology or authentic African text based on Kemetic sacred teachings. Occasional references were made to "the greatness of ancient Egypt" to prove Africa's ancient grandeur and human achievement, but a serious exploration of Kemet's spiritual terrain and legacy was neither ventured nor voiced.

It was Dr. Yosef ben-Jochannan who would in 1978 write a book specifically calling for the development of a Black theology and what he called a "Black Bible".[5] This call for both a Black theology and Black sacred text marked another phase in the evolution of the quest, involving the focus on what the major western religions owed to Egypt and the appeal to reappropriate that legacy.[6] This call carried, however, some internal tensions. Among them were the unanswered questions of the role of the Bibical texts in the formulation of the new sacred text given the appeal to appropriate what George James calls our "Stolen Legacy".[7] Likewise, in the development of an African theology, the question of how much deference will be given to the Judeo-Christian tradition is not fully answered. Ben-Jochannan rightly argues for a non-denominational African theology,[8] but a theology based on Kemetic teachings has already assumed a particular identity with its own moral and spritual postulates.

Moreover, the call for a "Black bible" instead of a Black sacred text reflects a conceptual rootedness in the Judeo-Christian religious tradition and inadvertently places the proposed African sacred text, not outside, but within the western paradigm. Thus, the category "Black bible" is problematic and should be replaced by the term "sacred text" since "bible" is a Judeo-Christian category not a generic one as is sacred text. The Quran is not a Muslim bible; nor is the Dhammapada a Buddhist bible nor the Bhagavad-Gita a Hindu bible. Thus to be truly authentic and original rather than inauthentic and derivative, an African sacred text must be self-referential and culturally representative, not modelled categorically or textually on another sacred text. Such a decision marks a clear rupture with the Judeo-Christian conceptual and textual framework, eliminates the tendency to refer to Kemetic sacred texts but read from the Bible and thus paves the way for an authentic African sacred text rather than a Black version of a white one.

Nevertheless, ben-Jochannan's call was and remains an essential one, and Jacob Carruthers and his colleagues at the Kemetic Institute began to answer it. Not only did they begin to translate, study and teach the actual Kemetic sacred texts, but they re-established a Kemetic Temple with priests and appropriate rituals. This marked not only a necessary and critical institutionalization of the quest for an authentic African spirituality and sacred text, but also an indispensable transition from simple and limited references to Kemetic texts while quoting extensively from the Bible to the actual study and teaching of the sacred texts themselves. At the same time, it was a critical transition from an almost exclusive dependence on secondary interpretive sources on Kemetic spirituality, however valuable, i.e., Gerald Massey, R.A. Schwaller de Lubicz et al[9] to independent systematic exegesis of the sacred texts themselves in the context of an African worldview.[10] It was, in fact, a response to a more ancient call, a call from Kemet itself, from the Book of Kheti which says, "Follow in the footsteps of your ancestors, for the mind is trained through knowledge. Behold their words endure in books. *Open them* and follow their wise counsel" (emphasis mine).

The fourth phase of the evolution of the quest for an authentic African spirituality and sacred text begins with this author's collaboration with Jacob Carruthers and his subsequent beginning efforts to restore the sacred literature of Kemet in the form of *The Husia,* beginning with a book of selections from this sacred wisdom.[11] The project assumed and responded to the need for a truly authentic African spirituality rooted in and reflective of an equally authentic African sacred text. This, of necessity, meant returning to Kemet, researching, rescuing and restoring the sacred literature as the foundation upon which we build our spiritual life. The challenge of the project was and remains both awesome and unending and the story of its beginning and development is the substance and purpose of this paper.

II. PURSUIT OF THE PROJECT

The project began with the collection and organization of the various texts available, found in exclusively religious texts like Alexandre Piankoff's Bollingen Series[12] and anthologies of general literature like those of Lichtheim,[13] Kaster,[14] and Simpson.[15] It proceeded with the classification of the various kinds of sacred texts I found in my research. These were: the texts of knowing the creations, prayers and sacred praises, a moral narrative, wise instruction, texts of contemplation, declarations of virtues, and the so-called coffin and pyramid texts which along with the Book of Coming Forth By Day I categorized as "Books of Rising Like Ra." This did not mean this was an exhaustive list of sacred text classification. It was, as the title of my book says, a "Selection" and categorization based on that selection. There are clearly more existing texts, i.e., the mystery, mythological and ritual texts whose symbolism and esoteric character seemed problematic in contrast to the clear moral and spiritual postulates in the books included.

The books not placed in *The Husia,* include the Book of Gates, the Book of Am-Duat, the Book of Breathings, the Book of Caverns, the Book of the Heavenly Cow, the Book of Traversing Eternity, the Book of the Two Ways, and the Book of the Opening of the Mouth; as well as the Mythological Papyri collected and translated by Piankoff.[16] It seemed to me that these texts should form a corpus unto themselves and be classified as "sesheta" or Mystery texts. They are clearly relevant, spiritual literature and should be retranslated and studied, but they should be separate from *The Husia* given their stress and use.

In selecting the texts for inclusion, I developed a rationale for selection based on four basic criteria. First, the writings selected and included should be clearly Kemetic, i.e., conceptually and authorially. In a word, a conscious effort was made to edit out foreign concepts and contentions, i.e., Greek hostility to the woman expressed in later periods. Secondly, the writings should be in harmony with general African ethics as we understand and accept them. This is an added test of cultural authenticity which again seeks to block and eliminate foreign intrusions. Thirdly, the writings should be supportive of our current moral judgement. This meets the progressive and necessary demand of synthesizing tradition and reason. And fourthly, included writings should project and support the personal and collective ideals and aspirations of our struggle for liberation and a higher level of human life. In a word, the texts must pass the dual test of tradition and reason and offer written witness to the Ultimate Ideal - divine and human, i.e., witness to its existence and the possiblity of achieving it.

The naming of *The Husia* was also a challenge of no meagre proportion. As there is no single or major Kemetic sacred text, it was necessary not only to collect writings from various sources and attempt to impose an effective order on them, but also to give these writings a name. The thrust here was to produce a major sacred text, inclusive of all fundamental sacred texts as well as of "created" texts like the Book of Declarations of Virtues which is composed of declarations which express virtues fundamental to understanding and appreciating Kemetic morality rooted in and expressive of service to others. The need, then, was to choose a name reflective of both the rich variousness of the spiritual and moral messages of the texts as well as one rooted in the dynamics and demands of the spirituality itself.

Given this, I chose the combined words, Hu (authoritative utterance) and Sia (exceptional insight or understanding) as the most appropriate title, i.e., *The Husia.* Together they mean "authoritative utterance of exceptional insight." Moreover, they are the two divine powers by which Ra (Ptah) created the world as expressed in the Shabaka Text generally called "the Memphite Theology by traditional egyptologists".[17] Thus, given the importance of authoritative utterance and exceptional insight in the realm of morality and spirituality, and their divine character in Kemetic theology, *Husia* appears as both compelling and proper as a title for a comprehensive text of Kemetic sacred writings.

In translating the sacred writings, I made necessary use of existing translations in English and French, but often disagreed with their translations and their conception of Kemetic culture upon which their translations are based. Appreciating the need for exact translations, I did not confuse exactness with literalness which in the hands of most translators, usually produced dull and often incorrect translations. Taking the liberty of being figurative where a literal translation would deprive a passage of beauty or meaning, I attempted to render the message in the spirit and conceptual framework in which the authors conceived and wrote it.

Also, I used one name for God, that is to say, Ra, using the names of other netchers like Ptah with Ra in order to standardize reference to the One God. The choice of Ra as the name of the Netcher of netchers or the One God was made based on its antiquity, preeminence and prevalence in Kemetic sacred literature as such. In other cases, I usually translated the name of other netchers as an attribute or praise name of Ra, i.e., Atum, the complete one. Likewise, I translated the names of "gods" and "goddesses" by their attributes and the words "god" and "goddess" as powers of heaven, divine powers or exalted ones.

This was done for simplification as well as in response to the Kemetic conception of netchers as attributes and manifestations of Ra. Even Amen, it can be argued, is a form and attribute of Ra, i.e, "the hidden one." In fact, a hymn to Ra in the Bulaq Museum, according to Renouf, has the phrase "...his name, which is Amon".[18] Thus, we also use Amen-Ra which regardless of its political history, nevertheless, has sound spiritual grounding. The sacred texts, Morenz points out, say of Amen-Ra, "his form (abwt) is each neter".[19] Moreover, Renouf who mistakenly calls this concept pantheistic, quotes a hymn on the walls of the temple in the oasis of El Kharegh which says, "Each god has assumed your aspect". And Budge quotes a hymn to Amen-Ra which praises him as "One, only One," who "is of many forms in his might".[20] Thus, it is homage to the One God in his many manifestations or forms which allows the Kemites to be monotheistic and at the same time recognize and pay homage to the many forms in which the One God appears.

The problematic of the word netcher has challenged egyptologists since the inception of their studies. Some see its essential meaning as "power", especially divine power and others assert that it means "divine" or "holy". However, Morenz concludes that "despite all the thought that has been given to this question, nothing can be stated with confidence."[21] Still he leans toward its origin in the concept of power. Therefore, netcher was used as power, but it was also used as principle since these two concepts overlap and interchange in meaning. As Frankfort notes, often "we meet a number of Egyptian terms which stand in one context for qualities while they appear in another as independent spiritual entities."[22] In conclusion, then, whereas netcher is often translated as god or God, I have translated it as God for Ra and power, principles and exalted ones for his many manifestations.

III. THE HUSIA: STRUCTURE AND CONTENT

The Husia is divided into seven sections according to the character and content of the book or goup of books involved. The seven sections are: 1) The Book of of Knowing the Creations; 2) The Book of Prayers and Sacred Praises; 3) The Book of the Moral Narrative; 4) The Books of Wise Instruction; 5) The Books of Contemplation; 6) The Book of Declarations of Virtues,and; 7) The Books of Rising Like Ra. A systematic discussion of their contents will reveal the rich moral and spiritual legacy which ancient Africa gave humanity thru its daughter Kemet.

A. The Book of Knowing the Creations

This book takes its title from "The Book of Knowing the Creations of Ra and of Striking Down Apophis (the serpent of evil and chaos) but it contains writing from other sources as well. The other sources include a section from "The Shabaka Text", titled "The Creation of Ra as Ptah" and which is often called the Memphite Theology; sections from the Book of Vindication (the so-called Coffin Texts) on "The Four Good Deeds of the Creator"; and a statement on "the Self-Definition of Ra" taken from the so-called "Legend of Isis and Ra". Since there is no single text which presents a composite of the Kemetic conception of creation, it was necessary to collect and synthesize passages from various sources.

This book, then, is a recreation in the spirit of its title. As the title suggest, the Kemites viewed creation as a continuous process. Therefore, we have "The Creations" rather than "The Creation". The first creation was the first event at the first time. But creation is repeated each day in nature and in human history.[23] In nature, sunrise and the new beginning it brings each day is a reflection of this. In human history, it is reflected in humanity's constant establishment and re-establishment of order and righteousness in the midst of chaos and evil in a role similar to that of Ra's.

In the section from the Shabaka Text, we read the earliest written record of the dawn of structured human consciousness concerning ontology and ethics.[24] These sacred writings predate Hebrew, Christian and Muslim ontologies and ethics by thousands of years and apparently contributed to them. Thus, we find for the first time in human history the concept of Logos, i.e., creation through conceptual thought and authoritative utterance. As it is said, creation is achieved "according to the command which is conceived by the heart and mind and brought forth by the tongue."[25] This, as Frankfort notes, means that "the tongue is realizing thought. It translates concepts into actuality by means of 'Hu' - authoritative utterance".[26] We also see the key humanist concepts of free will and human equality in Ra's statement of His Four Good Deeds. In terms of human equality, the *Husia* (p.7) teaches that Ra declared he "created the four winds so that every person might breathe in his or her time and place" and "the great flood for irrigation so that the humble might benefit from it like the great"; and he "made every person like his or her fellow".

Also, we witness, as Breasted notes, a reflective morality which indicates definite social judgments on that which is loved and that which is hated and belief that God would grant life for the righteous and punishment and death for the wicked.[27] The *Husia* (p.8) says, "Justice is given to one who does what is loved and punishment to one who does what is hated" and "life is given to the peaceful and death is given to one who violates the law". The loved here is equivalent to the right and the hated to the wrong.

A final and important point to note is that Ra created the universe thru Maat, a term with multiple meanings, i.e., truth, justice, propriety, harmony, balance, order, reciprocity, righteousness, etc. Its importance lies in the fact that it is a divine concept, power and practice which not only informed and aided Ra's action, but was established as the fundamental concept, power and practice for the organization, maintenance and development of human society also. Herein lies a concept of natural and divine law which must be observed in social life for maximum human fulfillment.[28]

B. The Book of Prayers and Sacred Praises.

In this book we find one of Africa's most distinct and undeniable instructions and achievements in the spiritual and aesthetic realm - the praise poem.[29] And the fact that these praise poems were equally vital in Kemet as in other parts of Africa, reaffirms the truth of the Africanness of Kemet. The praise-poem or the "songs of praising and glorifying" as they are called in the Book of Coming Forth By Day"[30] are acts of worship and offering, of Ra, a sharing in his strength and glory, his beneficence and beauty and in His creation and his active care of it.

We find here descriptions and praises of God that would later appear in Hebrew, Christian and Muslim sacred texts. Ra is the Good Shepherd fond of His flock which is in His own image. He rescues the humble and needy, hears and answers the prayers of the prisoner and the oppressed. He is "the helmsman that knows the water well" and the rescuer and "prime minister of the poor". He is the physician who cures without medicine and the judge that takes no bribes. It is this imagery of God and humankind's relationship and the use of human society and nature as realms of revealing the Creator's benevolence that served as a source of not only the Hebrew Psalms but, as we shall see of their theology in general also.

"Blessed is one who sits in the hands of Amen Ra", the *Husia* (p.14) states, "for it is he who directs the timid, who rescues the humble and the needy". This is reflective of the various verses which suggest a liberational ethics in favor of the vulnerable and poor. Also, we see monotheistic declarations thruout the poems such as "You are the only God and there is none like you" (p.14). Showing a merciful Lord tolerant of human frailty, it (p.17) says, "Though the servant be inclined to make mistakes, the Lord is inclined to be merciful."

Finally, it should be noted that this is a composed book, made up of collected praise poems and named accordingly. The thematic glue which holds them is the beauty and power of their homage to Ra and the image of divinity which inspires and uplifts.

C. The Book of the Moral Narrative

Although there are other moral narratives in ancient Kemetic sacred wisdom, none is so clear, beautiful and definitive as the Book of Khun-Anup. This Book is called "The Eloquent Peasant" by traditional egyptologists. However, I have chosen to call it by the name of the man who is its central character and spokesman, a peasant or farmer who is unjustly treated and appeals for relief, justice and righteousness from the High Steward, Rensi, who handled such matters. Rensi is impressed with Khun-Anup's eloquence and reports it to the pharaoh. The pharaoh impressed by the report asks Rensi to delay ruling on the case in order to benefit from Khun-Anup's beautiful speech which in ancient Kemet as in other parts of Africa was/is highly appreciated. Rensi was also ordered to take care of Khun-Anup's family for the days he kept Khun-Anup waiting for a decision and to meticulously copy down all he said.

What follows is a series of nine petitions made by Khun-Anup for justice and righteousness or as the Kemites called both, Maat. This treatise is clearly the earliest treatise on social justice inspite of the western claims of Jewish and Greek priority. In fact, when this was written, neither Jews nor Greeks were a nation. As stated in the introduction to the Book of Knowing the Creations, Maat in Kemet was seen as the foundation of both the natural and social order. Its core concept is rightness in nature and righteousness (which makes an order or system right) in human society. Although traditional egyptologists translate Maat mostly as justice in this narrative, I translate it mostly as righteousness. For among the three most used meanings - truth, justice and righteousness - righteousness seems to me to be the most comprehensive and inclusive term and suggests and necessitates both truth and justice. However, it is not incorrect to use either of the three words for Maat, for in Medu Netcher, the language of Kemet, Maat means these three things and more, as stated above.

Khun-Anup appeals to Rensi's sense of righteousness, truth and justice, for Maat was seen in Kemetic society as the spirit and method of organizing and conducting the relations of human society. The pharaoh and his society were the symbol and embodiment of Maat and judges, as the representatives of the pharaoh, wore on their chest an image of the divine power, Maat, pointing it toward the vindicated in a case. Khun-Anup begins by praising Rensi, pharaoh's representative, as one who destroys falsehood and brings righteousness, and challenges him to win eternal life by his righteousness. He subsequently criticizes him for not acting according to Maat. But in the end a judgement is rendered in Khun-Anup's favor.

Several key concepts are advanced in this treatise on social justice.

First, there is the concept of *reciprocity,* a central meaning and expression of Maat. There are essentially three forms of reciprocity advanced here. The first is a compensatory reciprocity, i.e., "a good deed returns to those who do it" (p.32). Secondly, there is an obligatory reciprocity based on the demands of justice, i.e., "Answer not good with evil and put not one thing in the place of another" (p.32). In a word, return in equal measure that which was given to you. And thirdly, there is an initiatory reciprocity that commands one to "do to the doer that he or she may also do." In a word, cultivate Maat in others by doing Maat to them. This we are told by the *Husia* (p.32) is "thanking one for what one may do, (and) blocking a blow before it strikes," i.e., preemptively removing the basis for hostility and negatives.

A second major concept in this treatise is the one discussed above, the obligation for the pharaoh and his officials to maintain and practice Maat. The assertion is that "the balancing of the land lies in Maat." Thus, Khun-Anup tells, Rensi, "Do not speak falsely for you are great; do not act lightly for you have weight; be not untrue for you are the balance and do not swerve, for you are the standard" (p.32). "Helmsman," he concludes, "do not let your ship go astray."

A third major concept is respect and justice for the poor. A prohibition is made against robbing the poor "for the poor's belongings are breath to them and to take them away is to stop up their nose (p.33). Finally, there is a hymn to Maat (truth, justice, righteousness). Maat is for eternity, the *Husia* teaches (p.34). "It goes to the grave with those who do it. When they are buried and the earth envelops them, their name is not erased from the face of the earth." On the contrary, "they are remembered because of their goodness."

D. The Books of Wise Instruction

Certainly one of the most important and well-written kinds of sacred literature of ancient Kemet are the Books of Wise Instruction. Although some traditional egyptologists would argue that the Instructions are more secular than sacred, evidence does not support such a contention.[31] One assumes they came to this conclusion because the Instructions offer explicit life-lessons on how to conduct oneself, alone and with others. However, if that is their main argument - and it seems to be from all readings - then they would have to rule the Book of Proverbs secular. For not only does it contain similar instruction, but also it was based on the ancient Kemetic model and borrowed whole passages from the Book of Amenomope.[32]

The Books of Wise Instruction are as sacred as any of the other books of *The Husia,* for the main focus is on Maat and the moral and spiritual obligation each person has in preserving and practicing it in and for the community. Thus, each person, not just the pharaoh, was urged to preserve and practice Maat. For he or she was judged by it and granted long life on earth as well as eternal life in Amenta (paradise) or death and non-existence based on this.

Therefore, Ptah-hotep says, "Maat is great, its value is lasting and it has remained unchanged and unequalled since the time of its Creator" (p.41). It is, he continues, "a plain path even for the ignorant and those who violate its laws are punished." Thus, he urges moral excellence in all one does "so no fault can be found in your character". Likewise, Kheti tells his son Merikare that "righteousness is fitting for a ruler" and that he should "do that which is right that you may live long on earth" (p.51). For "more acceptable is the virtue of the righteous than the ox of those who do evil" (p.52).

Clearly, then, Maat, the quintessential moral and spiritual concept of ancient Kemetic sacred literature, forms the core focus of the Instructions even though some rather secular situations and solutions are posed. Moreover, given the inseparable link in ancient Kemet and other parts of Africa between the sacred and secular, the attempt to separte them makes little sense and meets with even less success. Thus, the Seba teach their children and the people to think Maat, speak Maat and do Maat in secular and sacred situations. For this will not only insure a mutually beneficial community based on Maat, but also everlasting life.

"Speak truth in your house that the princes of the earth may respect you" teaches Kheti (p.51). "Destroy the desire to do evil within you," Ani says, "for the evil man has no rest" (p.54). Amenomope says, "Better is a bushel which God gives you than five thousand wrongfully gotten" (p.60). Ankhsheshonqi teaches service and gentleness. Phebhor teaches balance and calm and care for the unfortunate.

These are the books and wisdom of the ancient Seba (moral teachers), more precisely, Seba Maat, teachers of Maat, whose legacy we are compelled to honor and build upon. Their method was to give command and counsel to the people thru instructions to their children. As Seti I wrote "command was spoken for them to hear, and counsel was given for them to learn."[33]

E. The Books of Contemplation

These books contain three forms of contemplation: lamentations, prophetic assertions and meditations on death and eternal life. They reflect a skepticism, sadness and contemplative posture born of the collapse and transformation of the social order and the resultant chaos and loss of cultural center this brought.[34] The Books of Khakheper-Ra-Soneb, and Ipuwer represent lamentations on the low state to which the society had fallen. As Khakheper-Ra-Soneb says, "Maat, righteousness and order, has been cast out and isfet, evil and chaos, is in the Council Hall. The way of God is violated and His commandments are brushed aside. The land is in turmoil and there is mourning everywhere" (p.77). Under pressure, he counsels strength saying, "Another heart might bend or break, but a strong heart in the midst of difficulties is an ally to its owner" (p.77).

Ipuwer laments the reversal of the social order when outsiders have destroyed the internal harmony and stability of Kemetic society. "Behold now," he says, "how greatly the people have changed." "The robber has become rich and the honorable person a thief." The foreigners have imposed new ways and created new relations and the righteous "Kemite of yesterday cannot be found anywhere."

In the Book of Dialog with the Soul a man expresses despair at the changed social circumstances and contemplates death. This is the earliest known literary example of a soul in turmoil confronting unjust suffering and raising the question of why and what is to be done. It predates the Hebrew Book of Job approximately fifteen hundred years which represents a similar concern and question and to which it has been compared. "To whom shall I speak today," the man dialoging with his soul asks. "Brothers and sisters are evil and friends today are not worth loving. Kindness has passed away and violence is imposed on everyone." However, the soul refuses to allow the sufferer to give in to the urge to die. It counsels internal strength and durability, saying "cast your complaints aside.. and cling to life" (p.82).

The first three songs in Book of Songs focus meditation on the inevitability of death and the need to enjoy life now for the most part and suggests a posture that is expressed later in the Hebrew Book of Ecclesiastes. "Celebrate, then, the days of rejoicing and do not tire of them. For lo, none may take their goods with them and none who depart ever come back again" (p.83). The last song, however, focuses on praise of learning and the learned and argues it is learned achievement which causes one's name to last forever. "Man decays," it states, "his corpse becomes dust and all his relatives die. But a book causes him to be remembered...." Indeed, "Better is a book than a well-built house...or a stela in the temple."

Finally, the Book of Neferti offers prophecy of the coming of a righteous savior-king, a messiah to re-establish Maat and cast out isfet. This is the oldest and clearest messianic projection and antedates the Hebrew model of David by more than a thousand years. At least one traditional egyptologist has argued that such messianism was evident in Ipuwer, which is at least five hundred years earlier, but the passage he quotes to support it seems more an appeal to God than the pharaoh.[35] However, there are other passages in Ipuwer that suggest such a messianic hope and projection. Also, a note of interest in this prophecy is the prediction of a messiah king born of a mother from Nubia, which was the source of repeated Kemetic renaissances after periods of degeneration and despair.

F. The Book of Delcarations of Virtues

As stated earlier, the heart of Kemetic ethics and spiritual striving is

Maat. Kemetic ethics and spirituality, like all African ethics and spirituality, have and stress a practical dimension. Righteousness is real only in personal and social practice. As Seba Ankhsheshonqi says, "There is no good deed except a good deed that is done for one who needs it" (p.66). Maat, then, is a social as well as spiritual task for which the reward is an enjoyable and beautiful life in the community on earth and a spiritual life in the heavens as a living god (see below in the Books of Rising Like Ra). In a word, Maat is both a personal and social task and the promise and reward for completing it.

The Kemites, thus, developed an ideal character type rooted in and reflective of Maat which the Instructions urge and the Declarations of Virtues state as both an accomplished fact and a model to emulate. This ideal type was the *geru,* the self-mastered, i.e., calm, silent, controlled, modest, wise, gentle and socially active; and the *geru Maat,* who was truly the self-mastered. The first was the self-mastered, the second a kind of master of the self-mastered. The opposite of the self-mastered is the unrestrained person - hot-mouthed, hot-tempered, aggressive, and generally infused with isfet, the opposite of Maat. The contrast of these two types is found in Amenomope (p.59) who poses the unrestrained as "a tree grown in unfertile ground. Its leaves wither quickly and its unripe fruit falls to the ground." "But the self-mastered man or woman sets himself or herself apart. He or she is like a tree grown in fertile ground. It grows green and doubles its yield of fruit." A similar analogy would appear in the Hebrew Bible in both Psalms 1.3 and Jeremiah 17:18. Such borrowing of imagery and concept Griffith tells us was not abnormal, for "when the Hebrews were becoming civilized under Solomon and his successors, they looked especially to Egypt and Babylonia for instructions in the arts of life."[36]

What one sees, then in the Declarations of Virtues is the practice of basic values on the personal and social level which pose an ideal type and serve as a model of Maat for others to emulate. It is important to note that the personal is inseparable from the social, that righteousness and restraint are always, as in other African ethics and spirituality, achieved, tested and tempered in relations with others. Maat begins with family relations that makes one praised by his (her) father, loved by his (her) mother, and cherished by his (her) brothers and sisters. Maat expresses itself in a classic statement of Kemetic morality which appear thousands of years later in Hebrew Christian sacred texts: " I gave food to the hungry, clothes to the naked, water to the thirsty and a boat to those without one." The last part of this declaration of virtue, of course, reflects again the Kemetic sea-faring environment and reveals the essentiality of having a means of transportation on water.

Also, the virtues of kind-heartedness, gentleness, truth, justice, commitment to the poor and vulnerable, i.e., being "a friend to the poor" (p.96), "a shelter for the child and help to the widow" (p.93), honor for parents and respect for the human personality as a result of "know(ing) the God that dwells in man and woman" (p.94) are promoted.

These Declarations which were usually found on stelae, a kind of memorial plaque, form a parallel and complement to the Declarations of Innocence which appear in the Book of Coming Forth by Day (see below) and thus, express a consistent ethic of right thought and practice with focus on social service whose reward is found in this life and the next, i.e, being "one welcomed by others, widely loved and cheerful" (p.95) and "reach(ing) the city of those who dwell in eternity" (p.97).

F. The Books of Rising Like Ra

These books are singularly and together the oldest written record of the dawn of structured moral consciousness. They represent Africans leading the human rupture with the animal world and establishing not only an ethical standard of social behavior but posing the possiblity of resurrection, ascension and transformation into a living god. In this section, I have given these books titles different than those most traditional egyptologists have assigned them. The oldest texts which are from the Old Kingdom and are called by them the Pyramid Texts.[37] I have titled the Book of Rising and Transformation. The rationale for this is the focus and activity expressed in the text where the royal vindicated one, i.e., the pharaoh in this case, rises from the dead, ascends in the heavens and transforms into a living god. Rising here refers both to resurrection and ascension in the heavens. And transformation is achieved through having lived righteously, becoming one with God and then becoming a living god oneself, i.e., a power in the heavens.

The texts from the Middle Kingdom are called the Coffin Texts by the traditional egyptologists.[38] These I have titled "The Book of Vindication" which, as the first line in the book shows, is what at least one part of it, if not the total text, was called. Finally, I have rejected the title, Book of the Dead, and used also the title the Kemites assigned the book, i.e., The Book of Coming Forth By Day.[39]

Although the Book of Rising and Transformation was apparently first used mainly for pharaohs, it was, in my estimation, a model for human possibility represented by the person who more than anyone else symbolized the possibility of divinity. Moreover, this book and the others in this section were eventually appropriated by the masses and became the basic texts for "rising like Ra". Thus, I used "royal vindicated one", or "vindicated one" rather than the "N" or name of a particular pharaoh as is the practice of traditional egyptologists. For it is not just the pharaoh who rose and transformed, but any and all vindicated ones, all those who could say "I have stood up with my feather of *truth* on my head and my righteousness on my brow"(p.113).

I have put the books in an order that is reversed chronologically, bu' which logically fit according to the activity each contains. First a persor *comes forth* (resurrects), declares his (her) innocence in the Hall of Judg ment, is *vindicated,* and then *rises and transforms* into a living god. Although there is some of each in all, each book tends to have more of the activity by which it is named.

In the Book of Coming Forth By Day, I have used the title, Declarations of Innocence, for the thirty-six and forty-two declarations made by a person in the Hall of Righteousness to establish his (her) blamelessness. Although some traditional egyptologists call this statement, "the Negative Confession", others have used "the Declarations of Innocence" also. The Declaration is obviously not a confession either in content or context. It is not an admission of faults, but rather a denial of them. And the Hall of Righteousness is not a place where one confesses faults, but rather where one declares oneself innocent so that he or she may be vindicated and rise like Ra.

One of the major significances of these "Books of Rising Like Ra" is their emphasis on the Kemetic belief in the concept of the possibility of immortality and divinity for humans. In a word, they posit that thru right thought and practice, one could become a god and live forever at the right hand of Ra. This could be achieved as these books and others of *The Husia* state and suggest, in three basic ways: 1) achieved internal development; 2) excellence in social relations; and 3) significant sociohistorical service and achievement.

The Husia (p.107) says, "I worship God in heaven and I am given that which endures in the midst of things which are overthrown." "May I rise like a living god," the petitioner prays, "and give forth light like the divine powers in heaven" (p.106). "Let life rise out of death," the Kemites prayed, "let not decay make an end of me . . ." (p.108). And they were assured, "You are a god and you shall be a god" (p.114) thru your vindication in Maat.

Finally, it is important to note that in the Delcarations of Innocence, as has been pointed out often, we find a source of the Ten Commandments. The Declarations of Innocence of theft, lies, murder, adultery, blasphemy, violation of sacred days and covetousness show this source clearly (pp.109-110). In the Books of Rising Like Ra we find again the historical source of so many other concepts central to Hebrew and Christian theology, i.e., resurrection, the Risen Savior, the Beloved son, the Day and Hall of Judgment, immortality of the soul, etc. "The Heavens declare: *This royal vindicated one* is my beloved son in whom I am well pleased," says *the Husia* (p.119). The vindicated one "comes to (you) an undying and indestructible spirit" O Ra (p.119). "Have they killed you or said you shall die?", *the Husia* asks? "You shall never die, but shall surely live forever" (p.124). It is this and the other contributions cited above as well as those unmentioned above which form the rich and ancient moral and spiritual legacy Africa, thru its daughter, ancient Kemet, has given the world.

IV. CONCLUSION

It is clear that the quest for an authentic African spirituality unavoidably depends on the restoration of the central sacred writings of Kemet. And this is the mission and meaning of *the Husia*. The practice of restoration is an historical legacy from Kemet and we honor our ancestors by continuing and expanding that legacy. As King Shabaka said of the Memphite Text, "His Majesty found it as a *work of the ancestors*, it having been eaten by worms and not legible from beginning to end. Then his Majesty *wrote it out anew, so that it was more beautiful than it was before*" (emphasis mine).

The task, then, is clear: to restore that which was in ruins, to raise up that which was destroyed by the invaders who were ignorant and disregardful of Maat. It is a great challenge to dare restore the work of the ancestors; to dare raise up and re-establish that which has lain in ruins for thousands of years and to make it even better than before in the tradition of the ancient kings and queens, scribes, Seba, and peoples of Kemet. What will evolve from our work is an established discourse and critical witness in the form of *the Husia* to the historical and current richness and value of Kemetic spirituality. It will reveal and reaffirm the Way of Maat (Wat-n-Maat), a well-defined path and pattern of human life which offers an ascendant paradigm, not only for ourselves as Africans, but for both history and humanity in the true spirit of our Kemetic ancestors, the sun people, who were truly the light and warmth of the world.

* * *

NOTES

1. James Breasted,*The Dawn of Conscience,* New York: Charles Scribner's Sons, 1934, p. xv.
2. Ibid, p. 13
3. Cheikh Anta Diop, *Civilisation au Barbarie,* Paris: Presence Africaine, 1981, p. 12 translation mine.
4. See Gayraud S. Wilmore and James Cone (eds.) *Documents of Black Theology,* Maryknoll, NY: Orbis Books, 1979; C. Eric Lincoln, *The Black Experience in Religion,* Garden city, NY: Anchor Books, 1974; and E.U. Essien-Udom, *Black Nationalism,* New York: Dell Publishing, 1964.
5. Yosef ben-Jochannan. *Our Black Seminarians and Black Clergy Without a Black Theology,* New York: Alkebu-lan Books. 1978.
6. _____. *African Origins of Major Western Religions,* New York: Alkebu-lan Books, 1970.
7. George James. *Stolen Legacy,* San Francisco: Julian Richardson Associates, 1976.
8. ben-Jochannan, (1978) op. cit.

9. Gerald Massey. *Ancient Egypt: The Light of the World,* New York: Samuel Weiser, 1970; R.A. Schwaller de Lubicz, *The Temple in Man,* Brookline, Mass.: Autumn Press, 1977.
10. Jacob H. Carruthers. *Essays in Ancient Egyptian Studies,* Los Angeles: University of Sankore Press, 1984.
11. Maulana Karenga. *Selections From The Husia: Sacred Wisdom of Ancient Egypt,* Los Angeles: University of Sankore Press, 1984.
12. Alexandre Piankoff. *Egyptian Religious Texts and Representations,* Volumes 1-6, Princeton: Princeton University Press, 1957-1964.
13. Miriam Lichtheim.*Ancient Egyptian Literature,* 3 volumes, Berkeley: University of Press, 1975-80.
14. Joseph Kaster. *Wings of the Falcon: Life and Thought of Ancient Egypt,* New York: Holt, Rinehart & Wilson, 1968
15. William K. Simpson, *The Literature of Ancient Egypt,* New Haven: Yale University Press, 1973.
16. Alexandre Piankoff. *Mythological Papyri,*Princeton: Princeton University Press, 1957.
17. Henri Frankfort. *Kingship and the Gods,* Chicago: University of Chicago Press, 1948, p. 24.
18. P. LePage Renouf.*The Hibbert Lectures,* London: Williams and Norgate, 1880, p. 226.
19. Siegfried Morenz.*Egyptian Religion,* Ithaca, NY: Cornell University Press, 1978, p. 151.
20. E.A. Wallis Budge. *From Fetish to God in Ancient Egypt,* Oxford: University Press, 1934, p. 411.
21. Renouf, op. cit., p. 93ff; Budge, op. cit., p.138ff; Morenz, op. cit., p.19.
22. Frankfort, op. cit., p. 61.
23. Morenz, op. cit., p. 167.
24. Breasted, op. cit., chapter XVII.
25. Karenga, *the Husia,* op. cit., p. .From here on, the Husia shall be listed inside the text as the reference point for all Husitic quotes rather than the author in the Notes, bearing in mind that it refers to the author's selection and retranslation cited above.
26. Frankfort, op. cit., p. 29.
27. Breasted, op. cit., p.38-39.
28. Henri Frankfort. *Ancient Egyptian Religion,* New York: Columbia University Press, 1949.
29. Judith Gleason. *Leaf and Bone: African Praise Poems,* New York: Viking Press, 1980.
30. E.A. Wallis Budge. *The Book of the Dead,* Hyde Park, NY: University Books, 1960, p. 355.
31. Frankfort, (1949) op. cit., pp. 62-65.
32. W.O.E. Oesterley. *The Wisdom of Egypt and the Old Testament,* New York: The Macmillan Co., 1927.
33. Lichtheim, op. cit., Vol. I, p. 116.
34. Breasted, op, cit., chapter X.

35. Ibid, p. 199.
36. F.L. Griffith. "The Teachings of Amenophis," *Journal of Egyptian Archaelogy,* XII (1926), pp. 191-231.
37. R.O. Faulkner. *The Pyramid Texts,* 2 volumes, Oxford: Oxford University Press 1969.
38. R.O. Faulkner. *The Coffin Texts,* 2 volumes London: Aris & Phillips, 1972.
39. Thomas Allen. *The Book of the Dead or Going Forth by Day,* Chicago: University of Chicago Press, 1974.

ANCIENT EGYPTIAN THOUGHT AND THE DEVELOPMENT OF AFRICAN (BLACK) PSYCHOLOGY

WADE W. NOBLES

An understanding of the relationship between ancient Egyptian thought and African (Black) psychology requires first and foremost the recognition that the ancient African world was a world of symbolism and that much of what is meaningful in African psychology today has gone unrecognized and misunderstood because of our inability to understand the role of symbolism in the African mind—both ancient and modern. Typically for most of us today, symbols and symbolism represent the use of abbreviated designations which "stand-for" something. Symbolism thusly amounts to a kind of metaphoric device. However, symbolism in the context of this discussion must be thought of as the set of rules and methods for analytically interpreting ancient African thought. Through the use of symbols and symbolism the ancients intuitive vision approached the world of knowing with an attitude which perceived all the phenomena of nature as symbolic writing, capable of revealing the forces and laws governing the material and spiritual aspects of their universe. The use of symbols and symbolism in ancient times was in fact the means for transmitting a precise and exact rational, if not suprarational, knowledge which emerged from the intuitive vision. This, Schwalter de Lubicz contends, was the major aspect of ancient science.[1]

Unlike the "stand-for" connotation of the symbolic utilized today, the symbolic of ancient African times, and I would say the contemporary African as well, was a symbolism that went beyond the "representational-sequential-analytical" mode to the "transformation-synchronistic-analogic" mode.

Unlike reading where signs "stand-for" the object, the object and the symbol or sign become identical in African thought. In ancient Africa, for example, the symbol of an animal was worshipped as an act of consecration to the vital functions which the animal incarnated. The symbol of the animal was identical to the law of nature embodied by the animal. Through the use of symbols and the symbolic one can understand in this regard that so-called primitive animal worship was not in reality the worship of animals, but a method used to identify and clarify the essential function or law of nature embodied in the particular animal. Perceptually the symbol and the symbolic should be viewed as material representations of immaterial qualities and functions. The symbol is the objectification of things subjective in us and subliminal in nature.[2] Hence, the method of interpreting ancient African thought, thusly requires us to experience the symbol and the symbolic.

In this regard it has been suggested that in being grounded in the symbolic method and through its use of symbols, ancient Egypt educated the neurological structures of the brain so as to be able to maintain an active conscious connection between the bilateral lobes of the cerebral cortex and the impulses and subliminal information received from the more ancient and deeper brain centers.[3] In doing so the more ancient aspects of our nature were integrated into the activity of human reasoning and thought.

Parenthetically, support for this conception of symbolism and mental functioning is found in modern medical research regarding the anatomical evolution of the brain. Macleans proposes that the triune anatomical division of the brain into hindbrain, midbrain and cerebral cortex parallels distinct functions which developed during successive evolutionary phases.[4] Each new division of the brain grew as a peripheral structure enveloping and encasing the prior brain component. Each division of the brain though interconnected can therefore be distinguished neuro-anatomically (each contains different distributions of the neurochemicals dopamne and cholin-esterase). Each according to Macleans also has its own special intelligence, subjectivity, sense of time and space, memory and motor function. Macleans believes that even today the midbrain and hindbrain lying beneath the cerebral cortex still perform as they did in our most remote ancestors.

I. ANCIENT EGYPTIAN THOUGHT

As stated above, the symbolic attitude or mentality of the ancestors cultivated the intellect to the extent or degree that humans were accustomed to perceiving all the phenomena of nature as a symbolic script capable of revealing the forces and laws governing the universe.

It is the opinion of this author that the activity of ancient human reasoning and thought is only understood via an understanding of the symbolic method (i.e., transformation-synchronistic-analogic modality) and that is the inability to use symbol and symbolism effectively which complicates the appreciation and comprehension of ancient African thought.

Thought which emerges from the use of symbol and the symbolic can be called "speculative" or "imaginative" with the caution that speculative as used here should not be tainted with meaning similar to fantasy. Speculative thought is more akin to intuitive if not visionary modes of apprehension. *Speculative thought attempts to explain, order and above all else unify experience for the knower.*

Reality for the ancients was always conceived as the synthesis of the visible and the invisible, the material and immaterial, the cognitive and emotive, the inner and the outer. Accordingly, the phenomenal world was known through speculative thought as the representative of the subliminal.

Problem in the Study

In addition to the difficulties associated with attempting to understand one thought system with methods relevant to another thought system, the study of ancient Egyptian thought is also marred by the proliferation of information about ancient African life from the perspective of white vested interest. This latter point is understood if one understands that the political control of knowledge is a necessary condition for white supremacy; and, that in this regard as Diop has pointed out, the common denominator characterizing the study of ancient Egypt by white egyptologists has been their seemingly desperate pathological necessity and unrelentless attempt to refute ancient Africa's Blackness.[5] Consequently, information regarding ancient Africa has been destroyed, distorted, falsified, suppressed and intentionally made unclear.

Hence, given that the remaining discussion is obviously influenced by these two levels of concern, the analysis offered here is more an initial beginning step than a definitive conclusion. In order to overcome the dangerous limitations and misinterpretations associated with this dilemma, one must attempt to seek out and utilize the techniques of thinking practiced by the ancients. The ancient technique of thinking depended upon a fuller and richer integration of mind, body and spirit. Hence, we are proposing that we utilize this technique while simultaneously attempting to uncover the very system which one is utilizing in order to discover the thinking system.

The solution to this problem in part will be achieved when, as Professor Carruthers points out, the methodological problems are solved (i.e., evolutionary theory, spatial perceptions, linguistics and historiographical context, chronological perspective and identification) and the ideological accuracy associated with reformulating an African world view from ancient Egyptian data is adopted.[6] In regards to ancient Egyptian thought, this author accepts as irrefutable the data that demonstrate that the oldest records of human culture were found in Africa and that the people who created and invented the cultural foundations for and developments of religion, science, art, mathematics, medicine and education were Black.

In relation to ancient Egyptian thought one must recognize that of the thirty dynasties representing Egyptian civilization, it was during the indigenous Black dynasties (1, 12, 18 and 25) that the greatest creativity and achievements were accomplished. In fact, as noted by Clark, by the end of the sixth dynasty or what is referred to as the old kingdom, the pattern of African civilization (and I would interject African thought) was complete.[7] Clark goes on to maintain that there was no fundamental change in the philosophy of ancient Africa as represented by the Egyptian experience until the conversion to Christianity in the fourth and fifth Century A.D.

In recognition of the maxim that "ideas are the substance of behavior", the accomplishments (behavior) of Black dynastic Egypt provide us with a wellspring of insight and direction for understanding the thought (ideas) of Ancient Africa and the subsequent development of psychology. Even though this analysis will concentrate on Dynasties I through IV, 18 and 25 it should be noted that dynastic Egypt didn't simply materialize out of nothing. In fact one must recognize as did Chancelor Williams that the thinking reflected in early dynastic Egypt was essentially the formalization of pre-dynastic Egyptian thought.[8]

In extending this analysis, at another time, it would be important to also understand the ideas which were the substance of the behavior of Mentuhotep II of the eleventh dynasty who undertook to settle the white Asian problem by reversing the policy of integration and expelling whites from lower Egypt. Additionally it would be important to understand why a revival of learning, science, art and the crafts occurred along with or only with the expulsion of the whites. What ideas characterized this period of Black rule? What ideas or thoughts served as the substance of the behavior of Pharaoh Kamose who during the 17th Dynasty led a man of liberation against the Hyksos rule and helped to usher in the greatest Egyptian Dynasty (the 18th) since the fourth. What ideas or thought governed the age of the Ramses (19th & 20th) whose kings stamped their period of reign as amongst the most outstanding in the long history of Egypt? And finally what ideas or thought influenced the behavior of Pianki to Shabaka to Tanutamon who together stamped an undeniable Black presence on the twenty-fifth Dynasty. What in fact was the central idea or thought which governed Black behavior for close to 2,500 years?

If it is true as Clark suggests, that the philosophy of the latter Dynasties did not fundamentally change from that established during the old kingdom, then we can return to these early indigenous Black Dynasties for our understanding of ancient African thought.

Myth and Ancient African Thought

Interestingly enough an analysis of ancient African mythology shall serve as the starting point for explicating ancient Egyptian thought. The importance of mythology is of course that it is a form of documentation which transcends the human record in as much as it states "truth" rather than a fact. Myth can be considered a form of reasoning and record keeping which goes beyond reasoning and record keeping by providing an implicit guide for bringing about the fulfillment of the truth it proclaims. It connects the invisible order with the visible order.

Myth is therefore the form in which the experience of a people has become conscious and as such should be viewed as a carefully constructed symbolic cloak for their abstract thought. When perceived thusly myth is far more than the product of fantasy, legend, fable and fairytale even though each of the latter retains elements of myth. As symbolism, the imagery and thought reflected in the myth are inseparable from the laws of nature embodied in the drama. It, thereby, provides us with the metaphysical truths about reality.

As a reflection of the thought and experience of a people the analytical value of myth is that it serves as a measure and/or reflection of the human possibilities, probabilities and potentialities of a people. Myth should therefore be taken seriously because it reveals a significant if unverifiable truth.

Myth when taken as concrete and analyzed symbolically can accordingly provide us with an important tool for understanding ancient African thought as well as contemporary African and African-American conduct.

In the Memphite Theology, the ancient Africans spoke the language of myth and it is here that we shall turn to obtain an understanding of ancient African thought.

The inscription called the Memphite Theology is the text taken from a stone bearing the name of an Egyptian pharaoh who ruled about 700 B.C. The text itself is the documentation of African thought which comes from the earliest periods of Egyptian recorded history when the first dynasties made their capitol at Memphis in the city of the God, Ptah. The actual ideas found in the Memphite theological text obviously were present in other African texts; however, the importance of the Memphite text is that it brings together ancient African ideas about creation into a broad philosophical system about the nature of the universe. The text itself is also in part a theological argument regarding the primacy of the God Ptah and the centrality of Memphis in the theocratic state. [9]

Overall the Memphite text takes the earlier African ideas about creation (i.e., Atum coming into being out of the primeval waters, and then bringing forth the Ennead of Gods into existence) and places or subsumes them into a symbolic system which reveals the divine laws of nature.

In the Memphite theology, for instance "The Primate of the gods, Ptah, conceived in his heart, everthing that exists and by his utterance created them all". The god, "Ptah", is first to emerge from the primeval waters of "Nun" and emerges as a primeval hill. Next the god "Atum" emerges from the waters and sits upon "Ptah". In the primeval waters there remains four pairs of male and female gods: (1) Nun and Naunet (primeval water and counter heaven; (2) Hugh and Hauhet (the boundless and its compliment or opposite); (3) Kuk and Kauket (darkness and its compliment or opposite); and (4) Amun and Amaunet (the hidden and and its compliment or opposite). It should be noted that according to the Memphite theology, while the sun god, Atum, sits upon Ptah, the primeval hill, he accomplishes the work of creation. [10]

It is important to recognize however that the creation story for the Black ancients was not simply a record of a series of events of time. The creation story was a "speculation" about the principle of life and the order of the universe. From this perspective one can see that the theology of Memphis perceived God as a spirit and the fundamental or founding principle of the world's organization as ideas. [11]

When one examines this mythology as mythic symbolism a very clear system of ideas and a specific pattern of thought emerges. In this theology all the characters or actors in the primeval drama are aspects of Ptah, the supreme power. Ptah, in fact is not only the creator of the gods, he/she is the provider of their particular power. Symbolically, the Ennead of Gods are attributes of Divine Being and law. In re-noting that the imagery and thought reflected in the myth are inseparable from the laws of nature embodied in the drama, this myth provides us with an objectification of the subliminal.

In analyzing the myth as symbolism and speculative thought, one is able to see that, overall, the myth of the ancients accomplished two things. First it gave or outlined the steps whereby the universe was arranged; or created; and, secondly it provided a series of symbols to describe the origin and development of human consciousness. In the first regard, the Coffin text (VI, 342) for example, suggest that God while still motionless in the primeval waters had "thought" out the ideas of all the creatures in the universe before creation began. Wallis Budge notes that in the "Book of Knowing the Evolutions of Ra", the god Neb-er-tcher records the following story of creation and the birth of the gods: The text states:

"I am he who evolved himself under the form of the god Khepera. I, the evolver of the evolutions and developments which came forth from my mouth. No heaven existed, and no earth, and no terrestrial animals or reptiles had come into being. I formed them out of the inert mass of watery matter. I found no place whereon to stand . . . I was alone, and the gods Shu and Tefnut had not gone forth from me; there existed none other who worked with me. I laid the foundations of all things by will, and all things evolved themselves therefrom. I united myself to my shadow, and set forth Shu and Tefnut out of myself; thus from being one god I became three, and Shu and Tefnut gave to Nut and Seb, and Nut gave birth to Osiris, Horus-Khent-An-Maa, Sut, Isis and Nephthys, at one birth, one after the other, and their children multiply upon this earth". [12]

In ancient African cosmogony the "primeval waters" and Divine mind (intelligence) are fundamental to all creation. In the Memphite theology God is both a spirit and a fundamental principle of the world's organization.

The essence of God is revealed as thought (will) and command (intent). The symbols or signs of heart and tongue become the material representation of the immaterial qualities or attributes of will (thought) and intent (command). The essence of Ptah is therefore will and intent. One text states:

"In the form of Atum there came into being heart and there
came into being tongue. But the supreme God is Ptah, who
has endowed all the gods and their Ka's through that *heart*
which appeared in the form of Thoth, both of which were
forms of Ptah."

The heart is the organ which conceives thought and the tongue is
the organ which creates the conceived thought as a phenomenal actuality. As an attempt to explain order and unify experience, (i.e., serve
as speculative thought) the Memphite theology essentially states that
the natural attributes of the Divine mind was will and intent or divine
intelligence. In chapter 85 of The Book of the Dead, the creator is
heard to say:

"I came into being of myself in the midst of the primeval
waters . . ."

During another period Atum is conceived as the aboriginal deity.
Atum which meant self-created; everything and nothing, the all inclusive and the emptiness, was considered a demiurge possessing creative powers.[13] Atum was not only God but all things to come. In ancient
text Atum is seen creating from him/herself all else. In the pyramid
text, for example, (see Utterance 527) the text states:

"Atum was creative in that he proceeded to masturbate
with himself . . .; He put his penis in his hand that he might
obtain the pleasure of emission thereby and there was
born brother and sister - That is Shu and Tefnut".

In another myth, Shu and Tefnut came into being by being spat
forth from the creator's mouth. Utterance 600 of the pyramid text
states:

"You spat forth as Shu, you expecturated as Tefnut, you
put your arms around them in an act of Ka-giving so that
your Ka might be in them".

In noting the symbol and use the symbolism in the creation story as
well as the role of speculative thought, one is able to understand why
in ancient African mythology there is no story or drama of the separate
creation of Man. Conceptually or more accurately the intuitive vision
of the Ancients saw no firm and final dividing line between gods and
men. To the Ancients, all the elements of the universe were "consub-
stantial". That is to say the nature of all things was of the same spirit or
Ka. The Divine willed first itself to be and then manifested itself as

complimentary male-female gods who in having the attributes (the Ka) of the Divine manifested themselves as man and woman. Hence, all things are endowed with the spirit of God, (i.e., the Ka of God).

In remembering that mythology is symbolic writing designed to reveal the natural law and forces governing the universe, and that ancient thought was speculative thought, one can speculate that what is being revealed here is an account of creation as physical and spiritual generation. In terms of symbol and symbolic thought the masturbation version accounts for or explains creation in terms of physical self-generation where as the spitting version symbolically expresses creation as the entry of the breath of life or divine word.

It shall be noted that these two versions are not alternative explanations but complimentary text. The masturbation motif stresses the physical reproductive aspect of life behind which lies the spiritual essence of life. Hence the generation of Shu and Tefnut are described in terms of both masturbation (physical) and spitting (spiritual). The early Coffin text in fact clarifies this point. It states:

> "This was the manner of your engendering: You conceived with your mouth and you gave birth from your hand in the pleasure of emission.".

The underlying law being revealed here is (1) that Being, as represented by the creation story, is simultaneously "spiritual" and "physical"; and, (2) that the reality (creation) is the consequence of both the idea (conception) and the act (masturbation). Human reality results therefore from both thinking and doing.

If one looks closely at ancient African thought particularly as revealed in mythology, the underlying law which governs the universe becomes rather evident. For instance, the Jackal in ancient African thought was the symbol of judgement. However, as symbol and symbolism it represents "digestion" which in turn should be viewed as the precise act of innate discrimination and analysis. The process of eating, we all will note, is an act of ingestion and digestion wherein we separate out the elements capable of transformation (into energy) and future evolution from the elements that are untransmutable (waste). Digestion is a "destructive-productive" process of transformation and the Jackal which symbolically represents the incarnation of this thereby represents the recognition of "Form" in the universe being capable of breaking down into its constituent elements which in turn serves as the base for continued evolution (the process of transformation). In brief, death of the old gives life to the new. Other "underlying laws" revealed in the symbolism of ancient Egyptian thought are growth, assimilation, coagulation, decomposition and of course transformation.

A summary reading of mythology reveals that ancient Egyptian thought can be characterized as possessing (1) "ideas of thought" which represent the human capacity to have "will" and to invent or create; (2) "ideas of command" which represent the human capacity to have "intent" and to produce that which it wills. Parenthetically these two, will and intent, are the characteristics of divine spirit and would serve as the best operationalization of human intelligence.

Before attempting to apply the sets of ideas found in ancient Egyptian thought to the emergence of Black psychology, one must discuss the ancient notion of soul or spirit in Egyptian metaphysics. Psychology technically means the study of the soul or spirit. Thusly, Black psychology must be the study of the soul belonging to a particular group of people whose class membership is rooted in the historical and cultural experience of African people and who are euphemistically called Black.

II. SOUL IN EGYPTIAN METAPHYSICS

Ancient Egyptian thought was fundamentally concerned with the "essential" or "essence" of being which when codified became the "ontological principle of consubstantiation". This principle is in fact the primary principle underlying the universal laws of nature.

The African proverb, "whatever is is in the first place spirit" is an abstract (symbolic) codification of this principle as reflected in a more contemporary African experience. The principle of consubstantiality states that the elements of the universe are of one substance. With the essence of being of the same stuff, the ancient African law of transformation and the later practice of substitution (i.e., that which acts in the place of another, shares some of the personality of that other) makes sense. One can only have a conception of growth which results from the Jackal function if the essence of all things is the same. Similarly, one can only accept the substitution of one thing for another if the important aspects (i.e., their nature) of each is the same. The essence or essentialness of all things is spirit. Hence, it is very important that we understand the conceptualization of the spirit or soul in Eqyptian thought.

Division of the Psychic Nature

The psychic or spiritual constitution in ancient Egyptian thought was believed to be comprised of seven parts or divisions. (The Ka) or principle body was the first division of the psychic nature. It like all others had a formal structure capable of ultimate disintegration and would return to the elements from which it came unless it was Osirified or mummified..

The "Ba" (soul of breath) was the second division of the psychic nature. It represented the transmission of the breath of life. The

Ancients believed that there was only one power, which was symbolically represented as "the breath", and, that this power or breath was transmitted from the ancestors to the descendants. The Ancients believed that this power or energy has always existed and will always exist. The Ba is the invisible source (like electricity) of all visible functions. The Ba was in effect the vital principle which represented the essence of all things.

The Khaba or third division of the psychic nature was in fact a luminous intangible covering of the vital principle (Ba). In the Egyptian language Khaba means to veil or to cover. Among the phenomena which it produced are emotion and motion. The Ancients believed that human emotion and motion were produced by the Khaba. It was further thought to be responsible for sustaining the sensory perceptions and the phenomena of color, total harmony and the circulation of blood. It was also responsible for delusions and was sometimes called the sin body of the Ancients. Finally because it was the abode of the psyche pattern by which the body was afflicted, it was believed to play a significant part in disease.

The Akhu or fourth division of the psychic nature was the seat of "intelligence" and mental perception". It was in the area of Akhu, the Ancients believed, that the whole mystery of the human mind was to be comprehended. The mind was in fact, an entity in and of itself and only during physical life was the human mind the instrument of the human spirit. The concerns of the mind were primarily the survival of its own thinking processes. The Akhu was characterized by attributes like judgement, analysis, and mental reflection, all of which could be trained and disciplined so as to be dedicated to the service of higher being.

The Seb or ancestral soul was the fifth division of the psychic nature. It however, does not manifest itself in humans until puberty or adolescence. The evidence of the presence of the Seb was the power of the human being to generate his own kind. The Seb is in effect the self-creative power of Being.

The Putah was the sixth division of the psychic nature and represented the "first intellectual father". The Putah was associated with the mental maturity of the individual. The coming of Putah marked the union of the brain with the mind. It was the Putah which established the fact of the person and from the moment of its manifestation or attainment it was believed that intellect (i.e., will and intent) alone governed conduct.

The Atmu was the seventh division of the soul. It was considered the divine or the eternal/soul. In some text it is identified with the seventh creation, the god Atmu who inspired the breath of life everlasting. In ritual this division of the soul is represented as parenthood which symbolically stood for the presence of full creative powers and perpetual continuation.

Enwrapping and serving as the essence of all the divisions of the soul was the Ka of God. In some text the Ka is thought of as the sum of the above mentioned seven. However, this is only true if the sum is considered greater than the total of its parts. The Ka was the divine spirit which endowed all things and which survived past the physical life of the individual. The Ka, it was thought, had magical powers and could cause the dead to live again in the thoughts of the survivors and could even enter into a mummified being, animate it internally and likeness of the living. It appeared in the dream state and some believed actually traveled independently of the body during those times.

III. IMPLICATIONS FOR THE EMERGENT AFRICAN PSYCHOLOGY AND BLACK HUMAN CONDUCT

Admittedly this paper is diminished by the lack of a full discussion of the changes occurring in the intellectual history of humankind resulting from European and/or Western dominance. For instance, "The Mesopotamian shift" which resulted in a very different psychological mood, wherein man came to distrust the cosmic order is of paramount importance for a fuller appreciation of the intellectual history of human beings.

Similarly the Greek mutations are most informative. For example, the Greek so-called derivation of Atum from "alpha", the negative prefix meaning not and "temnein" the present infinitive active of "temno" to cut resulted in a meaning of Atum as "that which can not be cut" which in fact was distortion of the Ancient African meaning of "Atum" (i.e., the all and the not yet being). The shift in thinking and emphasis resulting from the exchange of Egypt with Mesopotamia and the distortion occurring alongside or simultaneously with the ascension of Judeo-Christian and Greco-Roman world dominance requires major analytical treatment. [14] In fact, an analysis of the Mesopotamian shift and the Judeo-Christian Greco-Roman distortion will be necessary if we are to truly understand what is wrong with Western Psychology.

Nevertheless, the implications that ancient African thought has for the development of Black psychology are clear and stateable. These implications are, in fact, found in the definition of "Beingness" and "Becoming".

Speculative thought would therefore suggest in this regard that human nature is in fact a symbolic presentation of divine Ka. Hence to be human is to possess "will" and "intent" (i.e., divine intelligence) and to have the capacity to develop and change. Humans have "intent" and are innately endowed with the capacity to ascend or grow to the higher condition. Implied in the capacity to grow (ascend) is the law of transformation. The implication, the ancient African ideas of transformation has for human psychology is the recognition that humans have the capacity to change.

"Beingness" would therefore be comprised of having the capacity of will and intent (Divine Intelligence), and the ability to command and produce that which it wills. "Becoming" in turn would be by definition the innate capacity to develop and change. Given ancient African thought, both Beingness and Becoming would be based on the principle of Ka or universal spirit. The fundamental basis of all things (as a state of being or the process of becoming) is spirit or energy.

African Psychology and Black Human Conduct

Hence, Black human conduct is or should be the behavioral representation of African thought. Ideas are the substance of behavior. Given the ancient African ideas discussed above, one can see not only a predictable and consistent value system, principle of identity and cultural common sense one can also speculate as the appropriate human conduct and social order emerging from the African philosophy and culture. For example, human purpose, the distortion of which is the root of almost all human mal-functioning short of biological or chemical based maladies, and the "meaningfullness" of one's action is revealed in the awareness of one's intent and will. Similarly, a sense of self as collective or extended (i.e., pars pro toto), the comprehension and respect of the sameness of self and others; the interdependence and synthesis of human beings, etc. all emerge from and are dependent upon the African ontological principle of consubstantiation.

African-American Mentality

Almost as if motivated by the ancestral spirit, several Black Psychologists began to develop conceptualizations of Black mental health which recognized that natural functioning was the result of being centered in and consistent with oneself. In an earlier article, this author noted for instance, that the natural consciousness of Black people is forced to relate to a reality defined by the cultural prerequisites of white people.[15] Such a situation it was argued was tantamount to Black people living in an insane environment.

That is, it is insane for Black people, where national consciousness understands the interdependence and harmonious aspects with a reality which is based on independence (selfishness) and conflict (competition) in the universe.

The cause of this insanity is in fact a disruption in the natural, harmonious relationship between the spiritual, material, conceptual, affective and connotive aspects of Black psycho-social and geophysical reality. One consequence of this disruption is a perceptual and emotional distortion. Hence, insane Blacks deny their self and kind.

Consequently, a Black who kills another Black doesn't realize his act is suicide and not homicide. Another consequence of this disruption is cognitive and political confusion. Here we find insane Black people deifying white people and dehumanizing Black people. Conceptually, whites are viewed by Blacks as omnipotent and this belief suggests, in effect, that if anything has to get done, it is they who must do it. Here we find Black people also denying our communality and epitomizing our individuality. Politically therefore, Black people should unite, affirm and protect their own.

The Black dope pusher, pimp and killer are only symptomatic of Black people living in white insanity. And, as long as Black people respond to and accept (without question) white reality we will never be able to see, think, feel and act in a fashion that affirms and protects our being.

Consistent with the above mentioned ancient African ideas, Akbar identified mental health as the affirmative identification and commitment to our African (natural) identity.[16] In utilizing one's own natural identity as the core being, he went on to conceptualize a system of mental disorders (anti-self, alien-self, etc.) which demonstrated that African-American insanity is the result of engaging in behaviors which deny ones African Identity and survival imperatives. The key, of course, to understanding abnormal and/or aberrant functioning is found in ancient thought, (i.e., know thy Ka). In knowing one's nature (i.e., having will and intent and the capacity to produce that which one wills), one is less likely to allow societal conditions to become internalized and in so doing become the agent of psychological maladaptation and mental dysfunctioning.

Features of Normal and Abnormal Functioning

Unlike the mathematical illusion of normality found in the west, normality which would be consistent with African thought is a normal which is equivalent to one's nature.

Human development is normally a natural and an orderly process. It in fact parallels and in many instances mirrors the growth and development of every thing endowed with a "Ka" (i.e., all living things). It is believed that what living things have in common, in terms of the developmental process, is (1) a sense of "self", which gives it some understanding of its own integrity; (2) Motion, which implies its changing nature; (3) Order, which defines the natural connections and separations of its integrity; (4) Form, which outlines its integrity and marks the point of distinction; and (5) Direction, which identifies its purpose and mission. These five characteristics can be thought of as developmental needs or conditions (not stages) in the human process. Human development, therefore is characterized by: (1) The *condition of self* wherein humans have a need to understand and define that which represents their own essence (integrity); (2) The *condition of motion* wherein humans have a need to be active, to grow or change; (3) The *condition of order* wherein humans have a need for balance between synthesis (connection), and contradiction (antagonism); (4) The *condition of form* wherein humans have a need to outline or define the essence of integrity of being human; (5) The *condition of direction* wherein humans have a need to define their purpose which is always a response to affirm one's humanity. Thus to be normal is to be consistent with the dictates of one's Ka. To be normal is to possess thought and command and to have the ability to produce that which one wills. Attitudinally and behaviorally normal or natural functioning is represented by (1) a sense of self which is collective or extended; (2) an attitude wherein one understands and respects the sameness in oneself and others; (3) a clear sense of one's spiritual connection to the universe; (4) the sense of mutual responsibility; and (5) a conscious understanding that human abnormality and/or deviancy is any act which is in opposition to oneself and kind which really means abnormality and/or deviance is any act which is in opposition to the Ka of God.

As noted above Akbar's notions of mental disorders are predicated on the notion of opposition or alienation from one's self. Abnormal functioning he contends can be the results of (1) an *alien-self disorder* wherein the person's thoughts and actions are characterized by an active "rejection" of themselves and of their natural and/or ethnic dispositions; (2) an *anti-self disorder* wherein the person's thoughts and actions are characterized by an overwhelming identification with the dominant/oppressive alien social group and the adoption of an active hostility to one's group of origin; (3) a *self-destructive disorder* wherein the person's thoughts and actions are characterized by engaging in practices (i.e., alcoholism, drug addiction, homosexuality, etc.) which are personally and/or culturally self-destructive; and (4) *organic disorders* which are behavioral dysfunctioning which results from major physiological and/or biochemical dysfunctioning or poisoning.

IV. AFRICAN-AMERICAN THOUGHT PATTERNS: IMPLICATIONS FOR CONTEMPORARY BLACK SOCIAL LIFE

The development of African (Black) psychology has, from the discipline's inception in modern times, been enriched by the recognition of the need to grapple with an understanding of the fundamental nature of what it is to be human.[17] Black Psychology's leading theoreticians (Wade Nobles, Cedric X, Naim Akbar, G. Jackson, Joseph Baldwin, and Semaj, 1980) have embraced a line of reasoning which views the behavior of African-Americans as having as its antecedents ancient African thought and philosophy.[18] In this tradition Matthews

has specifically noted that the African mode of thought has explana-
tive import for understanding how African-Americans come to know
and respond to their reality. [19]

In what, to some, is considered one of the "classics" in African
(Black) psychology, Cedric X, et al in their article "Voodoo or I.Q.: An
Introduction to African Psychology" have effectively argued that since
African psychology is based on an African conceptual or paradigmatic
framework for "knowing" the world, it, the discipline of African psy-
chology, must first explicate and understand ancient human thought. [20]

Implications for Social Thought, Action and Definition

Given the ancient African thought discussed above, one can simply
note that ontologically, the African belief system understood that the
nature of all things in the universe was the Ka of God or "force", or
"spirit". [21] It is logical, or at least consistent, therefore, that in believing
that all things, including man, were endowed with the same Supreme
Force, (i.e., the Ka of God) that one would also believe that all things
are "essentially" one or the same. For Africans, therefore, our most
comprehensive ideas about order (i.e., world-view) would be based on
the ontological identification of "being (existence) in the universe" as
being characterized by a cosmological "participation in the supreme
Force". Parenthetically, it is understandable that if ontologically the
African believes that the nature of all things is Force, then the African
would, accordingly, view the variety of cosmic beings as quantitative
alterations of the same Supreme Energy. [22]

What characterized African peoples' understanding of the universe
is, consequently, a simultaneous respect for the concrete detail in the
multiplicity of forms AND the rejection of the possibility of an absence
or vacuum of forms.

The African conception of the world and the phenomena within it
amounts to a set of synthesis (connections) and contradictions
(antagonisms) linked to the particular classification of beings as dif-
ferential quantifications of force. Combined, these "connectual" and
"antagonistic" participatory sets form the whole of universal relations.
Accordingly, relationships in the universe are determined by elements
belonging to the same metaphysical plane, "participating by resemblance" or by elements belonging to different metaphysical planes,
"participating by difference". [23] The dynamic quality of the total universe is, however, thought to be the conciliation of these various "participatory sets". In fact, the conciliation of, on the one hand, the unity
of the cosmos and, on the other, the diverseness of beings within the
cosmos make for the special features (e.g., dynamism, interdependence, variety, optimism, etc.) of the traditional African world-view.

Psychologically or in terms of social life, individual consciousness
becomes such, that the family or peoplehood constituted the refer-

ence point wherein one's existence was perceived as being interconnected to the existence of all else. The individual was an integral part
of the collective unity, i.e. the family. In recognition of this kind of
awareness, others (Mbiti, 1970; Nobles, 1973) have noted that the traditional African view of "self" is contingent upon the existence of and
interconnectedness with others (The Oneness of Being).[24]

Existence therefore is at the level of the family or peoplehood. That
is, family or peoplehood existence is more important than individual
existence. As an aside, we can note that in terms of the notion of
"genetic proximity", wherein simplistically, the "begetter is always
more powerful" than the offspring, the family entity constitutes more
power or force than the individual entity. Accordingly, family or people
existence is "paramount" to individual existence and to paraphrase
Satre, the *family essence* or *essence* of *peoplehood* preceeds the *individual essence*. The family, which includes the living, the dead, and
those yet-to-be born is, therefore, the center, the focal point wherein
the essence of the community (of peoplehood) is kept alive.[25] The
family or peoplehood is the center of existence. It is the center of the
universe. Our peoplehood then becomes the source of our definition.

Behavioral Responses and Dispositional Features

Just as African thought should and does influence our definition of
who we are, it should and does influence how we respond to our
concrete conditions. Given the ancient African thought and its modern
day replications, one would be remiss if one did not also point out that
there is a recognizable and identifiable African-American style of
responding to and manipulating our reality which has its roots in our
African Beingness. Psychologically the techiques associated with our
cultural disposition are "Improvisation", "Transcendence" and "Transformation". These techniques are all governed by the human possibilities defined by our indigenous African-American cultural substance
and mythic consciousness.

The technique of *improvisation* is a process of spontaneously
creating, inventing or arranging a known experience, situation or event
such that the known experience is extended into the unknown and
thereby results in a new experience.

The techniques of *transcendence* is the quality, state or ability to
exceed, go beyond or rise above the limits of an experience, condition
or situation.

The technique of *transformation* is the predisposition to recognize
that the condition, quality or nature of an experience or element has
the potential to change into a different experience or element.

The relationship between the social and psychological development of our people and the social structures and institutions (i.e.,

government, education, health, etc.) designed (in theory) to affirm our people's being, is ultimately a question of transformation. We would contend that where the social structures and/or institutions are (cultural) transplants and do not emerge from, and reflect the cultural definition of our people, that in those circumstances the social structures will serve only to change and probably dehumanize and oppress our people. It is further suggested that the emergence of counter ideologies and popular liberation movements in Black ruled communities/ countries is evidence of our people's rejection of the cultural transplants reflected in the adoption of foreign institutions. It is not enough to have Africans operate and control institutions emerging from and reflective of the cultural reality of foreigners.

V. CONCLUSION

As an active response to reclaim mastery of one's own "productive forces", liberation struggles implicity require the capacity to also control the nature, definition, and meaning of these "productive forces". At its simplest level, total struggle requires that one wages both a physical and a psychological war against oppression and the oppressor. If culture is the ulimate expression and definition of a people's capacity to create progress and/or determine history, then critical thought or science which is the reconstruction of that culture, must be one of the mechanisms for expressing and defining the people's capacity to create progress.

It is in the reclamation of culture and ancient thought and in the creative reconstruction of them as psychology, that one seizes control over the interpretation of reality; and, consequently, connects struggle with our human development. As the expression of all that constitutes the every day way of life of a people, culture defines and gives meaning to everything experienced by the living. Accordingly, culture defines and gives meaning to the notion of human development; and, science as its reconstruction, simply further refines the definition and meaning of that human development.

If social life for people who are oppressed is a social life motivated by liberation; and, if liberation struggles are, by definition, struggles to reclaim the right of culture (i.e., the right of an indigenous vast structure of languages, behavior, customs, knowledge, symbols, ideas, and values which influence the general design for living and patterns for interpreting reality), then liberation struggles must develop and utilize a system of critical thought emerging from our own ancient indigenous thought.

As a reconstruction of the systematic and cumulative ideas, beliefs and knowledge (i.e., common sense) of our people, the role of psychology in liberation struggles, therefore, must be to provide an analysis and understanding of our Beingness and Becoming which will further filter, organize and transform our natural "sensations" into particular mental, impressions and behavioral dispositions and/or responses that affirm our Being and resist our oppression. This in itself should be the essence of our social life.

Liberation, in effect, should be the fundamental reason or value in understanding ancient Egyptian thought for contemporary African peoples.

NOTES

1. R.A. Schwalter de Lubicz, *Symbol and the Symbolic: Ancient Egypt Science and the Evolution of Consciousness*, New York: Inner Traditions International, 1978.
2. Ibid.
3. Ibid.
4. Paul Macleans in Carl Sagan (ed), *The Dragon of Eden*, New York: Random House, 1977.
5. Cheikh Anta Diop, *The African Origin of Civilization: Myth or Reality*, Westport: Lawrence Hill and Company, 1967.
6. Jacob Carruthers, *Essays in Ancient Egyptian Studies*, Los Angeles: University of Sankore Press, 1984.
7. R.T. Rundle Clark, *Myth and Symbol in Ancient Egypt*, London: Thames and Hudson, 1959.
8. Chancellor Williams, *The Destruction of Black Civilization: Great Issues of Race from 4500 B.C. to 2000 A.D.*, Chicago: Third World Press, 1976.
9. Henri Frankfort, *The Intellectual Adventure of Ancient Man*, Chicago: University of Chicago Press, 1946.
10. George James, *Stolen Legacy*, San Francisco: Julian Richardson Associates Publishers, 1976.
11. Frankfort, op. cit.
12. Wallis E.A. Budge, *The Egyptian Book of the Dead: The Papyrus of Ani* New York: Dover Publications, 1967.
13. Frankfort, op cit.
14. W.W. Nobles, "Standing in the River, Transformed and Transforming: The Reascension of Black Psychology", submitted for publication, *Race Relations Abstracts*, 1984.
15. W.W. Nobles, "African Philosophy: Foundations for Black Psychology" in Reginald James (ed), *Black Psychology*, New York: Harper and Row, 1972.
16. Naim Akbar, "Mental Disorders Among African-Americans", *Black Books Bulletin*, Vol. 7, 2, pp. 18-25, 1981.
17. Cedric X, et al, *Voodoo or I.Q.: An Introduction to African Psychology*, Chicago: Institute of Positive Education, 1976.
18. Nobles, op. cit.; Cedric X, op. cit. 1976; Akbar, op. cit. pp. 18-25; G. Jackson, "The Origin and Development of Black Psychology: Implications for Black Studies and Human Behavior," *Studies Africaine*, 1,3, (1976) 271-292; J.A. Baldwin, "African (Black) Psychology: Issues and Synthesis," unpublished paper, Florida A & M, 1980; L. Semaj, "Meaningful

Male/Female Relationships in the State of Declining Sex-Ratio," *Black Books Bulletin*, 6, 4 (1980) 4-10.

19. Basil Mathews. "Black Prespectives, Black Family and Black Community," paper presented to the Annual Philosophy Conference, Baltimore, 1972.
20. Cedric X et al, op. cit. 1976.
21. P. Temples. *Bantu Philosophy*, Presence Africaine, 1959.
22. L.V. Thomas. "A Sengalese Philosophical System: The Cosmology of the Jolah People," *Presence Africaine*, 4-5, 1969.
23. Ibid.
24. J. Mbiti. *African Religions and Philosophies*. New York: Anchor Press, 1970.
25. K. Busia, "The Ashanti of the Gold Coast," in *African Worlds (ed.) Darryl Forde, London: Oxford University Press, 1954.*

SIMILARITIES BETWEEN EGYPTIAN AND DOGON PERCEPTION OF MAN, GOD AND NATURE

DAIMA M. CLARK

Let us direct our discussion on the religious perceptions of our ancient Egyptian ancestors so that we can (1) appreciate Egyptian religious ideas and values within the context of a total cultural process; and (2) ascertain how we can strengthen our protracted struggle for all African Liberation by making sure we incorporate the most essential of these ideas and beliefs in our own system of values. Egyptian religion like art, music, dance --- was a functional dynamic of African life. Religion was not separable from life anymore than pictorial arts, music, sculpturing. Religion was life in total.

The perceptions of the ancient Egyptians are still very much alive in the contemporary cultural constellations of the Dogon people even though the Dogons are separated from Egypt by a whole continent so to speak, The Dogons occupy Mali on the extreme west of Africa, living near the bend of the River Niger. The Dogons share perceptions very similar to the Egyptians, despite their temporal separation of several milleniums. Neither geographical distance separating ancient Egypt from the Dogons has diminished the obvious similarities in their theological rationale on the meaning of life; nor has separation by several milleniums effaced in any way the vitality of Egyptian precepts which are central to the Dogon worldview.

As we look at several African social institutions which developed into a viable system of high culture, first by the Egyptians, the evidence of which still survives today --- we shall see that these institutions networked in such a manner that to comparmentalize these institutions is to distort both their meaning and value. *Example:* Understanding of the purpose and function of the Extended Family Lineage System as part and parcel of the Egyptian and Dogon Ancestral Cults. As a system, Totemism is both the ground of and link between the African Family and the Ancestral Cult. The onto-theological rationale underlying the Rite of Passage or Circumcision --- is pivotal to perpetuation of the family and its ancestral foundation. Before surveying other ramifications of the family, lets see how the Extended Family and Ancestral Lineage became an integral part of the religious process.

THE ROLE OF THE WOMAN

Cultural historians have theorized that the African woman was the world's first agronomist.[1] We certainly know that Egyptians were the first people in the world to develop a sophisticated high culture founded on an agricultural base. At this point they ceased to be nomadic food gatherers and hunters. They developed a sedentary material culture where they could settle down to other civilizing pursuits such as: artisans, kings, priests, architects, stone masons, mathematicians, et cetera.

What proof do we have for the notion that the African woman first domesticated plants? For one thing we know that it required many, many years of testing and experimenting for the domestication of plants. So we are talking about generations of women transmitting their bits of new expertise and knowledge to those coming behind them.

We know that the woman, in time, became an indispensable economic partner to her husband by providing enough food to feed her family, thus freeing her husband to hunt and develop other skills. As indispensable partner, the African woman was deemed an equal to her mate. Now which one African woman or which several Egyptian women started the process of domesticating plants? There is no way to know since the process of domesticating plants through experimentation was a long ongoing procedure involving centuries of patient observation and testing. But women ancestors known for their noteworthy expertise and contributions were glorified in legend for their collective contributions. For the African woman to develop strength enough to dig, to plant, to harvest crops in addition to preparing meals for her family and nurturing her children's health and survival, these accomplishments alone attest to her greatness. This fortitude and keeness of mind and imagination, the African woman maintained while fulfilling her biologically analogous function as partner in the procreation of her children.

By the time woman's role as provider of food for the family became entrenched as part of tradition the centuries had obliterated the memory of who in particular got the process underway. Gradually the accretions of glorifying the beauty, physical, moral stamina and creativity of the African woman took on the quality of religious deification and in time the Egyptian woman was deified as a goddess and mythologized as goddess of fertility. She was named Isis, the goddess of corn. The African woman's husband helped her by clearing the land for gardening. He did other heavy agricultural chores. Likewise he was right there planting his seed into Isis womb. His name is Osiris. From this union was born a son, named Horus. Thus Osiris becomes the god of fertility and he too is associated with corn. On the basis of sexual equality and the heightened preeminence enjoyed by the African woman, we may infer that the African man and woman by mutual agreement[2] organized the Extended Family on a matrilineal basis with inheritance passing through the female to either her husband's sons in the case of Egyptian monarchal families or the inheritance passed through the wife to her brother's sons.

THE ORIGIN OF METALLURGY

In another example of the *sine qua non* role and function of the Ancestral Cult in Egyptian religion, we might ask, "Was it possible for legend to carry us back to a knowledge of which ancestors were responsible for the smelting of iron?" As a logical response we should ask, "Whose memory reaches back 7 thousand years, 10 thousand years in legend or written records to honor the discoverers of metallurgy?" With metal becoming essential to the material culture in everyday use as utensils, tools, decorative jewelry, weapons — again our Egyptian and Dogon-forebears took the history of metallurgy as far back as historical legend would go. From that point back, the ancestors responsible for the discovery of metallurgy were mythologized into Egyptian and Dogon religion, using stories as vehicle for impressing upon the minds of each succeeding generation, the living images, the dramatic religious significance or moral values in the uses and misuses of metals. There is no way the African could fabricate or fantasize that he invented the process of metallurgy without the various metals being present in his material culture for longer than anyone can remember. So Egyptians mythologized the god Horus as responsible for bringing metallurgy to Egypt from the south. But the historical fact is mythologized in this instance by crediting Horus with spreading this technology throughout Egypt. Dr. John G. Jackson reports that the Edufu Text on early history of the Nile Valley,

> "gives an account of the origin of Egyptian civilization (indicating that it) was brought from the south by a band of invaders under the leadership of King Horus. . . The followers of Horus were called 'Blacksmiths' because they possessed iron implements."[3]

The Dogons mythologized that they were taught the science of metallurgy by their 7th Nummo Ancestor who was a Smith and Master of Speech. Ogotemmeli, a late Dogon Chief Elder, indicated in one of his instructive discourses with the late Marcel Griaule, a French ethnologist, that the original ancestors had flexible joints, arms without elbow, making the ancestor ill-suited for the work of forge and field. ". . . hammering red-hot iron or digging land needs the leverage of the forearms," said Griaule.[4] "From the time of the smith's coming, men had joints," said Ogotemmeli. "Up til then they had flexible bones which would not bend enough."[5] Since arms and bare hands alone were inadequate for agricultural labor, the 7th Nummo Ancestor who was a smithy, gave men iron hoes which he helved. Thus the hoe extended man's arm and became the signal for agricultural labor.

The process of metallurgy was discovered first in Africa. This process is so ancient in African experience, oral history cannot pinpoint which persons in their ancestral lore discovered and taught the process of metallurgy to them. This is why the role of the Blacksmith in African history has been mythologized. Scientific verification that iron ore was first processed in Africa before borrowings by other parts of the world turned up in the N.Y. Times about 15 years ago, dated Feb. 6, 1970, stating that South African archeaologists discovered the NGWENYA IRON MINE in Swaziland; and radio carbon tests taken of charcoal in this mine revealed that smelting of iron dates back at least 43,000 years in Africa.[6] That the god Horus in the Egyptian pantheon and the 7th Nummo Smithy in the Dogon Pantheon are credited with the discovery of metallurgy, underscores the importance of Ancestral Cults in African religion.

THE ANCESTORS

Ancestors were and are a vital ambiance in the life of every living African whether he or she is aware of this reality or not. Centuries of traditions have been transmitted in their essence, to each successive generation as part and parcel of their cultural identity. Our Egyptian ancestors in their wisdom, perceived the value of cultivating functional unity between the body, mind and soul of their people. This heritage an African may ignore, but he/she cannot escape it. We have been talking about ancestors who have moved completely into spirit world and therefore became deified. However there are the living-dead ancestors who are closer to the living generations with respect to time and the fact that some living persons still remeber them. These living-dead ancestors straddle SASA time and ZAMANI time. John S. Mbiti explains that the African psychic experiences time only as a present event or action, not as an abstract linear concept. Thus SASA time is the act of experiencing an action NOW. ZAMANI time is a past event which one remembers. When you ask, "What's happening brother?" This is Sasa time. What is happening now? "Well yesterday I saw..guess who... Kamu at Reid's Records...you remember him...?" This is Zamani time, a past happening.

Living-Dead ancestors who are still remembered, are part of Sasa and Zamani time. Some living persons *remember* the ancestor; that's Sasa time. But the ancestor is no longer living; this places the ancestor into Zamani time. When there is no longer any living person who remebers a particular ancestor, that ancestor has passed over completely into the spriit world and Zamani time. Zamani time is the graveyard of Sasa time.[7]

TOTEMISM

We may postulate that through the practice of totemism the Egyptian tried to harmonize the one and the many at the physical, oral and spiritual levels, uniting God, man and animal into a close complementary relationship. It is conceivable that totemism may have given impetus to widespread development of agronomy, botany and animal husbandry among African families by the very nature of the function of totemism. The practice of totemism served to regulate marriages, both endogamous and exogamous. Another practical function of totemism was the regulation of food supply. Clans, sometimes whole tribes formed a covenant of mutual protection with animals and some plants. The life-force which characterized the animal(s) in question, infused and strengthened the life-force of clan members, a sort of double indemnity, we might say. The clan agreed in return, not to kill or eat its animal totem.

It has been suggested that clans often worked prodigiously to cultivate plants that were not prohibited to their consumption as well as plants that were. The same applied to animals which farmers domesticated. So we can see that an attitude of cooperation developed between clans and tribes for the purpose of assuring their mutual survival. At the same time this kinship to animals through an intermingling of man's life-force with the life-force of their totems, without doubt gave rise to the African belief in the relatedness of all life or "reverence for life". With totemism infusing the Egyptians' perceptions relative to reverence for our ancestors it becomes self-evident that belief in the brotherhood and sisterhood of mankind was bound to emerge.

So deep was the belief in the brotherhood of man, modern warfare was unknown to them. The object of traditional warfare in Africa was to get the battle over with as quickly as possible. Once several soldiers were maimed, the object was to call it quits.[8] Over-kill by piling up a lot of dead bodies on the field of battle, was unknown to our African ancestors. In otherwords, an affirmation of life developed out of African institutions. *The African celebrated life.* An incurable optimism characterized the African ambiance beginning in Egypt where the architect, philosopher-physician, Imhotep, coined the expression, "EAT, DRINK AND BE MERRY, FOR TOMORROW WE DIE."[9]

Totemism was so deeply embedded in Egyptian religion, most of the gods were partly animal representations. The god Thoth inventor of hieroglyphic writing and scribe of the gods, had the head of an ibis, holding a pen and a scribe's ink-pallette; and in another aspect Thoth wore the lunar disc and crescent upon his head. The god Horus had so many different animal totems, his descendants would have had a hard time finding meat that wasn't taboo for them. In one aspect Horus was a lamb, in another aspect he was a lion. You don't suppose lions made for good eating, do you? Horus was also a hawk, vulture or Eagle Hawk, a young ear of corn, a red calf, et al.[10] Osiris who taught the civilizing work of agriculture to man, seems not to have had an animal form. In the Dogon religion, Amma, the creator God's essence, which was the Nummo Twins, was seen in the aspect of part human and part amphibian. This Nummo Pair infused all life, including fertilizing and purifying of the earth's soil.

Ogotemmeli summed up the religious meaning of totemism this way, "The animal is, as it were man's twin."[11] Griaule explained, "An ancestor could use the animal which was, so to speak *his* twin, to make himself known to the living men whom he wished to help."[12] From this we understand that your animal totem is the same as your ancestor's totem(s) and my animal totem is the same as my ancestor's totem(s). The 7th Nummo Ancestor like Osiris, taught mankind speech/language and social/economic organization; both language and social/economic organization are physical aspects of the spirit just as the physical aspects of Amon-Ra and the 7th Nummo incarnate their spirits. We see the animal/spiritual avatars serve a dual function as teachers and protectors of mankind.

Our Egyptian forebears' perception of totemism seems to suggest that modern man as we know him, evolved from an animal species. Man's physiological-cultural ascent is emphasized and the notion that somewhere in the dim recesses of man's collective consciousness --- he is vaguely aware of this evolutionary experience. We find this totem idea as developed in the Egyptian and Dogon relgions, expressed among Navajo Indians in North America.[13]

Witn agriculture as the basic economy upon which developed the great cities of Egypt — we can see how classification of things and occupations emerged in an organized hierarchy under religiously controlled regulations. Such occupations as: animal husbandry, farming, gardening, mining, goldsmithing, silver and blacksmithing, weaving, pottery, stone quarrying, military personnel, shipbuilding, science, engineering, architecture, carpentry, mathematics, writing, medicine, astronomy, astrology, art, dance, music, travelling singers, griots, priesthood, scribes, teaching, sculpturing and painting.

Organized Egyptian religion not only regulated these occupations through political control, religion functioned as the mother of history. Griots, singers, poets extolled the great achievements of their contemporary makers of history as well as maintained oral and written archives, inscriptions on walls, altars and on colonades of Thebes (Nowe) the oldest city in the world. [14]

THE RITE OF PASSAGE

We observed in the practice of totemism the interdependent relationship between man and nature and man in nature. This interdependence was transposed by the ancient Egyptians to social relationship within the family to assure individual growth and development within the family as well as renewal and growth of the family itself and the community. The primary family unit was/is directly responsible for child's physical, mental and moral nurture and growth until the child reaches puberty.

Before the child can assume the role of an adult, he/she must go through the Rite of Passage, i.e., the child must *die* and be reborn an adult. At the point where boys and girls qualify to be reborn into the community as adults, they must shed themselves of their dual or bi-sexual identity by being circumcised/excised. The androgynous proclivity with which they were born, must be circumcised by shedding the prepuce (female organ) of the boy's penis and excise the clitoris (male organ) of the girl's vulva so that the boy's male qualities become dominant in him and the girl's femininity dominates her sexuality. The physical operation of circumcision/excision symbolizes the children's payment of their blood-debt to Mother Earth from which each of us is made. The fact of one's readiness to cross over from childhood to a mature, responsible adult, was not left to chance. CIRCUMCISION/EXCISION were the outward manifestations that the male/female child had successfully fulfilled all requirements for assuming their respective roles as mature, responsible adults, ready for marriage and procreation.

Inherent in the Rite of Passage is a deeper meaning than the mere ritual acts of initiation: (1) the initiates depart from their individual families as children and they return to their communities as children of the community.[15] From this point forward the community assists the initiates at each transition of their life-cycles with life-long learning which ends with the grave.[16] (2) Initiation institutionalizes the cycle of birth, circumcision, marriage and death. The uncircumcised do not acquire acceptance by society as mature persons. Therefore the uncircumcised may not marry, they may not procreate or increase the family. (3) The practice of circumcision is analogous to the theological perception of purification and sacrifice, both aspects of the cyclic rhythms of the universe.

Egyptian priesthood perceived in mankind a microcosm of the Supreme God-Image. The priests also perceived the need for removing the dual sexual propensity in humans through circumcision/excision in order to promote growth and development of a productive and viable culture. A child was thought to be born with two souls, male and female. In order for a child to mature with purpose and direction, the family started early to condition the child for its sexual role; otherwise the boy or girl would be left without rootage in a firm self-identity with his or her self-image and would have no interest in procreation.

While the 8 primal deified Egyptian ancestors were believed to be androgynous and capable of self-procreation their finite descendants cannot bear the burden of possessing in equal strength dual souls (male and female) without setting into motion the inevitable consequences of confusion and sexual ambivalence. Similarly the Dogon 8 original ancestors were androgynous, capable of self-procreation but for finite descendants, the burden of possessing in equal strength dual souls, male and female without circumcision/excision would defeat the purpose of perpetuating the human race.

HARMONIZING THE OPPOSITES

Our ancient Egyptian ancestors created a pantheon of deities, presided over by the uncreated, Self-Engendered Supreme Lord-God Amon-Ra, creator of the world and all there is Amon Ra's infinite manifold aspects are symbolized by many different attributes. Inherent in this Supreme Lord-God is the Principle of Creativity; that is, male and female essences. The Dogon identify this idea as the Principle of Twinness. In the Egyptian and Dogon Worldview the Creator God is androgynous. Starting with the uncreated supreme God, creation is complete: that is, creation is whole. Creativity is open-ended; creativity is ongoing, ad infinitum. When perceived rightly, this duality in nature need not be polarized into absolute, irreconcilable OPPOSITES. Rather opposite qualities should be seen in their functional, interactive or complementary relationships. Everything moves. To see things or values as rigid, unmovable, unyielding structural entities is to set oneself against God's universe of rhythmic harmony.

Dual engendering essences are manifest everywhere. The 4 source elements of energy: earth and water, fire and air: and the 4 basic qualities of energy: wet and dry, hot and cold were perceived by the ancient Egyptians as laws of opposites that operate throughout the universe . . . [17]

The idea of the one and the many are not exclusively either/or terms to the African mind. The one and the many are not irreconcilable opposites. The one and only Supreme Lord God, maker of heaven and earth is both two and one. If the generating principle of creation is twinness, i.e., male-female essences, the Supreme One and only God is both 2 and 1 with all other deities performing subordinate roles as different aspects of the One and only Lord-God.

Most western-minded authorities insist that the Egyptian pantheon is tantamount to polytheism. By the same token one may argue that the Christian pantheon of angels and other celestial spirits is tantamount to polytheism. The problem is not a question of whether the Egyptians were polytheistic pantheists; the problem stems from a refusal by the enemies of African culture, to accept the ancient Egyptian religious precepts as culturally valid for Africans, most of whom subscribed to the precepts we have discussed, using diverse forms of expression and implementation. The truth is that pantheism does *not* have to contradict the ONENESS of God. Just because you perceive some aspect of God in all things does not mean that automtically you are a polytheist.

It would appear that the *conflict is waged by adherents to a monotheism which has been abstracted from reality. They attempt to triumph over a monotheism predicated upon reality.* Furthermore, the problem becomes more sticky if the monotheism which has ben abstracted from reality, is propped up by a triad (trinity) also abstracted from reality.

The debate as to whether the Jew first perceived monotheism or Ikhnaton, doesn't make sense. Historically, monotheism was already in place in Egypt before the Jews got there. Ingredients forming a nucleus of Egyptian high culture, including the the perception of one God, had been set in place so to speak, by indigenous Black Africans long before the rise of dynastic Egypt. Indigenous Africans who occupied the grassland area before desiccation of soil and other climatic conditions turned it into the Sahara desert about 7000 years ago, contributed to the formation of Egyptian civilization. The populations of Ethiopia and Central Africa also contributed.

The Twa people, nicknamed Pygmies, of the rain forests in Central East Africa, are credited by Dr. ben Jochannan with being the first people to create religious signs and symbols. Long before there was dynastic Egypt, the Twa people designed this cross ⵣ which can be fitted within a circle. ⊕ This sign means "The one great spirit." To the Twa people this one great spirit is everywhere present or this one great spirit is imminent in all things. In theology this belief is called pantheism. So the Twa people and the Egyptians perceived God as everywhere present in the universe.

When Ikhnaton asserted that there was only one God which he perceived to be Aten, the sun --- Ikhnaton did not attempt to suppress Aten's manifold manifestations. The God Aten was replacing Amon-Ra, the God of much earlier Egypt who was perceived to manifest aspects similar to those of Aten. So when Ikhnaton sings in his "Hymn To The Sun" that Aten was the "sole God to whom no other is likened." When he speaks of the God Aten as the "living Disk" (beginner) of life "fillest every land with thy beauty, Thy rays (sun rays) embrace the lands . . .", he is not flying in the face of reality. Aten is represented as the sun disk, bringing light to the world when Aten rises in the east and darkness falls when Aten travels to the western horizon. Similarly, Amon-Ra, the older God was represented as the essence of life and creation. The rams' horns on Amon-Ra symbolize moisture and humidity.

Ogotemmeli stated that the Nummo Pair, representation of Amma, were in essence water and moisture . . . they are the sun' rays . . . they excrete light because they are . . . light.[18]

Again, Ikhnaton did not fly in the face of the Principle of Creativity which is a living reality, just because he wanted to reform Egyptian theology by systematizing its precepts. He did not try to eliminate the ankh, symbol representing life nor did he change the meaning of other forms of the cross. The trinity as symbolized by the cross underscores the Principle of Creativity at the level of the cosmos and within the human context. This Trinity is a construct predicated upon the unity of two in Egyptian cosmogony: Osiris and Isis. The son Horus, issues as third party to the trinity. The creative principle has always been the cornerstone of Egyptian and Dogon religion.

From this cornerstone stems the perception that all life is related . . . all things come together as one . . . there is no superior race nor is there an inferior race. There is only one race --- the human race. The Egyptians perceived the power of God as imminent in all life. "Creator of issue in women" sings Ikhanton, "Who preserveth alive the son in his mother's womb. Giving breath to quicken all whom thou created. When the chick in the egg cries in the shell Thou givest him strength to break out from within and he comes forth to chirp and walk on two legs!"

Monotheism which espouses only the Fatherhood of God, corresponds best to a society whose family structure is patriarchal. It has been the characteristics of partriarchally oriented societies that are anti-matrilineal — to perceive women as being "less than" — necessary primarily for procreative purposes — accessories — otherwise, rather expendable objects. We refer to accounts by Julius Caesar and Tacitus for historical verification.

Partly because climatic conditions have not been very charitable where patriarchal societies early took root, land for example, is viewed as real estate rather than a gift from God to be shared with others. Land must be subdued, forced to yield bounty. Private owenership of land becomes a logical consequence. The propensity toward conquest becomes a way of life. A goddess had no place in a thoroughgoing theology of monotheism. As a mater of historical fact --- the demeaning position of women in such societies permitted only a very late rise of women to prominence in the political life of such societies and that by exception rather than by rule of tradition. The very act of setting up territorial boundaries as contrasted with respecting the AURA of other peoples and other forms of life --- fragments rather than unites people. And where we have witnessed African policy makers buying into the territorial boundaries put in place by Europeans before and following the Berlin scramble of Africa, great indeed has been the consequences of disunity and political/economic fragmentation. And even the patriarchal societies which have carried the logic of EXCLUSION or EXCLUSIVENESS to its furthest limits "The ONE and ONLY God the Father" --- such societies are experiencing an acceleration of fragmentation from within. Compare the African swastika with the German swastika. One fits within the circle of unity while the other fragments the oneness of the circle.

CONCLUSION

In this discussion we have attempted to communicate the idea that Egyptian religious perceptions developed as a process of establishing a system of values by which people could work productively and enjoy life. Enjoy life in the sense of wholeness. The sense of wholeness and satisfaction that derives from meaningful productivity. Meaningful productivity for Egyptians was couched within the group context, the primary group being the family. "Because the group exists, I exist." The family includes our ancestors and those yet-to-be-born. The individual derives part of his psychic strength or life-force from the quality of his relationship to the group. That life-force is reinforced by his/her relationshp to other forms of life on this planet. His understanding of and functioning according to the guidelines of his understanding as established by the group' experience --- increases his vitality and power.

We see through all of this the cycle of beginning and return. Birth, initiation, marriage, procreation, death, rebirth. Everthing comes together. Everything galls into place through the process of renewal. We can renew cultural values derived by the Egyptian from their religious perceptions, values functionally necessary in our protracted struggle to liberate Africans. These values can be expressed in simple understandable terms.

At the height of our struggle in the 60's, a set of African collective principles were articulated by Dr. Maulana Karenga as representing our aspirations to achieve self-defining autonomy as a people. These principles represent the unity of 7. Certainly more can be added; but NGUZO SABA represents in catechismic form our African Value System. The test of its validity for us rests upon our decision to internalize these basic tenets as a way of life to be practiced 365 days a year. They cut across all political differences. They cut across all religious differences. A maximum of flexibility and diversity of expression can and will develop as we take hold of our minds and bring forth within ourselves --- CONTROL of our collective life by THINKING for ourselves and concretizing the results of our collective thought with a pro-active willing.

May we conclude with a word of admonition from our Poet

Laureate:
> it is true that nature in time will solve the world's problems and resolve the world's disputes however, nature and time are unpredictable and may not act in our lifetime. our understanding of life demands that we respect nature & time but our children's future demands that we help nature solve our problems today with the little time we have on earth [19]

NOTES

1. Cheikh Anta Diop, *African Origin of Civilization, Reality or Myth.* New York: Lawrence Hill & Co., 1974, p. 144.
2. Ibid., pp. 142 - 145.
3. John G. Jackson, *Introduction to African Civilizations,* New York: University Books, 1970, p. 93.
4. Marcel, Griaule, *Conversations With Ogotemmeli,* London: Oxford University Press, 1963, p. 44.
5. Ibid., p. 48.
6. Yosef ben Jochannan, *The Black Man of the Nile and His Family,* New York: Alkebu-lan Associates, 1972, p. 98.
7. John S. Mbiti, *African Religions and Philosophy,* Garden City: Anchor Books, 1970, Chapter 3.

8. Jomo Kenyatta, *Facing Mt. Kenya.* New York: Vintage Books, p. 200 ff.
9. ben Jochannan, op. cit., p. 254.
10. Ibid., pp. 124 - 126.
11. Griaule, p. 127.
12. Ibid.
13. Clark. Images of animal totems used frequently in Navajo folklore, are illustrated in the story "Brown Eyes" where the author narrates how a sick little girl was healed through the powers and medicines of "Talking Bear". Surrounding "Brown Eyes were her family, community and "Talking Eagle." pp. 36 ff.
14. Williams. op. cit., pp. 93 ff.
15. Kenyatta, op. cit., p. 145.
16. Ibid., p. 96.
17. ben Jochannan, op. cit., p. 320.
18. Griaule, op. cit., p. 19.
19. Haki Madhubuti, *Book of Life.* Detroit: Broadside Press, 1973, p.41.

PEDAGOGY IN ANCIENT KEMET

ASA G. HILLIARD, III

The surface has been hardly scratched in the study of history of Africa and its people. The rough outlines of that history are beginning to emerge as well prepared African and African-American historians have begun the painstakingly detailed work of documenting the African experience in antiquity. It is hard enough to race the broad general outlines of the African Experience. It is even more difficult to focus in on small aspects of that experience, such as pedagogy, with any degree of clarity. And yet there is the need for us to do precisely that.

Our concern with the connection to our African past is really future oriented. It is not merely for sentimental or aesthetic reasons that we return. While it is true that no one can or should live in the past. It is equally true that all futures are created out of some past. Ancient Africans not only existed, they developed a way of life the remnants of which continue to influence world development. As we view competing designs for human institutions and competing philosophies it is incumbent upon us to come to that process as fully disciplined, and especially as creative participants. A reveiw of our past will reveal that no people has a better place from which to start.

It is my task today to draw the best possible picture of one small aspect of a total development process of ancient Africans in the Nile Valley region and in the Great Lakes region. Simply put, how did the ancient Africans design and carry out the educational process? What were the aims, the methods and the contents of ancient African education? The best preserved records of cultural activity are to be found in Kemet (Ancient Egypt). As a result a great deal of our attention must be focused on that point. However, it is important always to keep in mind the fact that ancient Egypt was, as Gerald Massey said, "merely the mouthpiece for a more deeply rooted African birthplace".

Anyone who is familiar with the material on ancient Egypt is well aware of the fact that there exist few if any books on the educational system of Egypt. Consequently the reconstruction of what must have been a highly developed and vast system of education necessarily requires an approach that is highly inferential. Nonetheless, the inferences are not without empirical grounding. For example, the evidence which gives information about the educational system can be found in paintings, monuments, architecture, technology and above all in the hieroglyphic and demotic writings, which include stories, rituals, songs and so forth. In addition, the skilled eye can detect in the widespread African diaspora an extensive variety of cultural forms whose antecedents are clear matches to those

131

of the Egyptian and earlier ancient cultural forms. And so we are not short of evidence for the fact that educational systems existed. Rather the task is to sift through a plethora of direct and indirect data in order to reconstruct a picture of the past.

It is important at this point that a few words be said about the general orientation which I consider to be essential to any understanding of the raw data or summarized interpretation of data about ancient Egyptian education. First, in doing our analysis we must always keep in mind the *antiquity* of African culture. Second, and just as important, we must always keep in mind what Cheikh Diop has referred to as the *unity* of African culture.[1] For to explain the culture, and particularly the educational system of Egypt, we must appeal not only to data in Egypt but to data about education from the cultural antecedents of Egypt, as well as manifestations of the core African culture, not only in the Egyptian part of the diaspora, but in the rest of the continental diaspora and later in the inter-continental diaspora as well.

HISTORY

Briefly let me summarize some of the main points of African ancient history with which most of us are now quite familiar. It is clear now from the archaelogical record that the whole body of data supports an African origin for mankind. What is equally important is that the earliest record of what we call civilization developed first in the same areas where the earliest fossil remains of humans are found. That is to say, long before Egypt began, it was Black people in Africa along the southern Nile River valley, close to its source, who produced the first stirrings of "civilization", that can be documented. Albert Churchwood, is merely echoed by Richard Leakey when he says:

"That the first paleolithic man was the pigmy who was evolved in Central Africa at the sources of the Nile or Nile Valley, and that from here all originated and were carried throughout the world..."[2]

In fact, Albert Churchwood goes further, saying:

"The sources of the Nile - equiritial provinces - where the Great Lakes in the papyrus swamp were their Ta-Nuter, or Holy Land - i.e., "the land of the spirits of Gods", and the chief features of this earthly paradise were repeated in the circumpolar highland".[3]

It was Henri Frankfort, among other students of Egyptian history and culture, who recognized from the evidence that Egypt's historical and cultural antecedents were to be found *south* of Egypt, deeper in the Nile Valley. For example Frankfort tells us:

"The roots of Egyptian unity reach back into the most distant past. The population of the Nile Valley was homogenous, both physically and culturally, as much as a large group can ever be. The evidence of fauna or flint tools suggest that the inhabitants deconded in early neolithic times from the surrounding desert plateaus.... We know that the physique of the inhabitants of this valley from the delta deep down in the Nubia remains much the same from predynastic to late historical times. They also shared a common material culture in pre-dynastic times. There are indications that this culture, the Amaration, extended well into Libya and reached the Red sea in the east. Ansomatic and ethnological resemblances and certain features of their languages, connect the ancient Egyptians firmly with the Hamitic speaking people of East Africa. It seems that the phaoranic civilization arose on this northeast African Hamitic substratum. In any case, the prehistoric inhabitants of the Nile Valley must have possessed a common spiritual culture as a correlate of the homogenous physical and archaelogical remains."[4]

Of course we are all familiar with the fact that the very first unification of the two lands was initiated from the south and as John G. Jackson, has said:

"Egypt's first golden age was initiated by an invasion from Ethiopia, according to Petrie; a conqueror of Sudani founded the third dynasty, and many entirely new ideas entered the country. This new movement culminated the vast schemes of Khufu, one of history's most dominating personalities. With him the lines of Egyptian growth were established and in the course of events became the subject of the written records."[5]

And it is Yosef ben-Jochannan who often cites the records from the Papyrus of Hunefer where the Egyptians themselves announced that their home was to the south at the *source* of the Nile near the foothills of the "Mountains of the Moon" (or Mt. Kilimanjaro).[6]

Clearly what we are getting is the picture of highly developed civilized behavior long before Egypt began - to the south of Egypt. For example hieroglyphic writings existed long before the first dynasty in Egypt. Further the hard evidence from such great monuments as the great "Sphinx" of Giza (or as Africans called it, (Hor-Em-Aket), indicates that it was much older than the pyramids and probably much older than Egypt as a nation. As Jackson states:

"According to Sir Gastone Maspero, the Egyptians made their first appearance on the stage of history about 8000 to 10,000 B.C.... This estimate should not be considered excessive. The ancient statue known as the Great Sphinx has been estimated by another French Egyptologist, Professor Pierre Hippolyte Boussac, to be at least ten thousands years old . There is an inscription of the Pharoah Khufu, builder of the great pyramid, telling how a temple adjoining the Sphinx, which has for generations been buried under the desert sand, was discovered by chance in his reign. This inscription, now in the Boulak Museum in Cairo, informs us that the Sphinx was much older than the Great Pyramid and that the giant statue required repairs during the reign of Khufu".[7]

Citing the evidence once more we return to John Jackson who observed that:

"The Edfu text is an important source document on the early history of the Nile Valley. This famous inscription, found in the Temple of Horus at Edfu, gives an account of the origins of the Egyptian Civilization. According to this record, civilization was brought from the south by a band of invaders under the leadership of King Horus. This ruler, Horus, was later deified and became ultimately the Egyptian Christ. The followers of Horus were called "the blacksmiths" because they possessed iron implements. This early culture had been traced back to Somaliland; although it may have originated in the Great Lakes region of Central Africa. In Somaliland, there are ruins of buildings constructed with dressed stone, showing the close resemblance of the architecture of early Egypt. Professor Author G. Brodeur, in his *The Pageant of Civilization,* has conjectured that the ancestors of the southern Egyptians came originally from this region; that they entered the Nile through Nubia and brought with them a well developed civilization. It is estimated that this migration must have occurred long before 5000 B.C."[8]

Looking again to evidence for a southern origin of Egyptian civilization, we must note the recent evaluation of material from archaeological digs taken just before the waters behind the Aswan Dam flooded Nubia.

"South of Abu-Simbel, a group of curious conical mounds at Ballana and on the opposite bank of Qostol, caught their eye, and they decided to make a trial excavation....Further mounds were examined with similar results, and eventually at Ballana, the tumulous graves of kings themselves were found. They were tall men, with negroid features".[9]

And so it is very recently that establishment egyptologists such as Bruce Williams[10], at the University of Chicago, have begun to say that Egyptian civilization had a parent, perhaps more than one, and that the most likely candidate for immediate parenthood is the Nubian civilization of Ta-Seti to the south of Egypt. Finally as Barbara Mertz, has said:

"Let's look to the fair queens of Egypt to begin with. I discussed them in another book, but this point requires repetition. As far as I know, there never was a blond queen of Egypt. The famous fourth dynasty lady, who was believed to be blond or red headed, has been shown to be wearing a yellow headcloth. There never were any other candidates for the description".[11]

What emerges clearly from the evidence is that *indigenous Black Africans* developed the whole Nile Valley, including Egyptian civilization.

CULTURE

Diop's concepts of cultural unity is very important to us.[12] It is a powerful explanatory construct and it helps to guide empirical investigation. The concept of cultural unity helps us to bridge from Egypt (East Africa) to the rest of Africa to the inter-continental diaspora. It cannot be emphasized too strongly that we are not limited to mere speculation on these points, as Diop's book on the cultural unity of Black Africa has demonstrated. There is abundant evidence for the cultural unity, both in antiquity and in the present. For example, in West Africa

> "Ethnologists who have studied Bozos believed that this tiny island of fishermen came from Egypt 5000 years ago and settled in the Niger bin. They have not moved since or changed their ways, which are derived from the river people of the Nile, under the early dynasties, as is their language. The Bozos have maintained their spiritual independence from Islam and Christianity and kept alive traditions that originated before the fall of Memphis. Watching a Bozo ceremony, the dancer's heads covered with animal masks, is like watching living hierogylphics".[13]

I must emphasize that it was the *empirical* evidence which led DeGramont to such a conclusion. Similarly, study of Voodoo religion in West Africa reveals its similarity to ancient Egyptian religion, and to its offspring, European religion.

> "The role of the mystery named Legba, for example, corresponds to that of Hermes in Helenistic mysteries, so many of their symbols being identical that the analogy cannot be dismissed, either as incidental or as a consequence of what anthropologists term "convergence." They comprise the total image of the god, and are furthermore, symbolically consistent, whether rendered in the rites and myths or as interpreted by qualified *Houngans* - with a sufficient number of whom Milo Ligaud has been for years well acquainted on the best of terms. In any case, no matter what the explanation may be, the parallel between the myth and cult in contemporary Haiti and those not only of 17th century Africa but over antiquity are undeniable and abundant".[14]

We can look at another culture in West Africa. DeGramont in his book, *The Strong Brown God* was fascinated by the ancient West African city of Djenne, a companion city to Timbuktu in Mali which he called an "African Venice".

"When the river is high it can only be reached by boat, protected by water. Djenne is said to have resisted 99 sieges in the course of its history. If the Pharaoh awoke there today, he would think he was in ancient Egypt. The clay houses have decorated facades with trapezoidal porticos, pointed glens and columns in low relief. The Mosque, as large as a gothic cathedral, is all inspiring in its use of primitive materials on a monumental scale. The people of Djenne are fishermen and traders attached to their city, seldom leaving it".[15]

It is amazing how often scholars who wish to understand ancient Egyptian culture especially its religion, are driven to the study of other Black African populations who are descendants of ancient Egyptians or who descended from a common source as the ancient Egyptians. This was expressed explicitly by E.A. Wallace Budge and also by Henri Frankfort in his book, *Kingship and the Gods* as he states:

"There are two ways to penetrate behind the words of our text. In the first place, there are alive today in African subgroups of people who are the survivors of that great East African substratum out of which Egyptian culture arose. Among other things we can study how deeply the divine nature of kings affects both the ruler and his subjects. Yet, this evidence requires correction for we are dealing here with savages, who either by tenacity or by inertia, have preserved through several thousand years the remnants of a primeval world of thought, while pharaonic culture was the most developed and most aggressive of its age."[16]

Once again, the essential point to be made here is there is an overwhelming abundance of *empirical* data to show both the historical and contemporary cultural connection between East Africa, including Egypt, and its continental and its inter- continental diaspora.

We need the linguistic terms from Noam Chomsky of "surface structure" and "deep structure" to explain the apparent diversity which exists throughtout the African continent and, indeed throughout the diaspora. Foreign explorers have been fascinated by what they considered to be significant differences among Africans, differences in the physiognomy of peoples, in ways of worship, etc. However, they have been attracted to the surface structural manifestations. Clearly an impartial investigation based upon empirical facts will demonstrate as Diop and others such as Thompson[17] and John[18] have done, that cultural unity is far more signifcant than is superficial diversity.

If time permitted, it would be instructive to examine the records of African neighbors in what we now call the Middle East, in Asia, and in Europe. In doing this we would see that during the early part of development of civilization the source of civil ideas was almost completely African. Three thousand years of unbroken development along the Nile valley positioned Africans to have a major influence on the world, an influence which still continues.

EDUCATION

This brings me to my major task which is to attempt to sharpen our picture of Egyptian education. We are hampered in our attempt to learn about ancient Egyptian education not only by the widespread loss of documentary materials, by the destruction of social institutions and civilizations, including their library records, and by years of prejudice and neglect; but we are also hindered by the fact that some of the most important parts of the educational process were conducted in "secret". Much of the tradition was passed on orally to the prepared initiate.

We are indebted to such writers as George G.M.James,[19] R.A. Schwaller DeLubicz,[20] Thompson,[21] Albert Churchwood,[22] and others for helping to pull back the veil on some of this "secret" tradition. George James studied the reports of the establishment historians and collected fragments of accepted information, placing them in a new perspective. R.A. Schwaller DeLubicz studied the ruins of the Temple at Luxor and Egyptian symbolic writing and thought. Thompson studied cultural patterns of existing Bantu tribal groups, especially their religious practices. Churchwood studied the evolution of the use of symbols from their source in the Great Lakes region and Nile valley to the dispersion of the use of those symbols through the world. What I'm trying to show once again is that there is an *empirical* base for emerging descriptions of an ancient Egyptian educational system.

As we look at the ancient Egyptian cultural patterns we see that there was not only a cultural unity *among* apparently diverse groups of people. There was also an essential unity *within* the culture which was reflected in the intimate and harmonious ties between and among education, politics, economics, religion, and so forth. It would make no sense whatsoever to consider the educational process apart from a deep study of the world view and religion of ancient Egypt. Ancient Egyptians lived close to nature, basically as a sedentary population under highly favorable environmental conditions. They were in a position to make repeated observations of natural processes over thousands of years. As clearly as anywhere else in the world, it can be seen in the Nile valley that nature has regular processes of birth, growth, aging, death, decay, and rebirth. All nature seems to tell the same story. The behavior of the mother Nile was cyclical. Within general limits, this behavior could be predicted. Indeed, the successful predictions of its rise and fall determined the degree to which its bountiful resources could be exploited.

The skies were almost always clear, providing an unparalleled opportunity for long term systematic observation of the behavior of heavenly bodies. The enduring repetitive cycles obviously made a profound impression upon the ancient dwellers on the Nile. Since the Nile River in Egypt is but a thin ribbon in a vast land with a full population. Egypt is, and from its beginning, was crowded providing the basis for easy transportation up and down the smooth Nile river. The transportation on the Nile was assisted by winds that blow from the north to the south, enabling travelers to take a current downstream to the north to the return aided by the light breezes from the north.

The ancient Egyptians observed movement, change and life itself. What seems to have impressed them most was the degree to which a grand design appeared to be evident throughout the universe, enabling one who studied any part of the universe to understand the rest of it through the play of analogies. For example, the Nile was a river on the earth and the Milky Way was a "river in the sky". The observation of plant and animal life provided the opportunity to reflect on human life as well as with cycles of birth, growth, death, decay, and rebirth.

A major technology arose in the northern end of the Nile valley. That technology is reflected in thousands of temples, tombs, pyramids and in writings and scientific developments and discoveries. The observational technology produced the first Zodiac such as that seen in the Temple of Dendera or in the Tomb of Seti I in the valley of the kings at Waset (Luxor to the Arabs and Thebes to the Greeks), gives evidence of a long line of development. The construction of the Great Pyramid at Giza, attributed to Pharaoh Khufu, with its 2,200,000 limestone rocks averaging two tons each, some weighing as much as forty tons, gives ample evidence of a high level of technical development. This is especially true when we realize that until the present time, no one appears to have been able to repeat the feat.

But given these and many other examples of high level technical developments in Egypt, what is important is not so much the level of technical development as the *philosophical orientation of the users of the technology*. The purpose to which technology was put was to develop a greater understanding of man's relationship to nature and mankind's place in nature. This is in stark contrast to some contemporary expressions about purposes of technology. Today we seem to seek technical developments for the sole purpose of *exploiting* the environment for personal gains in wealth and power. Sometimes the goal of technology is expressed merely as one of helping people or nations to know, but toward *what end?*

At this point we need to return to George G. M. James who has given an excellent summary description of the Egyptian Mystery System. The ultimate aim of education in Egypt was for a person to become "one with God" or to "become like God." The path to the development of god-like qualities was through the development of virtue. A person was seen as being essentially spiritual whose essence was housed in a finite body. It was the spirit that had an eternal existence. The capacity of a person to become god-like was determined by the degree to which the person was able to overcome certain natural impediments of the body, these were character flaws. Virtue was the antidote to character flaws. But virtue could be achieved only through special study and effort. According to George G. M. James, the following ten virtues were sought by students in the ancient Egyptian Mystery System.

1. Control of thought
2. Control of action
3. Devotion of purpose
4. Faith in the Masters ability to teach the truth
5. Faith in ones ability to assimilate the truth
6. Faith in our self to wield the truth
7. Freedom from resentment under persecution
8. Freedom from resentment under wrong
9. Ability to distinguish right from wrong
10. Ability to distinguish the real from the unreal

Even a brief study of this list of ten virtues will reveal just how different it is in character from typical educational objectives with which most of us are familiar. In *Stolen Legacy,* George G. M. James goes into much greater detail to explain and to interpret the meaning of these ten virtues.

George James also tells us that the center of the higher education system in ancient Egypt was located at the ancient Egyptian city of Waset, which means "the septer", after the town or nome or province from which this small city sprang. It was sometimes referred to as the city of Amun which was the name of the great god. Apparently, Waset was so important that it was sometimes simply referred to as "The City". Waset was later given the name Thebes by European invaders, and after that, the name Luxor by the Arab invaders. Various sections of the city of Waset had their own names. One section of the city was called Ipet-Isut which means "Most Select of Places." Later populations would refer to it as Karnak where a great temple now stands. Another part of Waset was called the Southern Opet or sanctuary. Later populations would refer to this section as Luxor the name by which the whole city is now called.

And so, it was at Waset (Thebes or Luxor) at which we find located the oldest records of a university headquarters. We may think of this as the main branch. Speculation places the age of this headquarters as far back as 3000 B.C. There was another "grand lodge" in lower or northern Egypt dedicated to God in the name of Osiris. It was called the Osiriaca. This lodge had branches in other parts of the Egyptian sphere of influence. According to George James, several were located as follows: There was an Ionian Temple at Dydma; there was Euclid's Lodge at Megara; there was Pythagoras's Lodge at Cortona, and there was the Orphic Temple at Delphi.

We begin to get some inkling of the high level of esteem and for the Egyptian civilization and all that Greek and Romans felt for it by a review of the activities of the Europeans when confronted with African civilization. It is hard to account for the behavior of European conquerors of Kemet except to note that they must have felt themselves to be in the presence of a superior civilization. They tried to imitate it. Kamil notes that:

"The rule of the Ptolemies is noted for its architectural activity and the Greeks conscientiously endeavored to add to the splendor of national buildings after a priest had told Alexander that he was the son of Amon and should revere him. The Romans too repaired ruins and built temples in the traditional style, each retaining something of the earlier grandeur. But it was a losing battle, the past was not to be recaptured. Thebes could hardly hide its well worn wrinkles and a time weathered quality lay over the Metropolis."[24]

Not only were buildings copied, European kings and people joined the African religions in Africa and in Europe. It was this *African religion* of Isis, Osiris, Horus and Amen (Amon or Amun) that remained one of the major religions of Europe until the National Government of Rome installed Christianity as the state religion, after the council of Nicea, nearly three hundred years after the death of Christ.

Parenthetically we can illustrate at this point the close connection between education and religion. We can also show some antecedents of western religion. In doing this, we take our material directly from the remains of the monuments themselves, in this case the Temple of Luxor. As Kamil states:

"The story of the birthroom is depicted in three rows on the left hand wall. From left to right in the lower row the God Khnum molds the infant, Amenhotep and his guardian spirit or *Ka,* and fashions them on a potter's wheel. The Goddess Isis sits in the presence of Amon. In the center row, Amon is led by Ibis-headed God of Wisdom to the queen's bed chamber, where he approached her to beget the child already moulded by Khnum. The pregnancy and confinement are attended by Bes and Thoueris, the patron dieties of childbirth. After the delivery Amon stands with the child in his arms in the presence of Hathor and Mut. On the much damaged top row are the suckling of the infant king, his guardian spirits, and his presentation to Amon by Horus who promised him "million of years like *Ra.* In the corner the grown Amen-Hotep stands as King."[25]

Here we have then in the 18th dynasty a visual record of the virgin birth of Amen-Hotep. We find the same scene portrayed in the mortuary temple of Hatshepsut. Once again, it is in the birth colonnade of that temple.

"The birth Colonnade corresponding exactly to the Punt Colonnade is already mentioned, it was constructed to a lay concern about Hatshepsut's right to the throne. The theory of divine origin was above discussion, let alone dispute, and this is shown in a scene of the rams headed Khnum shaping Hatshepsut and her Ka on the potter's wheel under instructions from Amon who has impregnated the queen's mother Ahmose, full with child. She radiates joy, stands dignified in her pregnancy, smiling a smile of supreme contentment as she is led to the birthroom. Unfortunately, most of the scene in which Amon and the queen's mother are borne to the heavens by two goddess seated on a lion headed couch, is badly damaged."[26]

The careful listener may wonder why we skipped from a period in the 12th dynasty over as far as the 18th dynasty. It must be noted there that during this period of time the government of Egypt was in the hands of invading kings, the Hyksos from Asia. However, their reign is less important than it might be for a very simple reason. They seem to have had little to offer to Kemet. As Riefstahl observed:

"Since the Hyksos has scant culture of their own, they readily adopted Egyptian arts, and customs, even to some extent Egyptian religion. The new rulers took over the Titulary of Egyptian kings; like the latter, they were "sons of Re", the ancient Egyptian solar god from which all pharaohs claim descent. In their capitol at Avaris in the Delta, they set up their own thunder god, who was identified with the Egyptian God Seth. Sparse remains indicate that they added to and embellished Egyptian temples, while despoiling others. Though what little survives from the Hyksos periods in the way of art and architecture shows a decline in skill, extant papyri indicate that the ancient learning continued undiminished in the temples."[27]

Certain authors have looked at the initiation system which still exists in West Africa. It is good to do this because that system is a direct outgrowth of the more ancient initiation system which was utilized in the Nile Valley. Contemporary information and historical study of the initiation in West African reveals that the process operated in the following way. According to Pierre Erny in his book, *Childhood and Cosmo*[28] the following things were included in the initiation process.

1. The initiates were physically segregated from the regular activity of daily life.

2. They retreated from their familiar environment to an environment that enable them to get more directly in touch with nature. This symbolized a move from the infantile situation into a situation which would allow for more maturity.

3. The initiate joined with other initiated of the same age and shared their lives in common, since the common living experience was also a common learning experience.

4. The initiates were separated from their parents in addition to being separated from the large community.

5. The initiates had to renounce all that recalls the past existence.

6. The initiates were then taught by the old men and old women of the village or town.

7. The initiates frequently went nude or wore clothes made of grass to symbolize the clothes of the first men or women.

8. The initiates underwent purification baths.

9. During the course of initiation a number of tests of audacity, courage, fasting, flogging, hazing, mutations, scarifications were conducted. (The purpose of the test was to give the opportunity for the initiate to demonstrate a refusal to take life as it is given as a way of opening the mind to beauty, joy and ecstasy.)

10. Initiates learned a new and secret language.

11. Initiates were given new names.

12. The initiation processes symbolize a rebirth.

13. The initiation process included a number of exercises and things to be learned such as physical and military training, songs, dances, how to handle sacred things such as math and tools.

Dadisi Sonyika summarizes the initiation process into seven steps.

1. Separation.

2. Location in a sacred place.

3. Symbolic death and burial.

4. Testing or revelation.

5. Testing.

6. Ressurection (symbolic).

7. Reintroduction or reincorporation of the initiate into the larger community.

It can be seen from the study of Schaller DeLubicz's work *Her-Bak* (2 Vols)[29] that the West African initiation as described by Sonyika and Erny are quite congruent with the initiations which are described by Schwaller DeLubicz, based upon the study of documents, carvings, and paintings from ancient Egypt. At its base, initiation is a comprehensive education system. In addition to the narrowly vocational aims one can discern in the ancient Egyptian and ancient African educational system, the goals were:

1. *Unity of the person, unity of the tribe,* and *unity with nature.*

2. The development of *social responsibility.*

3. The development of *character.*

4. The development of *spiritual power.*

It was these higher aims which drove the educational process. Vocational skill training was merely a small part of the whole process.

In the ancient Egyptian educational system little thought seems to have been given to the question of the "inept intellectual capacity" of a person. Much more attention was given to character as an impediment or as a facilitator of educational development. While learning obviously was done by individuals, the picture that we get of the method used is that it was a collective rather than an individual effort. The educational process was designed in such a way that it seemed as a true rebirth which occurs through a successive series of personal and social transformations.

Initiatives were deeply emersed in a comprehensive process. It was an interactive process. There were interactions among students and interactions between student and teacher. The process was full including much time for stories, examination of signs, symbols, the use of proverbs, the use of songs, dances, and so forth, all combined to convey values and to convey a special view of the world. Teachers or "masters" *modeled* the behavior that they expected the initiates to learn. The masters were alert and in a position to react to and to nurture the direct experience of students in order that they could experience to learn higher level lessons.

At its base, the educational process was a religious process in the broadest sense of that word. The entire living environment was organized and constructed down to the smallest detail as a teaching environment. The architecture was symbolic down to the smallest detail. Even the layout of buildings within a city carried symbolic meaning. Clothing that was worn, names that were given, everything had multi-levels of meaning. This indicated a full time commitment to the goal of personal *transformation* through education.

The best single description of education in ancient Egypt is given by Isha Schaller DeLubicz. In two books, she presents her findings through the eyes of an initiate, Her-Bak. DeLubicz and her husband R.A.Schaller DeLubicz spent nearly fifteen years in detailed study of the Temple of Luxor and its environs. R. A. Schwaller DeLubicz has written numbers of important books on that work. Among them, *The Temple in Man* and, *Symbol and the Symbolic*. Both DeLubiczs tried to "enter into the mentality of the Egyptians" by in-depth study of their records, both written and archeological. In Isha Schwaller DeLubicz's books, almost all narrative is supported by illustrations of temple carvings, drawings, relief carvings, and building configurations, primarily at Luxor and Karnak Temples in Waset.

It must be kept in mind that both Luxor Temple and Karnak Temple are built on the site of older Temples! For example, The "White Chapel", the oldest part of the 18th dynasty temple at Karnak, is a reconstruction from fragments which were made by crushing the old Chapel. The small pieces were then used as "seeds" from which the new Temple of Amon would grow. The fragments were found in the third Pylon of the Temple of Amon. The older Temple, the White Chapel, was built by Sesostris during the 12th dynasty (1950 B.C.) as an offering to the great Black God Min.[29] Both represent extensions of religious and educational practices which were known from the beginnings of Egyptian civilization.

While no one can be certain of all the details of ancient Egyptian culture, one must respect writers such as the DeLubiczs who do not stray far from primary sources, as best they can be understood.

The Aims of Egyptian Education

We must keep in mind that the Egyptians made no separation between "church and state", or for that matter between religion and life. They lived a totally religious life, just as is the case with traditional African religions today. Therefore, education was religious at its base.

The lower education system, no matter how unstructured, allowed for a natural progress along a path that reached certain choice points. Having started along a path of advanced education, a learner could reach the major choice of his or her life, according to Isha Schwaller DeLubicz, the *choice between leadership and high positions or knowledge and wisdom.* The learner who chose ambition also chose limits. It was said that "ambition does to intuition what weevils do to wheat." On the other hand, for one who was able to sacrifice personal ambition, the act of sacrifice was said to "defend consciousness against the deadly effect of the search for satisfaction." For that person the path leading to wisdom was open. The initiate could reach the outer Temple or "Peristyle" where *utilitarian* knowledge was mastered. However, once admitted to the Inner Temple the initiate learned about symbols and came to know him or herself. Undoubtedly, as George G. M. James, has so clearly shown, Greek students of the African "mysteries" came to respect this goal, "man know thyself," which has been falsely attributed to the Greek late comer of latest dynastic times, Socrates.[30] The highest aim of Egyptian education was for one to become God-like through the revelation of ones own "Neter", of how God is revealed in the person.

Method in Egyptian Pedagogy

Serious education began by putting the initiate on the path of observation of nature. Usually the initiate would be assigned to a master as an apprentice. But the purpose of the apprenticeship was for the student to learn the laws of matter (materials). It was the knowledge of these laws that separated the master craftsman from a mere worker. So, the "observation" of nature was really a participatory observation. Revealed in any craft were nature's laws. During the apprenticeship, the initiate was confronted with problems of conscience. This would allow for the development of a sense of responsibility and judgment. At the end of a successful apprenticeship, the initiate was offered the chance to choose between the two paths, *political power* and *wisdom.*

Heavy use was made of proverbs, songs, and stories. Direct or symbolic lessons were taught through these. It was the fundamental belief in the unity or interconnectedness of all things which made the use of analogies such a powerful pedagogical tool "for *above* is exalted by below".[13] The use of proverbs and analogies permeates African and African Diasporan culture till this very day.

Parenthetically, it is interesting that racist psychologists claim that

Black people are not capable of "Level II thinking," the kind of abstract thinking which is reflected in proverbs and analogies. To the contrary, this is our strong suit. It is the mis-match in experiential content between such psychologists and African-Americans which causes them to miss the extensive use of proverbs and analogies among us.

The African reader of ancient Egyptian writings will find familiar methodology in the use of such things as the sayings of Ptahotep, V Dynasty, (Circa, 2350 B.C.):

> "Do not be arrogant because of your knowledge, but confer with the ignorant man as with the learned, for the limit of skill has not been attained, and there is no craftsman who has (fully) acquired his mastery, Good speech is more hidden than malachite, yet is found in the possession of women slaves at the millstones."[32]

Then there are the teachings of Kagemni which are contained in the same Papyrus, Prisse, that contains the sayings of Ptahotep, of which the above is a sample.

> ". . . the submissive man prospers, the moderate man is praised, the tent is open for the silent man, and the place of the contented man is wide. Do not talk (freely), for the flint knives are sharpen against the one who strays from the road; there is no hastening, except indeed against his misdeed."[33]

The instructions of Amenomope are estimated to have been written during the 18th dynasty just before the Amarna period, possibly during the reign of Amenhotep III. These sayings have close parallels to later Hebrew scriptures in the Book of Proverbs.

> "The hot-headed man in the temple is like a tree grown indoors; only for a moment does it put forth roots. It reaches its end in the carpentry shop, It is floated away from its place, or fire is its funeral pyre. The truly temperate man sets himself apart, He is like a tree grown in a sunlit field, But it flourishes, it doubles its yield, It stands before its owner; Its fruit is something sweet, its shade pleasant; and it reaches its end as a statute."[34]

When we look at the "Memphite Theology" Lichtheim, 1975), writings which are estimated to have been composed at the beginning of the pyramid age, we see something remarkably similar to the method of Karl Marx, the dialectic, complete with the use of contradictions. In the Memphite Theology, writings on stone at memphis in Egypt, we find the doctrine of the four elements and the four qualities (James, 1976). This "law of opposites" (the relationship between pairs of elements) sets up the conditions under which creativity occurs. The Pyramid texts also use the principle of opposites in the description of the African "pantheon", or place of "the Gods". Like the later Greek and Roman copies, there was an

Ennead - a pantheon of nine Gods, or more correctly, a diagram of nine aspects of the one Great Neter (God).

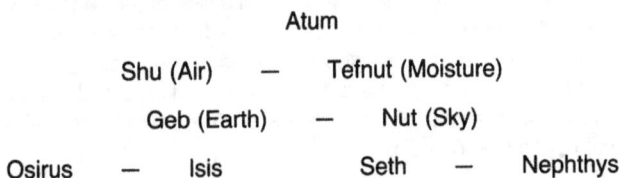

Atum

Shu (Air)   —   Tefnut (Moisture)

Geb (Earth)   —   Nut (Sky)

Osirus   —   Isis   Seth   —   Nephthys

In early times the Sun-God had his own family of gods which was also the supreme council of the gods. This group, which had its chief center at the temple of the sun at heliopolis, was the Ennead, "the Nine," consisting of four interrelated couples surmounted by one common ancestor. This Ennead or "Nine" may be placed in contrast to the "Eight", for "Eight" comprised elements of cosmic disorder, whereas the "Nine" contained only progressive steps of cosmic order: air and moisture; earth and sky; the beings on earth.

The Content of Egyptian Pedagogy

I have already referred to George G. M. James' list of curriculum content. Those courses, grammar, rhetoric, logic, arithmetic, astronomy, geometry and music were the liberating or liberal arts. They supported the quest of the initiate for the highest form of self knowledge. The initiate would study for *form, name, place,* and *symbol* of things. Having done that, it was believed that the *function* of things would be revealed.

The important thing to remember is that *nature itself,* the environment or the person, was the basic content for study. In addition, the study of nature was facilitated by the study of symbols, stories, proverbs, songs, puzzles, rhythm, and the sacred writings of the Mdw Ntr (Hieroglyphics). These studies also gave insight into human nature, which was as shown before, merely the study of one aspect of nature.

CONCLUSION

In the final analysis, the ancient Egyptian sought MAAT (truth, justice, and order) to be more correct, I should say that they sought to become one with MAAT, the cosmic order.

Our window on what was a well developed education system is through ancient Kemet. Even though the best records in antiquity are found in Keme' the picture is not yet complete. Suffice it to say that ancient Kemet was an African culture and that it shared then and shares now in the greater cultural unity of the African continent and in the diaspora of ancient African people.

A careful study and reconstruction of this aspect of our African past can give guidance to the reconstruction and development of educational aims, methods, and content appropriate to the children of the sun. As Gerald Massey has said, Truth is all powerful with its silent power / If only whispered and never heard aloud / But working secretly almost unseen, except in some excommunicated book / Truth is like lightning with its errand done before you hear the thunder.

HOTEP

NOTES

1. Cheikh Anta Diop, *The Cultural Unity of Black Africa*, Chicago: Third World Press, 1978.

2. Albert Churchward. *Signs and Symbols of Primordial Man*, Westport, Conn.: Greenwood Press, 1978, p. 3.

3. Ibid, 201.

4. Henri Frankfort. *Kingship and the Gods*, Chicago: University of Chicago Press, 1969, p. 16.

5. John Jackson. *Introduction to African Civilizations*, Secaucus, N.J.: Citadel Press, 1980, pp. 97-98.

6. Yosef ben-Jochannan. *Africa: Mother of Western Civilization*, New York Al-kebulan Books, 1971.

7. Jackson, op. cit., pp. 95-96.

8. Ibid, p. 93.

9. Margaret Drower. *Nubia: A Drowning Land,* New York: Atheneum, 1970, p. 65.

10. Bruce Williams, "The Lost Pharaohs of Nubia," *Archaeology*, (September/October, 1980).

11. Barbara Mertz. *Red Land, Black Land.* New York: Dodd, Mead & Co., 1978, p. 13.

12. Diop, op. cit.

13. Sanche DeGramont. *The Strong Brown God: The Story of the Niger River,* Boston: Houghton Mifflin, 1977, p. 30.

14. Maya Deren. *Divine Horsemen: The Voodoo Gods of Haiti,* New york: Delta, 1951, p. xi.

15. De Gramont, op. cit., pp. 32-33.

16. Frankfort, op. cit., p. 6.

17. Robert F. Thompson. *Four Moments of the Sun*, Washington, D.C.: National Gallery of Arts, 1981.

18. Janheinz Jahn. *Muntu: The New African Culture*, N.Y.: Grove Press, 1961.

19. George James. *Stolen Legacy*, San Francisco: Julian Richardson Associates, 1976.

20. R. A. Schwaller DeLubicz, *The Temple in Man*, Brooklin, Mass.: Autumn Press, 1977.

21. Thompson, op. cit.

22. Churchward, op. cit.
23. James, op. cit.
24. Jill Kamil. *Luxor: A Guide to Ancient Thebes,* New York: Longman's, 1976, p. 18.
25. Ibid, p. 32.
26. Ibid.
27. Elizabeth Riefstahl. *Thebes in the Time of Amunhotep III,* Norman: University of Oklahoma Press, 1964, p. 22.
28. Pierre Erny. Chilhood and Cosmos.
29. Henri Stierlin. *The World of the Pharaohs,* New York: Sunflower, 1978.
30. James, op. cit.
31. Bika Reed. *Rebel in the Soul,* New York: Inner Traditions International Ltd., 1978, p. 85.
32. William K. Simpson (ed). *The Literature of Ancient Egypt,* New Haven: Yale University Press, 1972, p. 161.
33. Ibid., p. 177.
34. John Wilson. *Ancient Egyptian Culture,* 1972, p. 246.
35. Henri Frankfort, et al. *The Intellectual Adventure of Man,* Chicago: University of Chicago Press, 1977, pp. 52-53.

IV. CREATIVE PRODUCTION

THE UNITY OF AFRICAN LANGUAGES

REKHETY WIMBY

PREVIOUS THEORIES OF AFRICAN LINGUISTIC UNITY

It was said among Africans that their people came, in early times, from the Nile Valley. People in the West spoke of migrations East to West; people in the Southern part of Africa spoke of migrations North to South; those in the East spoke of migrations from the central Nile Valley. Until recent time, African folklore was ignored by linguists. This tradition many anthropologists and linguists disputed when they thought of Africans as thousands of different tribes, hundreds of different kingdoms speaking 800 to 1000 different languages, having almost as many distinct origins.

The present thesis is that there are not hundreds or even four, as has been suggested, language families on the continent of Africa but rather one great genetic family composed of six branches, all which are ultimately related. I propose that the languages of Africa all derive, by evolutionary processes, from an original parent, to which I give the name, suggested by C.A. Diop in *Parente genetique,* Paleo-African.[1]

The genetic relationship of Egyptian to the African tongues has been demonstrated by numerous correspondences on every level of grammatical structure. Many detailed comparative studies have been made which attest to this fact. Three of the most noted studies will be briefly discussed here for the benefit of those who are still doubtful or uninformed of the relationship of ancient Egyptian to modern African languages. They are the studies of Homburger (1912), of Greenberg (1946) and of Diop (1948).

Cheikh Anta Diop has written a history of ancient Africa, and of the world; but since it would be quite impossible to enumerate all the things he has done in African linguistics in a sentence, or even a paragraph, let us proceed to point out some major points of his work.

As early as 1948 he presented us with comparative analyses of Egyptian and Walaf, his native tongue. In *Etude de linguistique oulove, origine de la langue et de race Walaf* (1848), then in voluminous other works, *Nations negres et culture; L'Afrique noire precoloniale; Anteriorite des civilizations negres,* these analyses are further developed, and a theory of the origin of many African languages and cultures is established. One of the things he speaks of in these works is the origin of the so-called classes of the "class languages". Of this he writes the following: "In conclusion to Chapter One, let us establish definitely

151

(1) that the relationship between Egyptian and Walaf is of the genetic type (2) that for the first time a tangible line, likewise genealogical, has been established between Egyptian demonstratives and the 'nominal classes' of African languages (one could not exaggerate the importance of this fact because of the light it throws on all African linguistic studies, and because of the new unexpected perspectives it opens up to researchers who might wish to delve into such areas); (3) that it appears possible to re-establish, by degrees as the research advances, the bases of a relative chronology extending into the prehistory of the Class Languages."[2]

Secondly, he discusses the need for a common African language, and guides us along the path of establishing one. In *Nations negres* he also lays out a format for resurrecting ancient Egyptian. (One of his main concerns now is finding a means of vocalizing this ancient tongue). Thirdly, he demonstrates beyond a doubt the genetic relationship of Walaf to ancient Egyptian, showing that both languages derive from a single parent, which he calls "Paleo-African". (We refer the reader at this point to *Parente genetique).*

Miss Lilian Homburger in 1912 proposed that indigenous African languages represent the evolution of dialectal forms of Egyptian or of Coptic (which is a later development of Egyptian).[3] According to Miss Homburger, "Nubia and Meroe, kingdoms to the south of Egypt, spoke an adulterated form of Egyptian. Dialects of Egyptian had developed in all the surrounding areas, as well as in Egypt itself (Hieratic, Demotic, Coptic). It was from this area that the migrations began. Popular traditions speak of movements east to west, or north to south, Most historians agree that Black Africans spread over Africa from the Upper Nile, and a 'primitive' unity of modern languages is generally admitted."[4] We know that caravans from Egypt crossed the Sahara and travelled (and settled) all of West Africa; and, furthermore, Egyptians for more than four thousand years travelled to East Asia as far as India. Despite her confused Pan-Africanism, Miss Homburger's studies are exhaustive and extremely valuable, wherein many definite correspondence were scientifically established and a "general unity" was, for the first time, admitted by the world outside Africa.

In more recent times Joseph H. Greenberg, has radically changed his system of African language classification.[5] In his article "The Classification of African Languages", which appeared in *American Anthropologist* (50, 1, 1948), he classified the languages of Africa into sixteen families. In another paper he reduced the number to twelve (S.J.A. 10,4,1954). Then in 1963, after further research, Greenberg reduced the number to four independent language families. This means that all African languages are merely 1000 different branches of the four currently accepted language families of Africa, which are: (1) Afro-Asiatic, (2) Nilo-Saharan, (3) Niger-Congo, (4) Khoisan.

Since the first appearance of his reclassification, there have been objections raised, mainly disagreements with the method of mass comparison of lexical items used by Greenberg. In the light of additional information, some of Greenberg's conclusions have been proven false. However this classification still proves correct in its essential details. With the new evidence relating ancient Egyptian to the West Atlantic sub-group of Niger-Congo (including such languages as Walaf, Serer, Dyola, etc.), its place in Afro-Asiatic needs to be reconsidered, and the status of Afro-Asiatic on the continent re-evaluated. This new evidence demands a new classification, which would probably result in a further reduction of the number of subgroups. And if we re-evaluated the work of Homburger, who demonstrated the affinity of Nilo-Saharan languages to Niger-Congo and ancient Egyptian, we would be left with the question: How many languages as families, independent genetic families, are there in Africa? Perhaps only one!

The remainder of this paper will be devoted to establishing the unity of the African languages, in order that we may become more aware of our common personality, as well as of our differences.

STATEMENT ON METHODOLOGY

Genetic relationship is the recognition that the resemblances of certain languages to one another are to be explained by "common descent", and upon finding certain shared features, recognizing that they may have developed from the same source. In comparing languages one should reject typological or ill-defined structural criteria, i.e. whether the language in question might be categorized as inflectional or isolating, or otherwise, or have gender and case systems, or manifest certain types of phonemes or phoneme sequences, etc. In comparing vocabularies in the search for common morphemes, two groups of words must be carefully excluded as irrelevant: borrowings from other languages and mere chance resemblances.

It is necessary to include many languages in the comparison, and, if possible, those that extend over a large geographical area, in order that the significance of the similarities can properly be assessed. For example: A descendent of Proto-Language "P" can be expected to have features of Language "P" which have been lost or have changed in other descendents within its own group; yet the feature might occur in other branches of Language "P". (Mass comparison, the method applied by J. Greenberg, establishes the validity of the entire system).

Languages change in the course of time and one of the principle types of change occurs in the sound system. Such changes may be due to assimulation, dissimulation, a desire for symmetry, or any of a number of complex factors. Because of sound change, the comparative method is established on the basis of "sound laws". When sound change is regular and recurrent, this also verifies the system.

After relationship is established, diachronic studies are done which aim at determining the Proto-Language and its possible reconstruction. However the problem in African linguistics is the rarity of older written texts, and therefore diachronic studies are difficult. Here we must devise new methods which would fit our particular (African) situation. I would suggest (1) using ancient Egyptian, Meroitic and other older texts as a basis for African diachronic studies; (2) using other sources, such as ancient Arabic texts on Africa; (3) using migration histories of peoples; (4) employing anthropological evidence of cultural similarities, especially regarding vocabulary; and (5) seeking the assistance of archaeology.

Karl Meinhof attempted to reconstruct Proto-Bantu, but actually ended up with "common" Bantu forms.[6] His failure derived from an inability to believe that Bantu could possibly be related to one of the older languages of the Nile Valley.

Now since Greenberg's classification is currently accepted in its essentials, it will be used here to form the basis for our classification in supplying the fundamental groupings of related languages. In our acceptance of the language groups themselves, we will retain the names given them by Greenberg simply to avoid the confusion that arise from assigning them new names.

As previously stated, it was indeed a great step to reduce the number of African languages to four families; however this classification presents real problems for us, in that the continued claim of Afro-Asiatic seems not based on sound linguistic principles but rather on racial theories.[7]

The main objective in looking for a relationship between ancient Egyptian and the African languages has been the purely racial hypothesis of a "Semitic" invasion into North Africa from Mesopotamia, or from South Arabia of a "Hamitic" speaking "caucasoid-pastoral" people. Due to this hypothesis, it has always been assumed that the origin of the Egyptian language lies in the lands of the East, and not in Africa.

Greenberg's rejection of the term Hamito-Semitic because of its racial overtones, did not change the picture, since the classification itself remained exactly the same, and after all, the new name, Afro-Asiatic, though not designating race, implies principally an Asiatic influence in Egypt and North Africa. It is just a new name for the same old idea. Hence we reject the concept of Afro-Asiatic, and from hereon out will refer to Hamitic and Semite languages, in, however, the original sense of the terms.

The linguistic terms Hamitic and Semitic were inspired by the Biblical story of Noah. Noah had three sons, Japheth, Ham and Shem. The early church fathers associated the sons of Noah with the three races of men, Japheth with the Caucasian race, Ham with the Blacks, and Shem with the Asians. "Hamitic" is derived from the name of the second son of Noah, Ham (or Kam). Km is an Egyptian root which etymologically signifies blackness, or solar fire. The Egyptians called themselves Kmtyw and their land kmt. The hieroglyph represented therefore is a piece of charcoal (or burning wood).

Hamitic was used as a linguistic term by Karl Meinhof to designate the languages of Africa which had affinities with the so-called Semitic tongues. Meinhof's hypothesis was certainly influenced by his notions of the racial history of North Africa. This was the only hypothesis which could account for the relationship of Semitic and African tongues. Meinhof was obviously unaware of the etymology of the word Hamitic, otherwise he would have chosen a name more agreeable with his thinking. The etymology had long been confused by his time (1912), since the hieroglyph which signifies Km had always been taken to mean the scales of a crocodile.[28]

We know then, that the people of the oldest attested Black nation called themselves Km (whence Ham), and no confusion caused by mistaken notions of race should cause us to reject this proper designation.

SUB-FAMILY 1: EGYPTIAN (OLD NIGER CONGO)

Joseph Greenberg established as a genetic family Niger-Congo, basically following the Sudanic studies of Westerman.[9] Westerman showed the linguistic unity of the languages of the Western Sudan, west of Lake Chad with one another and suggested their relationship to the Bantu languages. This stock he called "Western Sudanic".[10] Greenberg made changes upon Western Sudanic by including Fulani and excluding the Songhai languages of the Central Niger valley.

Niger-Congo is divided into seven distinct groups, which are (1) West Atlantic (Walaf, Serere-Sin, Fulani, Pajade, Bulom, only to name a few); (2) the Mande group (Soninke, Malinke, Bambara, and Dan); (3) the Gru group (Minianka, Lobi-Dogon, Puguli and Mossi); (4) Kwa (Kru, Logba, Ewe, Yoruba, Akan, Nupe, Ibo, Igala, and Bini); (5) the extensive Benue-Congo group, which has four major divisions (Kambari, Dukawa, Jukun, Efrik, Ukelle, Tiv and Bantu); (6) Adamawa-Eastern (Adamawa, Vere, Teme, Gbayaand Tagbo); (7) Kordofanian (Languages spoken in the Nuba hills of Kordofan).

The thesis presented here is that there is nothing particularly difficult about the genetic classification of Egyptian among the above African languages since the evidence presented by Diop in *Parente genetique* is sufficient to show the genetic relationship of Egyptian to Walaf, and hence its inclusion in the entire subgroup of West Atlantic.

Egyptian is the language of the ancient Egyptians, as revealed in their hieroglyphic writings. The language is now extinct; however its descendent Coptic is still spoken among Coptic Christians in Egypt and Ethiopia (mainly in its role of the lithurgical language of the Coptic Church). Earliest inscriptions go back as far as the First Dynasty. The hieroglyphic script was employed into the Christian Era.

Sir. Alan Gardiner has identified Egyptian language by five stages,[11] namely, (1) Old Egyptian, the language of Dynasties I-VIII, which passes with but little modification into, (2) Middle Egyptian, the vernacular of Dynasties IX-XI (2540-1990 B.C.), later "contaminated" with various popular elements, (3) Late Egyptian, the vernacular of Dynasties XVIII-XXIV (1573-715 B.C.), (4) Demotic, the language used in books and documents written in a script known as "Demotic", during the XXVth Dynasty (715 B.C.-470 A.D.). (5) Coptic, the Old Egyptian in its latest development, written in the Coptic script, from about the third century onward. Coptic as a vernacular, is now extinct; however several dialects descended therefrom are presently spoken.

These designations, however, reflect not so much stages in the development of Egyptian language *per se* as, rather stages in the evolving political history of the various dynasties. What Gardiner called "Late Egyptian" was the dialect of Upper Kemet, traces of which were already noticed in the Old Kingdom in Upper Kemetic sites.[12] In Dynasties VI-XI, the vernacular called "Middle Egyptian", was predominant in Kemet. During the First Intermediate Period this dialect spread northward. By the late XIth and early XIIth Dynasties so-called Late Egyptian forms occur on all types of monumental inscriptions. When the Nubian regime regained power in the XVIIIth Dynasty, the vernacular of Upper Kemet spread with the establishment of the New Kingdom. Amen Hotep II (1450) composed a letter to his viceroy in Nubia and in it he used what has come to be called Late Egyptian; in other words, his language was that of Nubia or Upper Egypt. It is essential when doing comparative studies of Egyptian to understand therefore that Late Egyptian is very different in its grammatical structure from Middle Egyptian. This fact was taken into account in this comparative study, and Late Egyptian forms are cited where they help to explain certain grammatical developments.

Morphological resemblances have the greatest value in proving genetic relationship, and indeed in the morphology of Egyptian and Niger-Congo (including the Nilo-Saharan group), the correspondence are numerous and the following are examples thereof. The evidence presented herein is taken from several sources, especially from the Walaf language of Senegal (forms cited from *Parente genetique*) and from my own material on the South African Bantu group.

(1) The primary linguistic feature which distinguishes the Niger-Congo languages from the other branches is its peculiar system of noun classification, such as that of the Bantu class languages. The system of noun classes did not exist in ancient Egyptian, but have their origin therein.

The nouns of a class language are composed of a theoretically invariable radical to which is adjoined an affix.

mtu: a person — watu: people (Swahili)

Pul-lo: a Pul — Pul-se: people of Pul (Fulani)

In some languages the affix occurs in the form of a prefix, as in the Bantu languages, and sometimes as a suffix, as in some languages of West-Atlantic and Adamawa-Eastern groups. C.A. Diop has determined the origin of the various African noun classes from Egyptian interrogative and demonstrative forms.

Egyptian had a series of 27 demonstratives which distinguished gender and location. These serve to define and localize a noun. All the demonstratives consisted of two elements: the demonstrative *per se* and the locative particle. For example:

pw: this — pwy: this (in close proximity to something else)

The definition of a class language given by Diop is "Les langues africaines qui possedent un nombre variable de consonnes pouvant se substituer chacune au p du demonstratif egyptien pw sans modification de sens, sont appelees des langues a classe. Ces consonnes ou semi-consonnes sont, pour le walaf, au nomber de huit (b, m, s, w, k, g, d, l); cela veut dire que l'on peut, dans les formes walafs ci-dessous, remplacer par une permutation circulaire, le p des exemples cites, successivement, par chacune de ces huit consonnes et le sens grammatical reste le mene, seul la valeur 'euphonique' change."[13]

	Egyptian	Walaf
pw		bw, mw, sw, ww, kw, gw, dw, lw

The African noun classes are demonstrative forms which define a radical as a noun. In Meinhof's Proto-Bantu (UrBantu), there are eleven demonstrative consonants which define a noun; they are yw, va, i, li, ya, ma, vu, ki, ka, ki, tu. They are employed in the same way as the consonant-classes of Walaf.[14]

(2) The construction of nouns, verbs and adjectives from a nominal radical by the addition of affixes occurs in most of the languages under consideration.

(3) Causative verbs are formed by the morpheme "s" ("sh", "z"), e.g. nfr "beauty" and snfr "Make beautiful"

Walaf: (Causative prefix is di, from Egyptian rdı — di)

Swahili· (s opr z before the final a of the radical) kujua "to know" and kujuli-sh-a "to inform"

Kongo: (isa, esa) i.e. wasumbi-s-a "cause to be brought"

Sotho: (caus. suffix — isa) i.e. lio luli-s-a

Kushitic: (Beja) nefr "be agreeable" and snafir "render agreable"

Coptic: (caus. prefix is tr — pronoun)

Nubian: (caus. ending g)

Somali: (causative in -si or -i) shakhei "work"; shakhei-si "make to work"

(4) The passive is formed by the morpheme "w" in the following languages:

Egyptian: kef.i "I seize"; kef-w.i "I am seized"

Walaf: kef-na "I seize"; kef-w-na "I am seized"

Swahili: ku-penda "to love"; ku-pend-w-a "to be loved"

Kongo: tonda "to love"; tond-w-a "to be loved"

Sotho: Tseba "to know"; tseb-w-a "to be known"
(5) A genetive particle n
Eg.: remet n Kemet "people of Kemet"
Walaf: nit non Misra "people of Egypt"
Nubian: genetive morpheme na (ne, n, e) sing. a., Coptic genetive n.

SUB-FAMILY II KUSHITIC (OLD SEMITIC)

I include the Chad languages within Greenberg's "Semitic Branch" in light of the close relationship between those tongues and the languages of ancient Arabia, Mesopotamia, and espcially Akkadian. Evidence for this will be presented later in this section. Greenberg excludes Chad altogether, considering it to be a separate Branch. To this Branch consisting of the Chad languages, spoken around Lake Chad and in central and northern Nigeria, Akkadian in the east, Canaanite and Phunic in the north, and Ethiopic in the south; I have adopted a more appropriate name Kushitic, in view of the African connection. In fact four of Greenberg's proposed Hamito-Semitic Families are found on the continent of Africa while only one, "Semitic" is found in a small portion of the New East outside Africa.

Kushitic is a proper designation for this Branch. The name Kush comes from the Egyptian root K 3 S which etymologically signifies that which is spiritual or ingenious. Kush was the Egyptian designation for the Kingdom of the Central Sudan, south of Kemet. This Kingdom later comprised the Hausa Bakwai (seven historical states of Kano, Katsina, Daura, Zazzau, Biram, Gobir, and Rano). (The name "Semitic" was never truly justifiable, for according to the Bible, the languages called Semitic today were originally spoken by the descendants of Ham, a Black race. The languages which were spoken by the descendants of Shem or "Semities" are: Sumerian, Elamitic, Lydian, Persian, Syric, Hebrew, Aramaic, etc.)[15]

Chad can be divided into nine distinct groups, which are (1) The Hausa and related languages (Gwandara, Ngizim, and Bede); (2) The Kotoka group (Logone, Ngala, and Shoe); (3) The Bata group (Margi, Fali, and Sukur); (4) Hina (and Gauar); (5) Gidder; (6) Mandara; (7) Musgu; (8) Bana; and (9) Somrai. Morphological resemblances are quite numerous between these languages, and were early noted by such as Meinhof (1863), F. Mueller (1866), and M. Cohen, who also determined their relationship (especially the Hausa group) to Hamito-Semitic.

Akkadian, the Eastern most group, is the ancient language of Mesopotamia. It is attested from the Third millennium B.C. up to the first Century A.D. There are three principal dialects namely, Akkadian, Babylonian and Assyrian, each has a number of discernible stages of development. Ethiopic is the designation for the languages spoken in what is today Ethiopia. Some Ethiopic tongues are (1) Ge'ez, a purely liturgical language; (2) Tagre, spoken in the north; (3) Tigrina, (a written language having some historically significant literature to its credit); (4) Amharic, the official language of Ethiopia, and an important literary vehicle; (5) Argobba, now nearly extinct but still spoken in Ankober; and (6) Gurage. It has generally been thought that the Ethiopian tongues akin to Akkadian (or "Semitic" languages) were derived from migrations of a Semitic people from Yemen-South Arabia. This hypothesis was first voiced by Job Ludolf in the XVlth century. All the facts show, however, that the original inhabitants of South Arabia were Black. Any migration was in the earliest times from Ethiopia to Yemen (Ethiopia is possibly the homeland of Paleo-African). There were five dialects of Yemen known from inscriptions, the major one being Sabaean. Five modern dialects are Soqotri, Mehri, Shahri, Bathari and Harsusi. Leslau (1968) showed the close relationship of the languages of Yemen and Ethiopia. Beyond this, others have noticed the affinity of Hausa and related tongues Sabaean, Akkadian and Ethiopic.

The following morphological resemblances attest to the unity of the Kushitic languages and their place in Paleo-African.

CHARACTERISTICS OF KUSHITIC SHARED WITH EGYPTIAN

A. Characteristics normally cited to affirm the relationship of Ancient Egyptian and Kushitic languages.

   (1) Guttural or laryngeal letters having unique sound in Egyptian and Kushitic. The most characteristic is the 'yin'.

   (2) There are approximately three hundred etymologies common to the two languages (Kushitic and Egyptian). Among the common roots are distinguished those, in great number, having three radicals; this phenomenon is called "triliteralism".[16] However, the most ancient roots have been found to be biliteral. Fabre d'Olivet sought to prove that all Semitic roots were originally biliteral, and that words composed of more than one syllable are derivatives, either two words united, or several signs joining to the root which modifies it.

   Let us note here that the African radical is formed on different principles than the Semitic root. In Semitic, the meaning of a word is determined by vocalic alternations (the vowels are grammatical elements) and a few affixes. In modern African tongues, essentially affixes alone determine whether the radical is a noun or verb.

   (3) In Egyptian and Kushitic the causative is formed by the morpheme s or s. In Kushitic the prefix varies somewhat from

language to language: sa - sa - ha (hiph'il form). Egyptian also had a prefix n for the causative.

Egyptian : 'nh "live" and s'nh "cause to live"

Akkadian: magatum "to fall" and sumqutum "to make fall"

(4) The Egyptian Pseudo-Participle, commonly referred to as the "Old-Perfective", is usually compared to the Semitic Perfective. The endings of this form are strikingly similar to those of the verb (see below). Affinities have also been found with the Akkadian permansive.

In all situations the Old-Perfective defines motion/action at a glance (at one specific moment).

Diop considers the Pseudo-Participle to be a mode, which was already disappearing in Old Egyptian.

"L'egyptien a trois modes: l'acheve, l'inacheve' et le pseudo-participe; ce dernier qui etait deja en voie de disparition en egyptien ancien n'a survecu en walaf que tres partielle-ment. . . . en walaf, il en est de meme de la 3 personne du masculin singulier et la premiere personne du singulier, et de la 3 personne du masculin pluriel."[17]

	Hebrew	Egyptian	Akkadian
Singular			
1st:	ty	kwi	ku
2nd (m):	ta	ti	ti
2nd (f):	t	ti	ta
3rd (m):	/	w	/
3rd (f):	ah	ti	t
Plural			
1st:	nu	win	ni, nu
2nd (m):	tm	tiwni	tunu
2nd (f):	tn	tiwni	tina
3rd (m):	u	w (u)	w (u)
3rd (f):	u	ti, t	w (u)

The Hebrew (Semitic) Perfective is identifiable with the "Old-Perfective" of Egyptian; however the function and meaning vary from language to language and are no longer always comparable.

(5) The Genetive is formed by the morpheme n.

Hausa: Possession is signaled by the morpheme -n/-r suffixed to the first nominal, -n is suffixed to masculine plural nouns, -r to feminine nouns. This n is a particle of 'belonging to'.

Mata-n-Bornu "women of Bornu"

Eg.: Remet n Kemet "people of Kemet"

Ethiopic has no distinct form.

(6) K/T opposition masculine/feminine

Hausa: t prefix for feminine possessives
n prefix for masculine possessives

nawa (masc.) mine and tana (fem) mine

Akkadian: feminine formative t.

belum "master" and beltum "mistress"

sarrum "king" and sarratum "queen"

Tigrigna: feminine formative t.

(7) Formation of an objective from preposition or substantives by adjunction of an ending "y"; the adjectives thus formed are never used predicatively, but only as epithets.[18]

Diop notes that the Egyptian form is not truly identifiable with the Semitic form. He concludes that the Egyptian form is identifiable with that of Walaf, by suffixation to a substantive of an adjunct morpheme, or of the enclitic "y"; the term obtained is a substantive which can serve as a predicate.[19]

LINGUISTIC UNITY AND ETHNIC CONSCIOUSNESS

The recognition of the unity of African languages is important in establishing the "common personality" or ethnic consciousness of a people; and upon recognizing that common linquistic unity (as well as cultural unity), commence establishing an ethnic African commonwealth. Unity is founded upon the recognition of certain common ideas and needs. Linguistic analysis has proven that all African languages are genetically related. Now this fact can be a foundation to build upon, and also offers insight into the choice of a National language for Africa, which is absolutely essential since language is the primary vehicle of culture; which in itself suggests that a people without their own language would be in essence a people without a culture. The use of indigenous African languages cannot be separated from the idea of an ethnic African state or group of states combined to make up an ethnic commonwealth.

Ethnic consciousness in its truest form cannot be born if the language of an oppressor or conqueror be used exclusively. A people are truly free only when they can determine and express by the use of their own language, with its ideas and subtleties, their own ideas and purposes. Every people's culture is embodied in their particular language structure. The way a man conceptualizes the universe is reflected in the grammatical structure of his language. It follows, then, that to give up one's language and adopt that of a foreign people is to forsake one's culture, perhaps forever. Since most of our conscious modes of conceptualizing, acting and moving about are conditioned in part by our language, to use the language of another culture is to use that culture's ideas; and to use another culture's ideas in place of one's own is to relegate the latter to a position of *de facto* inferiority. After all, one of the very first things conquering races have done on entering the domains of other, politically or militarily weaker, cultures, is to make their languages mandatory, and with them their ideas, whether they are correct or false, moral or immoral, helpful or destructive. This, then, should be a call for all Black people to concentrate on learning an indigenous Black language with which to communicate, and to choose among themselves an ethnic language.

Now obviously the basic purpose of language, beyond its immediate role of utterance pure and simple, is the communication of ideas and feelings together with the passing of information on all possible levels; and this to me signifies *education* in the broadest sense of the word. Thus it is perhaps the most important aspect of an indigenous ethnic language that it be in all ways a medium for *education*, edification, conscious intellectual development of a people; and therefore that it engender books and other writings that there might be generation upon generation of ethnic consciousness, the only truly permanent binding force that a people can possess — all mere material possession, such as natural resources, etc., being by comparison, and by nature, ephemeral.

However, certain so-called intellectuals who study language (but who often do not understand it) and who call themselves linguists, declare that indigenous African languages are not suitable for highly technological or theoretical thinking and learning. Were it not for the fact that some of my own people, African and Afro-American, have been misled to believe such a notion, I would not even consider responding to it. Probably such a statement was made as well by the Romans concerning the Goths, Picts and Celts (the original ancestors of the German, English and other northern European peoples). To put it bluntly, such intellectual trivia can only be generated by linguistic ignoramuses. Language, as *the* living, cultural phenomenon of a people, cannot help but grow with cultivation, and die with the lack of it: all languages are capable of developing what they need to meet the demands of the times, and losing what they do not need.

The language of technology today is English (albeit an English whose vocabulary is chiefly Greek and Latin) but before it was English it was German, then French, and before French, curiously enough, it was Arabic. All of which is only to say that whenever major scientific discoveries along with important technological advances are made by a particular people, and thus expressed in their language, that language then becomes *the* technological language of the day. It follows that people elsewhere will wish to learn such a language. And so, if tomorrow Africans began to employ their indigenous languages to express their new technology, then other people in the world would aspire to learn these tongues.

But beyond conveying our new technology (which would be in harmony with the African way of life), there is also a need for translating or incorporating into African languages the scientific terminology of other tongues. (Here we ought mention that C.A. Diop, in his *Nations negres,* has already begun a lexicon of scientific and philosophical terms translated into Walaf; surely this could serve as the nucleus of a scientific dictionary of African terms). Besides, the problem of rendering modern scientific concepts into African tongues is not really a problem but only a matter of dedicated labour. African languages have many diverse means for incorporating and translating new words, based on the rules of African morphological construction; and these rules are, generally speaking, as flexible and as capable of facilitating the current international scientific and technological jargon, as are any such analogous morphological systems existing in the world today. And the linguistic bigotry that claims otherwise can now easily be refuted by the true philological facts and that lie before us: language in its very essence is but one universal phenomenon wherever it occurs and whatever the divergences among its purely linguistic particulars.

THE CHOICE OF A LANGUAGE

We would choose a Kemetic language most closely related to ancient Egyptian as the classical language of Africa, in the same way Latin was chosen as the classical language of Europe. As with Latin, Egyptian (or a dialect thereof) would be resurrected as a literary vehicle only and used as such to provide all Africa with an historical literary unity, something which neither English, French, nor even Arabic could ever give it, i.e., a binding force for African intellectualism. By this is meant that not only Africans but all of African descent who bear Africa in their hearts and minds, would learn to speak an African tongue. For only in this way could we develop the most genuine form of ethnic consciousness.

Ancient Egyptian would be our first choice for a classical language since it is a truly historical language rooted in the very foundations of African culture. "Egypt is to Black Africa what Greece and Rome are to the west," says Diop. In other words, the birthplace of all African cultures, whose language is therefore the only true universal and classical language of Africa.

Besides the need for a classical language is the need for an intellectual "lingua franca" for all African peoples. The current proposal that Swahili be used is indeed well grounded; Swahili has long been the lingua franca along the East Coast of the continent, and has over 60 million speakers. Swahili is spoken from Zanzibar, the Commores Islands and Northeastern Madagascar to Tanzania, Kenya, Zaire and farther south among the Rwanda, as well as in Uganda and the Sudan.

Some have argued that Swahili has become thoroughly corrupted with foreign elements, principally Arabic. These allegations have to have been made in ignorance of the nature and grammatical structure of this language Swahili has a pure, strong, Bantu structure; there is nothing Semitic about it except that, in consequences of intercourse with traders from various parts of the world among the indigenous populations, it has evolved an extremely rich vocabulary which includes many words of foreign origin, notably, of course, Arabic.

However, all languages do in fact incorporate foreign terms when needed, and this ability is rather an asset. Indeed, this is what language is all about: it is a living process, always undergoing transformation.

The Egyptian language, under foreign rule and after the Middle Kingdom, incorporated many foreign words maintaining, however, its peculiar structure. (And, after all, genetic relationhship cannot be determined solely on the basis of lexical correspondences but rather by relationships on the essential levels of grammar, i.e., morphology and syntax).

To argue that Swahili is strongly influenced by Arabic is not to the point. Many of the foreign words in its vocabulary are not Arabic at all, but derive rather, since the earliest times, from Sumerian, Elamite,

Phoenecian, Omani, and later from various Indo-European tongues.
Swahili belongs to the Bantu sub-group of the Egyptian-Niger Congo
Branch of Paleo-African, which is spoken over three-fourths of the
continent, having over 60 million speakers. Swahili is now the major
representative of Bantu. The genetic relationship of the Bantu languages
to Egyptian, lends further support to the choice of Swahili. We will not
discuss here other problems, in considering an ethnic language, such
as the number of speakers, or of petty nationalism. These issues have
been adequately discussed elsewhere.

Let us say, in conclusion, that the three major choices for an ethnic
language are: Swahili, Walaf and Hausa. Now of these Swahili and
Walaf happen to belong to the Egyptian Branch. Another strong point
for Swahili is that it already has a vast written literature, stemming from
an early period. The language we would choose for a classical and/
or intellectual language must be purely indigenous, and must have
sprung from the very roots of Africa, unfettered by Indo-European
structure; and thus Egyptian and Swahili are to a high degree; and
those who champion them, of course, comprehend this.

NOTES

1. Cheikh Anta Diop, *Parente genetique des egyptiens pharoniq ue et des langes negres africaines*, IFAN, Dakar, 1975; see also, *Etude linguistique oulove, origine de la langue et de race walaf; Nations negres et culture*, Paris, Presence Africaine, 1954; *Anteriorite des civilisations negres: myths ou verite historique?* Presence Africaine, 1967.

2 Ibid, *Parente genetique*, p. 24.

3 Lillian Homburger. *The Negro African Language*, Lond, 1949.

4. Ibid, pp 221-225.

5. Joseph Greenberg, *Languages of Africa* Indiana: Indiana University Press, 1970.

6. Karl Meinhof *Die Sprachen der Hamiten.* Hamburg, 1912, p. 2

7 Ibid, p. 2; see also Charles G. Seligman, *Races of Man*, Cambridge, London, 1929, p 61

8. Alan H. Gardiner, *Egyptian Grammar*, 3rd edition, Indiana: Indiana University Press, 1966, p 6.

9. Joseph Greenberg, *The Language of Africa*, 3rd, edition, Indiana: Indiana University Press, 1966, p. 6.

10. Westerman, *Africa*, 22 p. 253, 1952.

11. Gardiner, Ibid, pp. 3-4.

12 Late Egyptian inscriptions in the Old Kingdom: Pierre Montent, "Les Tombeaux dits de Kasr-el-Sayad," *Kemi*, (1936, pp. 91, 97, 177; Aylward M. Blackman *The Rock Tombs of Meir*, Parts I, III, V, Archeological Survey of Egypt, Memoirs, 22, 24, 28, (London, 1914, 1915, 1953)

   First Intermediate Period inscriptions with late Egyptian forms: Blackman, ibid, vols. XI, XII (Dsir-el-Gebrawi),

   Middle Kingdom inscriptions with late Egyptian forms: N. Davies and Gardiner, *The Tomb of Antefoker and His Wife Senet*, Theban Tomb Series, No. 2, London, 1930.

13. Diop, op. cit., p. 4

14. Karl Meinhof, *Bantu Phonology,* (edited, N.J. van Warmelo), 1932.

15. For a synopsis of the process of Semitization, we refer the reader to *African Origins of Civilization,* Wesport, Conn.: Lawrence Hill & Co., 1974; pp. 100-128, and Parente genetique, op. cit., pp. xxix - xxxvii.

16. Gustav Lefebvre, *Grammaire de l'Egyptien Classique,* Cairo, 1940, p. 4

17. Diop, op. cit., p. 43.

18. Lefebvre, op. cit., pp. 93-94.

19. Diop, op. cit., p. 12.

THE NATURE AND ELEGANCE OF ANCIENT EGYPTIAN LITERATURE

W.J. HARDIMAN

This paper is intended as a contribution to the theory and pedagogical application of Ancient Egyptian Literature. It presents and discusses the hypothesis that the study of Ancient Egyptian Literature is an important medium for empowering the Black adult learner. It suggests that the processes of imaging and re-imaging leads to shifts in attitude and self-perception. This paper is a direct result of my research into how to teach "classical literature" to a group of Black adult learners enrolled at the Evergreen State College's Tacoma campus and is applicable, I believe, to other learning situations.

As a *Neophite* in the study of Ancient African Civilization, it feels a little presumptuous for me to be on the same program as seasoned scholars in the field. But I come, because too often scholars, mentors, warriors in the struggle do not get the chance to see the second and third generational fruits of their labor and I wish to thank them for planting the seed. My paper is intended as an offering, as a testimonial, as an acknowledgement of the scholarship of my colleagues and the elders and of the transformative powers of the ancestors.

> "What became of the Black people of Sumer? the traveller asked the old man, "for ancient records show that the people of Sumer were Black. What happened to them?" "Ah," the old man sighed, "they lost their history, so they died . . ."[1]

Storytelling and story making are two of the most critical activities for a people's survival, endurance and transcendence. Without the story, there is no continuity, there is nothing to grow to. There are no connections with previous or future truths.

There is a children's rhyme that says, "Sticks and stones may break my bones but names can never hurt me." That is not true. Names can hurt. Names can damage. If you call a people stupid long enough, they will think they are stupid. If you call a people dumb long enough, they will think they are dumb. He who controls the image controls the premise. That is why it is imperative to control the images of our lives, and one way we can do that is by reconnecting the literature of and about our ancestors with the literature of and about our lives.

Such a reconnection, in truth, a reclamation, is not an easy process. Literature, like most disciplines in the Euro-centric educational system is normally taught in such a way as to re-enforce the idea that world civilization started with the Greeks. In this way, it is asserted that other cultures might have produced folklore or mythology but the Greeks produced the *classics*. In few places is it openly declared that world civilization first reached its apex in Black Africa, or that Black Africans developed Egypt and were responsible for her periods of renaissance. In few places is it openly said that African civilization was the primary foundation for Western civilization. The works of ben-Jochannan, Diop and James are exceptions.[2] In few places is it openly said that ancient Africans developed an influential body of literature that includes autobiographies, historical inscriptions, praises and prayers, instructions, orations, school texts, and love lyrics[3]. And in few places is it openly said that the first recorded versions of the creation story, the flood story, the resurrection story, the story of Job (the eloquent peasant), the story of the prodigal son (Sinuhe), the story of the fall of Troy (the talking of Joppa), and even the Cinderella story (the girl with red slippers) are to be found in Ancient Egypt.

In few places in Euro-centric educational experience is it openly said that Ancient Egypt has had any relationship to the lives of Black Americans. And it not being said is dangerous because there is so little out here to balance the bombardment of negative images of Black people that abound in the American consciousness.

This paper describes an on-going effort, one that is to image, re-image, and *SHIFT* the premise of Black inferiority. It is a description of an effort to reclaim and reconnect Black classical "Ancient Egyptian" literature to the lives of a group of Black adult learners enrolled at the Evergreen State College's Tacoma campus.

The Evergreen State College's Tacoma campus was founded twelve years ago by Dr. Maxine Mimms to meet the educational needs of first generation Black adults who for reasons, such as job commitments, military service, family or personal responsibilities, have had to delay their college education. The current student body consists of retired military personnel, returning homemakers and working women, and younger 27 to 37 year old students of color. The students range in age from 27 to 64. The proportion of people of color has always been between 60% and 83% of the total enrollment, with men outnumbering women about two to one. The average age is 42 and the current enrollment is 120 students. The students attended school three days or three nights a week; most of them also hold full-time jobs. They are people who are rich in experience, with significant life stories. The fact that what's taught in class on Tuesday is often heard in the barber or beauty shop on Thursday, and in the pulpit on Sunday, is an indication of the connectiveness of the curriculum to a larger community. They are a group of students who take their learning seriously and teaching them is an exciting and rewarding proposition.

My investigation into Black classical (ancient Egyptian) literature was a direct result of a charge given to me four years ago by Dr. Mimms. I was told by her that my assignment was to teach classical literature to the adult students enrolled at the Tacoma campus. I was reading Dr. ben-Jochannan's *Africa, Mother of Western Civilization*, George G. M. James' *Stolen Legacy,* and Chancellor Williams' *Destruction of Black Civilization* at the time and so decided to start my investigations with the *African* origins of the classical tradition instead of with the Greek. I thought that using an Afro-centric perspective would make the material more approachable, more meaningful to the students. I had also been doing some reflection on the nature of Liberal Arts education. Dr. ben-Jochannan's *Ta-Merry's Mysteries System*, James' *Stolen Legacy*, and Dr. Asa Hilliard's paper on "Indigenous African and African Diaspora Education" were instrumental in my decision to incorporate the African pedagogies of modeling and initiation into the curriculum design. In this way, the students could not only reconnect their lives with the literature of their African/ancient Egyptian past by reclaiming their heritage, but they could create their own literature after they had studied classic examples of the form.

After consulting with Dr. Jacob Carruthers, reading his *Essays in Ancient Egyptian Studies*, reading Miriam Lichtheim's three volumes of *Ancient Egyptian Literature, Breasted's Ancient Records of Egypt*, Erman's *The Ancient Egyptians,* Myers' *The Oldest Book in the World*, Dr. Karenga's *Selections from the Husia*, and Diop's *The Cultural Unity of Black Africa*,[4] it became apparent to me that (1) Western literacy forms like the tragedy, comedy, farce, and melodrama had no comparative form in ancient Egyptian literature, and (2) if classical literature was to be taught from an Afro-centric perspective, I had to create an Afro-centric context and process and I had to use Afro-centric literacy forms/genres. Dr. Karenga's *Selections from the Husia* was especially helpful here in delineating indigenous ancient Egypt genres.[5]

The results of my four years of research have been more than satisfying. The introduction of the ancient Egyptian origins of a literacy form, plus the study of specific models of that form and the creation of contemporary versions of that form, led to (1) learner ownership and involvement with the subject matter, (2) a sense of historical continuity and personal authority, (3) an appreciation for storytelling and story making, and (4) changes in attitude and self-perception. Students moved from passive to active learning, from external evaluation, to self-evaluation from unquestioning acceptance of authority to critical analysis of data. The effect of the reclaimed information on the younger students was more dramatic because they were for the most part looking for the answers that the study of ancient Egyptian literature provided. For the older students, the effect was more subtle, but they were less fearful, more confident. A sample of students comments are as follows:

> "This class was the highlight of the quarter. Every hour spent in class was very uplifting and caused a thirst for knowledge on my part. Rather than the classics being stories written in a strange language that is difficult to understand, I find not only do I understand what they are about, but I am able to apply them to life in these United States today . . . one lecture from a book by Doctor George G.M. James, *Stolen Legacy*, was so interesting that I feel that it should be taught as a separate subject to all literature students before studying the classics because it will provide the connection to the beginning of civilization."

> "It was in my literature class that this quarter really jellied . . . as I read several books and familiarized myself with the many contributions of the Egyptians, I had the profound realization that these people were African people and, therefore, my forefathers. It occured to me that my goal was not just creating new images for myself, but to take possession of those positive images that are mine by birthright. It is my legacy to be intellectually, spiritually, and creatively brilliant and productive."

> "The literature classes, I can't say enough about the enjoyment and knowledge I experienced. I learned that reading can be just as relaxing as having a cold beer and sitting down in front of (the) television."

> "The study of ancient Egyptian history (has) brought class to a more balanced level than I had learned during my elementary and high school classes . . . I plan to read more of the new discoveries by Black authors on Black history and philosophy."

> "For centuries we have been told that the Egyptians (and other people who developed civilizations in the past) are not really any part of us. But I never believed that and this (ancient Egyptian literature) class has confirmed that belief."

My research has convinced me that a large body of ancient Egyptian literature exists and needs to be acknowledged beyond the confines of museums, anthropology, and archeology. It needs to be recognized and disseminated in the public domain and by public information systems such as schools, colleges, libraries, and the mass media. It needs to be seen as viable, valuable, significant, and *African*. It needs to be explored in terms of its relationship to concepts of literature and contemporary living situations.

To study ancient Egyptian literature is to expose one of the most dangerous misrepresentations in the Eurocentric curriculum of miseducation, the lie *that Black people cannot write*. Black people have been writing for centuries. For the ancient Egyptian "the speaking of the word" and "the writing of the word" were valued, complementary, and significant activities.

The idea that thoughts can manifest themselves in physical terms was a fundamental concept to the Egyptians. The ancient Egyptians believed that creation occurred through conceptual thought and authoritative utterance as evidenced in this quote from Dr. Karenga's *Selections From the Husia:* "Indeed every word of God came into being through that which the heart and mind thought and the tongue commanded."[6]

Books were important vehicles for passing on the wisdom of the ages. Again from the *Husia*, "Follow in the footsteps of your ancestors, for the mind is trained through knowledge. Behold, their words endure in books. Open and read them and follow their wise counsel."[7] Books were insurance for everlasting remembrance. "Man decays; his corpse becomes dust and relatives die. But a book causes him to be remembered through the mouth of those who quote it."[8] Further proof of the ancient Egyptian appreciation for the functional, sacred and aesthetic value of words and of writing lies in the high honor given to scribes.

My research has also convinced me that ancient Egyptian literature is a body of literature that is spiritual and transformative in nature. It served the ancient Egyptian as a means of transmigration; as an instructional guide for character development, social behavior, and community service, and as a record of an *exemplum* for human virtues and achievements.

It is a body of literature whose central concern and focus was Maat. It was -according to Dr. Maulana Karenga in his outstanding compilation and retranslation of Ancient Egyptian Wisdom Literature, *Selections From the Husia* - both a divine concept, power and practice, and a fundamental concept, power and practice for the organization, maintenance, and development of human society.[9] Maat for the ancient Egyptian, was the foundation of both natural and social order.[10]

It is a body of literature in which all parts re-enforce the center, which is Maat. The prayers were requests for blessings and for good reception in the afterlife.

Praise literature provided opportunities for worshipping, for participating and sharing in the qualities and action of the praised.

The private autobiographies and historical inscriptions articulated the ideal. The life lived in harmony with Maat served as models of service and commitment for others to emulate.

The instructions focused on the moral and spiritual obligations each person had in preserving and practicing Maat in and for the community.

Love lyrics and orations were formulaic celebrations of Maat. Moral narratives were exquisitely constructed exemplems about the consequences of living a righteous or a non-righteous life.

The comtemplations talk about the imbalanced world without Maat. In narratives of homecoming, like *The Memoirs of Sinuhe*, in stories of family estrangement and reunion, like *The Two Brothers*, in the urgings toward self-knowledge and self-mastery, service and achievement, toward hospitality and reciprocity found in the Instructions of Ptah-hotep, and in the celebrations of life and humanity in its praise songs like the Song of the Harper, we find works of literature that speak to the human condition and the Black experience with maturity and elegance.

Studying ancient Egyptian literature is a homecoming experience. It gives heritage to one's life and perspective to one's future. The act of reclaiming one's history, of reconnecting to the source of one's genius ensures that no one will ask, "What happened to the Black people of America?", and to be told, "They lost their history and so they died."

In conclusion, I just want to say again to my colleagues, my mentors, my elders and to the ancestors, "Thank you for planting the seed so that we all might be. I trust you are pleased with the fruits of your labor."

NOTES

1. Chancellor Williams. *The Destruction of Black Civilization*, Chicago: Third World Press, 1976, p. 15.
2. See Yosef ben-Jochannan. *Africa: Mother of "Western Civilization,"* New York: Alkebu-Ian Books, 1971; Cheikh Anta Diop, *The African Origin of Civilation: Myth or Reality*, Wesport, CN. Lawrence Hill & Co., 1974; George G.M. James, *Stolen Legacy*, San Francisco: Julian Richardson Associates, 1976.
3. Miriam Lichtheim, *Ancient Egyptian Literature,* 3 Vols. Berkeley: University of California Press, 1975, 1976, 1980.
4. Jacob Carruthers, *Essays in Ancient Egyptian Studies*, Los Angeles: University of Sankore Press, 1984; Lichtheim, op. cit.; James Breasted, *Ancient Records of Egypt*, Chicago: University of Chicago Press, 1927; Adolf Erman, *Life in Ancient Egypt*, London: Macmillan & Co. 1894; Issac Myer, *The Oldest Books in the World*, Baltimore: John F. Osbourne, 1935; Diop, op. cit.
5. Maulana Karenga, *Selections From the Husia: Sacred Wisdom of Ancient Egypt*, Los Angeles: University of Sankore Press, 1984.
6. Ibid, p. 6.
7. Ibid, p. 50.
8. Ibid, p. 84.
9. Ibid, p. 4.
10. Ibid, p. 29.

PARALLELS BETWEEN EGYPTIAN ART AND SOUTHWESTERN NIGERIAN ART

CLAUDE L. CLARK

Egyptian civilization has ceased to exist but contributions made by Egyptians and earlier African civilizations live on in cultures that followed in Asia, Middle East, Europe and the rest of the world. No one living today has ever talked with an Egyptian scribe or Pharaoh, yet we know about them through the works of artists. Most of the information obtained about scribes, pharaohs and Egypt, has been received through Egyptian art and architecture. Most of that information is contained in the hieroglyphic art media, best described as a complicated, detailed pictograph system of images or highly sophisticated development of language tramsmitted by pictures.

All African art is a functional and social art. It is first social, dominated by religious values, yet religion enters the creative process first though social avenues, reflecting people's emotional needs and values. Hence Africans identify with their art. African sculpture, for example, feeds on itself and on ideas contributed by people involved in the creative process. Craftsmen found that by creating a line and developing certain geometric shapes based on the line, they were creating space and volume which appeared to be unprecedented in their natural surroundings; yet indicative of their thoughts and behavioral activities.

Another form of art was Egyptian hieroglyphs, used for design as well as writing. African artists identify with nature and products of human culture through use of *plastic art images. These images are* a direct *product of human culture.* It is design and structure of the images which determine the visual perception of all plastic shapes and form in African art, writing, weaving, sculpture, painting. *Images are obtained through ideas and ideas stem from human experiences,* perceptions of nature, environment, culture, other ideas and abstractions of ideas.

An image may consist of geometric forms such as a cone, sphere or cylinder. Geometric shapes such as a triangle, circle or parallelogram. Thus human geometric shapes and forms are some of the most elementary art structures in which none are totally identical with similar prototypes in nature.

Starting about 5,000 B.C., Egyptians put the line to use by constructing triangles and parallelograms. They constituted a multitudinal variety of linear shapes and forms, using the straight line. When one adds to and modifies such structures, the difference between nature's creation and human perception is usually quite apparent.

Images come in the form of hieroglyphs, symbols or designs such as an ankh (the Egyptian hieroglyph representing life.), *akua-ma* (an Akan word and carved image referring to something similar to an ankh); *aro ni* (Yoruba design for lame leg) *owo eyo* (Yoruba design for cowrie shells), a Yoruba design representing eyes of a pigeon and a design representing the porcupine.[1]

None of these aforementioned images have the faintest resemblance to any of the objects they represent in nature. In fact, even the sounds and noises humans make to designate these images, sound different from sounds we hear in nature. Again we emphasize that Africans translate their experiences into ideas: *mind images*. They then translate these mental images into words and plastic images which are used for communication.

African art became a social mechanism for developing itself. The most extreme use of this art as a social, cohesive mechanism for developing itself in Egypt can be seen in their writing. There are *painted and incised* forms of *hieroglyphs; cursive hieroglyphs* done with reed on papyrus; cursive literary hieratic; *official hieratic* and *cursive literary demotic*. The art hieroglyphs were integrated into the architecture. Other forms of Egyptian writing appeared on the papyrus linen and potsherds.[2] One can see traces of hieroglyphic birds, eye, sun disks, ankhs and human figures in the literary hieratic writing.[3] Both types of writing appear to have influenced each other and developed from the same source of images.

Official hieratic appears to be later development of literary hieratic script. The *Egyptians used existing forms of writing to create non-existing forms of writing. They* also *used existing forms of art to create other forms of art*, but with less radical changes than they did in the writing. Both art and architecture seem to parallel closely the art hieroglyphs.

Image as Language in Egyptian Art

Egyptian art like all other African art was language. All human endeavors were/are perceived as language by African people. Work, play, dance, music, drama, etc. Egyptian hieroglyphs appear mostly in art; they double as pictoral art and writing. Hieroglyphs were considered as art images or as language of the art. At times it is difficult to tell the difference between an art image and an image hieroglyph. The Wepemnofret Stela, Victory Tablet of King Narmer and Tutankhamun's Cartouche Shaped Box are examples of integration of art image and hieroglyphic image.[4]

Images in sculpture, paintings and relief art appears to have been developed from hieroglyph prototypes. In 'Victory Tablet of Pharaoh

Narmer', the key figure resembles hieroglyph image of Seher, the god who terrifies and in 'Return of the Herd and Donkeys' from the tomb of Ti at Saqqara, Seher appears again-as herdsman 'to drive away.'[5] The Step Pyramid of King Zoser at Saqqara resembles the hieroglyph double staircase: 'to go up.'[6]

Many images of the pharaohs and other figure types are repeated frequently; dynasty after dynasty, with different names of people and slightly different facial features. The Seher hieroglyphs in the Victory Tablet of Pharaoh Narmer and King Tutmosis III smiting Asiatics, appear to be similar.[7] The structure of the written image appears to govern and control most of the art.

Egyptian Hieroglyphs And Yoruba Symbols Used As Design

The use of the hieroglyphic sign Ra or Sun-god, can be seen in several Egyptian bas reliefs and Egyptian statues. Each time this symbol appears in the form of a patterned design, it appears on the same object, the Blue Crown, or Xepers.[8] The Yoruba and Egyptians give names for their designs. Many of the Egyptian symbols appear in design and in hieroglyphics. In either case generally, a hieroglyph shown as a design or shown as a written symbol, is expected to be read. Yoruba symbols used as design are not expected to be read. However, Yoruba symbols used as images are expected to be read. Both symbols and design constitute language. Similarly the Ghanaian Adinkra hieroglyphs are expected to be read as design and language.

We know that art is often used to substantiate legend. Yoruba traditions for example are traced to the Nile Valley through their legends and through their art forms which reflected Egyptian ideological influences which the Yoruba took with them when they migrated to West Africa. The people from the Nile had helped shape Egyptian images for thousands of years, and the influence of Egyptian images was transferred to the Ife. It was decided that geometric forms would still be used for translating ideas into images; but this time, instead of using polygrams which was the custom in the Nile Valley, the craftsmen would use three basic curvilinear volumes native to the region near Ife for over one thousand years.

Symbol and Design in Yoruba Art

Symbols and design in Yoruba wood carving are calligraphic. The wood carver is concerned with legibility of each symbol as well as its aesthetic appearance. There are cross hatch and textured designs in Yoruba art as well, but the formal calligraphy is preferred to the loose configuration. A series of selected examples show little difference between styles of different artists carving these designs because the carver is concerned with legibility when he is doing this type of work. If an artist wishes to make a name for himself, he makes changes in formal gestures and develops new classical poses for acceptable figure types such as a circle chicken, mother with twin images (ere ibeji) holding circular fans, and a mother feeding her baby water from the palm of her hand.[9] Occasionally an artist has an opportunity to create a new acceptable image which is a rare feat. The most noticeable feature which distinguished Yoruba artists from each other are the sculptural images' overall form and features; such as shape and or placement of ears, eyes, mouth, neck, head and breast. With the exception of breast and neck, all of the other features lie in the head, the head being the most important part of the sculpture.

The lame leg (aro ni) design is identical to 'n' or water surface design in Egypt. An axe (ogun) is carved by the artist showing the design used on the first level of the hat band of the two heads in the carving. This design can be used in many areas of a carved image.[10] The cowrie design (Owo eyo) is shown on the crown and skirt of a sculpture in the Fisk University collection, carved by Lamidi Fakeye of Ila Orangun, Nigeria. The porcupine symbols are pyramid shaped. The design consists of pyramid clusters placed tightly together. Yoruba designs are used for decorative and practical purposes, either to characterize or to fill in surface areas of carvings. The design lili has been used by Fakeye to depict hair. This is an example of "practical characterization" of a surface area.

Another example of the same principle can be seen in a scene depicting the Christian scene of the Last Supper. One of the dishes has a lili design to represent food. The ram on the large dish lets the viewer know that someone of very high rank will be present. The lili design used on the man's hat to the left and the clothing of the person to the far right, is an example of design used as a "decorative fill" for surface areas. The cowrie design functions as a practical use of surface area of the bird carved by Fakeye. Short feathers located near the neck of the bird are represented with cowrie. This same principle can be seen in the upper left corner of the palace doors depicting a chain.[12]

Designs in Egyptian and Yoruba art are applied to surface images, to represent many things translated into ideas. In Yoruba art the designs lili and cowrie used to represent hair and bird feathers, has absolutely nothing to do with human hair having the characteristics of porcupine quills, nor bird feathers looking like cowrie shells. *The world of cultural images is an entirely different world from that of nature's creatures. Principles used in cultural creations, are based on ideas and abstractions of ideas — not seeds and chromosomes.*

Neither Egyptians nor Yoruba have sought to confuse human created culture with the great works of Ra and T'Olodumare. These people have created an image and language system of symbols which deal with their cultural creations, social purposes and human destiny.

The materials from which they created symbols and images derived from human ideas about nature, not attempts to copy nature.

Secret Objects and the Social Image Creative Process

The basic visual product in Yoruba carvings which separates social religious art from social secular art is object. The object adds one more link to the human communal creative process. Material objects are products from nature with the natural orientation of its reserves left in tact. An object also becomes a social mechanism through which unseen forces may communicate with the human world.

Palm nuts (ikin) are used as a social mechanism through which the *babalawo* (father of mysteries) may communicate with a deity connected with the ifa orical.[13] Sango is the deity of thunder. Sango is personified through *okuta* which are thought to be thunder bolts. Okuta or thunder stones can be found scattered over the ground after thunder storms in Yorubaland. These stones in fact were the stone tools of the stone age culture of many thousand years ago.[14] An abstraction of an idea concerning human association with the material object "thunder stones", appears in the form of an image referred to as the club of the god of thunder, *ose sango*. Odo Sango is a carved upside down motar image. Images of ideas concerning Oris practice are depicted on utensils connected with worship.

Some of the images of *Ifa* are as follows: a divination chain, a phallus instrument used for tapping a tray called *opo n Ifa*, through which divination is practiced. The ritual object known as the *inkin*, is kept in the carved cup known as the *Awo Ifa*. The thunder stone has given rise to a vivid expanse in the communal religious experience through use of this ritual object. These communal experiences are shaped by cultural practices celebrating the deity, Sango, in which his ritual object *okuta* appears. Images such as a type of drum (*odo Sango, Sango sere* and *bata*) are incorporated into the orisa Sango system. Community involvement is illustrated with images of orisa priests and Sango worshippers. Domesticated animals are depicted as images in the Sango art form.

Through the communal celebrations the wood carver strengthens and deepens his own cultural awareness, sufficient to develop ideas for Sango imagery. *When the sculptor's work is used as ritual object, it becomes a basis for developing further social imagery and ideas. Some of this material being used to form other art images. The thunder stone is the most dominant feature of Sango imagery. It is usually shown at or near the highest point in a carving and in an ose Sango* (drum). The thunder stone is larger than anything else in that particular sculptural form. *As symbolic imagery, the thunder stone (okuta) is similar to calligraphy.*

When the name *okuta* is applied to symbolic imagery used in an *ose Sango*, that does not mean that the image *okuta* is the same as ritual object or symbol — for they are not at all the same. One is a communal religious product for the Yoruba culture and the other is a religious ritual object, product of nature. The image *okuta* and the material *okuta* are then depicted differently. Image *okuta* usually appears as a double image, symmetrically balanced and ritual object *okuta* is asymmetrical, sometimes jagged on one end and round on the other end.

According to legend, during rain storms the two giant colossals bump heads and kiss, causing chunks of enamel to fall from their teeth. The large ones fall hard enough to put holes through buildings and bury themselves deep in the earth, while small ones knock people in the head, thus perpetuating the belief that stone-like thunder bolts indeed do fall from the sky during rain storms.

Again, images are only products of human ideas about human experiences. Although these experiences stem from physical/social environment and nature, they are used to shape human thoughts when dealing with human contingencies. In the Ifa culture, the ritual object of the *ikin* does not have a single recognizable symbolic imagery of its own as is the case with the Yoruba *okuta*. As a result, the Ifa must borrow recognizable symbols, thus its recognizable communal art imagery comes from several sources. The most dominant image of Ifa art culture is the *opon ifa*, a flat tray which is rectangular, circular or semi-circular in form; It is always made of wood.[15] *Esu* has a long backward arched hair-style. This image is carved in wood. *Esu* is covered from either the neck, waist or feet down with strings of cowrie shells.

This last image of the ifa, is house of the head which symbolizes destiny and fate. The symbol for the house of the head is the cowrie. It takes exactly one strand of 41 cowries to make the ritual object for *ori* or (house of the head). The ori religious art consists of 3 items which comprise the *ile ori* image. Two cones made of leather, decorated with cowrie, and one cone small enough to fit inside the other cone. The third item is a leather basket surfaced with cowrie. The larger cone containing the smaller cone inside, fits over the basket like a lid, thus completing the *ile ori* image.[16]

Orisa ori is the only orisa practiced by all the Yoruba people who still practice Yoruba communal religious culture. Every Yoruba bears an *ori* by carrying it between the shoulders. *Ori* is the Yoruba word for head. When a Yoruba worships *ori*, he or she is giving thanks to their own heads or ori-inu. *Ori-inu* means internal head. The internal head is a person's soul. *Whereas ori inu means soul in Yoruba, by contrast the Egyptian term for soul is ba.*[17]

Ifa is universal to all Yoruba city states and towns. People consult the Ifa oracle at some point during their lives. Ifa is the oracle and deity of wisdom. Babalawo, the father of mysteries, conducts or administers all activities and functions concerning Ifa are. While *Orisa ifa* is not consulted universally by the Yoruba, many people consult the orisa in order to learn their fate. For a description of how the *Orisa ori* and *Orisa ifa* are supportive of each other, we have a quote from Wande Abimola who says, "when a person goes to an Ifa priest for divination, he is simply trying to find out through Ifa the wishes of his own Ori (internal soul) who is his personal orisa (divinity) who regulates the affairs of his own life. *Whatever has not been sanctioned by a person's ori, cannot be approved by the divinities Ifa and other orisa.*" [18]

In West Africa about 900 B.C., the Nok of Nigeria began bending the line of which we spoke earlier in reference to Egyptian geometric forms and shapes — the Nok bent the line to create 3 basic curvilinear structures: the cone, the sphere and cylinder. They began using these basic structures to create abstract images stemming from ideas dealing with human and animal forms. The Nok would create an image of man with a sphere shaped head, another with a cone shaped head and still another with a cylinder shaped head.

For portrait sculpture the Yoruba used 3 basic forms: the cone, egg-sphere and cylinder. All 3 shapes were used separately to designate the head. Each shape was assigned to a certain area of the head or the neck and the cone shape represented the crown or house of the head. The Yoruba do not have names for these forms and it is not known what they said in order to designate such images. The dominant form was the egg-shaped sphere. This form was always depicted straddling the top end of the cylinder with the small end pointed down. This sphere was set at a 45 degree angle across the open end of the cylinder. Most of the illusions of realism center around the eyes, nose, cheeks and lips. There is very little attempt to produce realistic features anywhere else on the head and neck. The ears are tacked half way between the face and back of the head, completing the human image illusion. The rest of this art experience is developed in the human mind.

In conclusion: I have tried to show how African people expressed their social environment apart from nature in their art. Yet their environment was in harmony with nature. In harmony and in an interdependent relationship with nature. Certainly independent when developing creative ideas. Their art served to coalese these ideas.

African art has an indispensable role to play in our grand design of reconstructing and reconstituting our classical African history, for *African art was functional and social; serving as a social mechanism for developing itself and interpreting religious and social values revered in the culture by the people.* African art was and still is part of but not subject to nature's environment for African art develops itself. African art has strong image impact as visual and social language.

African people have created an image and language system of symbols which deal with cultural creations, social purposes and human destiny. The materials from which African artists create symbols and images, derived from human ideas about nature, not attempts to copy nature. African art is an essential development in our great traditions. We should study these traditions seriously; for as Maulana Karenga says, "To go back to traditions is the first step forward."

NOTES

1. Conversations with Lamidi Olonade Fakeye in 1976. *A Dictionary Of The Yoruba Language.* Ibadan. Univ. Press Ltd., 1979, Reprint, 1982. Conversations with Adebisi Aromolaran, 1985.
2. "Potsherds" is broken pottery, used like scratch paper is today. Papyrus paper was very expensive, but potshreds were cheap. For more information see *Life In Ancient Egypt* by Adolf Erman. New York, Dover, 1971, Chap. XVIII.
3. Alan Gardiner, *Egyptian Grammar* Oxford Griffith Institute, Ashmalean Museum. Third Edition, Revised 1982, ps 7-8 Hieroglyphic writing received its source for images from hieroglyphs and itself — all products of human culture.
4. Albert B. Elsasser and Vera-Mae Fredrickson, *Ancient Egypt* Berkeley, Univ. of Calif., 1966 ps. 42, 60, 62, 63 and 65. See also *Egypt Architecture, Sculpture; Painting* by Kurt Lange and Max Hirmer. London. Phaiden, First Edition, 1956 Revised, 1968. Plate 4 the "Thinite Period" and plate 5, Victory Tablet of King Narmer. *Treasurers of Tutankhamun.* New York. Metropolitan Museum of Art, 1976. See Cartouche shaped box, plate 17, cat. no. 28, plate 15, cat. no. 21 and plate 18, cat. no. 31.
5. Gardiner, Op. Cit., p. 445 A 59 "A man threatening with a stick."
6. Jean Yoyotte, *Treasures Of The Pharaohs.* Cleveland. The World Publishing Co., 1968, p. 11 "Step Pyramid of King Zoser" This may be a double staircase.
7. Kurt Lange and Max Hirmer, Op. Cit. Plate 139, "King Tuthmosis III Smiting The Asiatics." Though his right arm is missing, it is obvious what Tut is doing. C/f Gardiner, Op. Cit. p. 445, A 59, "A man threatening with a stick."
8. Ibid., p. 504 S No. 7, "the blue crown (hierglyph)" p. 485, No. 5 "sun hieroglyph)" Yoyotte, Op. Cit., p. 143 "Ramsses II Black Granite Statue" wears Xepers and the Xepers has a Ra design covering its surface. Pg. 125, "Tutankhamun Shooting Fish With A Bow And Arrow" with the same foregoing description of Xepers and Ra." Cheikh Anta Diop shows a side view of a Black Granite Statue of Ramsses II and a side view depicting the hair style of a person living in former Ruanda-Urundi in Central Africa. This hair style is worn by a Watusi male and is almost identical to the blue

crown of Egypt. *The African Origin of Civilization Myth or Reality.* New York, Lawrence Hill & Co., 1974, p. 11. Vincent A. Kofi shows the front view of the flattened head of an Ashanti girl. Her disk shaped head suggests the sun disk. See *Sculpture In Ghana.* Accra. Ghana Information Services, 1964, plate 33.

9. Kevin Carroll, *Yoruba Religious Carving.* New York, Frederick A. Praeger, 1969. Plate 35 depicts an *epa* mask, plate 59 has a circle chicken also. Both carvings were done by Areogun-yanna.

10. In Ibadan, Nigeria in 1976, I was given the following names for Yoruba designs: "lame leg, eyes of a pigeon, and cowrie (lili) which I was told was a game.

11. Carroll, Op. Cit., p. 53 figure 41, Doors at Ijero carved by Areagun.

12. The door of a Yoruba palace carved by Olowe with the *epele* chain shown in the upper lefthand corner. Frederick Lumley, *Nigeria The Land Its Art And Its People.* London. Studio Vista, 1974, p. 37.

13. *Ifa An Exposition of Ifa Literary Corpus,* Wande Ambimbola. Ibadan. Oxford Univ. Press, 1976 See notes on Plate no. 1, *ikin Ifa.*

14. Rev. Samuel Johnson says, "The emblems of worship representing Sango are certain smooth stones shaped like an axe head commonly taken for thunder bolts." The History of The Yoruba. London. Routledge & Kegan Paul Ltd., 1921, reprinted, 1973, p. 34.

15. Johnson says the word *opon* actually means bowl, not tray. He says that in the old days the Babalawo would make markings on the flat surface of a bowl. If one examines a present day *opon*, you will notice that part of the inside portion which is assumed to be a tray, is actually carved out. The carved out section is flat. When one turns the bowl upside down, the flat appearance gives the illusion that there is no depth at all. In fact the pictures around the edge of the bowl have given us the illusion that we have been looking at the face of something when actually we have never seen the face, but have been looking at the back. This back side has a slightly rounded smooth surface in the center and the sides of the bowl with the design have been pressed out flat, parallel with the bottom of the bowl; so that the design can be viewed all the way around the bowl from one place, or viewed without having to turn the bowl. Ibid., p. 33.

16. Ibid., p. 27. (ori and *ile ori*)

17. F. Omasande, Yoruba Beliefs and Sacrificial Rites, Longman Group Ltd., 1979, p. 54. See use of word *ori-inu.*

18. Ambinbola, Op. Cit., See "Notes On Plates, end of plate II.

THE EGYPTIAN ORIGIN OF RHETORIC AND ORATORY

MOLEFI KETE ASANTE

Maulana Karenga has written in *The Husia* that "Husia" signifies "the two divine powers by which Ra created the world, i.e., Hu, authoritative utterance and Sia, exceptional insight."[1] Rhetoric, the theory of authoritative utterance and oratory, elegant utterance, are intricately related to Egyptian life. In fact, despite the significance of the hieroglyphic, hieratic and demotic scripts which have given us so much information about ancient Africa, the Egyptians were primarily an oral people. The spoken word was the essential means of cultural and spiritual transmittal of values. Even the transmittal of the dead to the spirit world was accompanied by the spoken word. It is therefore no wonder that the Egyptians conceived of the concerns of oratory, the functions of rhetoric, and the nature of the systematic investigation of both the practice of public speaking, oratory, and its theory, rhetoric.

Reference to primary texts, however, provides us with our evidences since the spoken word was not preserved in ancient time. Actually, *The Coming Forth by Day* is itself a veritable expression of Egyptian style and rhetorical disposition. If we examined the canons of oratory established by the Egyptians under the tutelage of Thoth, the lord of divine speech, we will have the fundamental categories for oratory as contemporary as a Malcoln X or Martin Luther King, Jr.

For example, the origin of the introductory salutation is found in the "t'etet," oratorical expression of "adoration of Ra who rises in the eastern skies." The aim of such a salutation, later made by the Hebrews and Arabs introductions such as "to the God of Abraham, Isaac and Jacob" or "in the name of Allah, the most merciful" is to open a public speech.

Based on the historically correct position of Africans, the introductory salutations were intended to connect the present audience to the past. The speaker, in this case, was a nexus for the past and present. In order for an orator to carry out his functions he had to know the special duties of the speaker which related to *Maat*. No orator could effectively speak with the eloquence of Thoth unless he understood the special character of *Maat*.

"Know thyself," the admonition written on the temple at Karnak, reverberated deep in the heart of the ancient Egyptian orator. After the union of the two kingdoms, the Egyptians attained a high degree of knowledge of their material surroundings. They had erected pyramids, carved sphinxs, graded roads, introduced geometry, studied the stars, and built beautiful temples. By 2600 B.C. the last great pyramids had been built. And yet it is not the monumental material contributions of

182

ancient Egypt which only attract our attention. Egypt was always in search of immortality. In fact, immortality is the principle theme of its massive temples and pyramids. The quest for wisdom and truth occupied the lives of the elders but it was also a quest actively pursued by initiates who knew it as the pathway to establishing the proper order. Life was meaningless without this order. Consequently the priests as orators exercised considerable control over the philosophical thoughts of the society.

There is an account in *Her-Bak* that "the sage sat for a long time in silence. When Her-Bak showed uneasiness he said, "If yesterday's lesson suggests no questions we have no starting point for today's." Whatever the initiate studied, nothing was so important as achieving total knowledge of self. Let me explain. The Egyptian gods gave no divine guidance. Frankfort says that the gods were known to require that a person respect *Maat* but there were no specific divine commands which shaped human action.[2] What we know is that it was considered "right" to maintain unity of heart and tongue, conviction and speech, "right" to respect authority and right to enjoy inheritance. Yet human wisdom alone gave direction, there were no directives from gods. The whole oratorical enterprise was one which followed the signposts of the sages and sought not struggle or confrontation but harmony.

On the whole, even when a person erred it was not conceived of as rebellion against god. The person did not commit a crime against god; the person was moving against the established order and the responsibility of one god or another was to see that the order was vindicated. In Egypt as throughout Africa there is no violent conflict between gods and humans; there is also no image of the individual hero. The concept "the wrath of God" does not appear either and consequently the aberrations of the Egyptians are not sinful as against god; they are the results of ignorance and the poor fellow must be disciplined. The truly ignorant knows neither good nor evil. Such a person violates the principles of *Maat.* Ignorant orators are violators of *Maat*, bringers of disharmony.

Although the book, *The Coming Forth by Day*, often called *The Book of the Dead*, deals with passage from life to death, in its deeper meaning it is a book about *Maat. Maat*, when applied to public speaking is the product of existential tension. A speaker achieves it only when he self-consciously knows that he is indeed alive. *Maat*, ultimately a spiritual concept, is the central notion in the questing life. Yet an orator can only become truly *Maat*-oriented in the company of a thousand gods. The one is not separated from the other, and the other cannot exist without the one. A speaker needs an audience. In fact, as Isha Schwaller de Lubicz says, it is only "by the heart of Osiris" in us that we can become *Maat*-oriented. What is it then?

Maat is a social, ethical, and rhetorical term. The Egyptians understood it as the divine order of creation, of society, of nature. Since the cosmos was one they had no difficulty with *Maat* meaning justice, truth, harmony; the categories and contrasts are ours. Even today in traditional African societies medicine, ethics, and rhetoric are connected. In the west one may believe that nature is cruel and that belief does not affect anything else. This not true in Africa. All things are connected. In Yoruba a child is not a person until the name is spoken.

Maat becomes a symbol of the search for existential peace, it preserves whatever union with the Egyptian "deep sources" are necessary to reveal the modalities of the spirit which manifest truth, justice, and wisdom. Everything in rhetorical expression reveals unity between the person and the cosmos. This cosmos is a unified spiritual totality different from the materialized universe of a technocratic perspective which does not yield cosmos.[3] Richards is correct when she says "spirit is not separate from matter."[4] In effect, *Maat* apprehends spirit in matter. There is no oppositional element in the spiritual and material as in the western oppositions of body/mind, knowledge/opinion, male/female, science/religion, and so on. To the Egyptian the cosmos had complementary pairs. That is why the divine being in most African cultures following Egypt is androgynous, therefore able to reproduce itself. Thus, the orator searches for harmony in conflict.

The African view is little changed from this idea of unity with the cosmos. I am river, I am mountain, I am tree, I am love, I am sex, I am emotion, I am beauty, I am lake, I am cloud, I am sun, I am sky, I am mind, I am one with one. There is no difference between human beings in-knowledge-of-themselves and the cosmos-becoming. The symbols which suggest *Maat* provide existential connections to those who would decipher the orator's message.

Maat's special character seems to have been *righteousness* and *rightness* in the person. Justice, truth, and righteousness were often used to denote *Maat*. However, righteousness is more that the rightness we find in nature; righteousness is a transpersonal experience within the human order. One cannot *be* righteous, it is a continuous process by which we align ourselves with the harmony we find in nature. Thus, righteousness is processual and when we say "be righteous" we only mean it as a process for the moment, for the particular context. One may have integrity but one cannot have righteousness.

The orator's search for soul becomes a search for cosmic unity, better yet, cosmic union. Like the entire enterprise of the death mystery in the Egyptian pyramid narratives oratory is an effort to address the cosmic union. One merges with the past and in this merging with the past finds the pathway to the future. There is no discovery, no transpersonal insight, without according the past its proper place. This is why the most advanced psychotherapies attempt to have a person make peace with the past in a quest for present and future peace. The ancient Egyptians understood this and endeavored to ritualize the transpersonal experience by using symbolic representations of the experience. One travels as Ra travels and emerges as Ra emerges. The dead person is committed to the "womb" of the pyramid, much like the initiate is made to remain in an isolated hut, prior to receiving qualifications to enter into life. Therefore, the ancient Egyptian, as other African peoples, did not carry on a widespread practice of cremation. The aim was to have the person emerge as whole. The womb, the tomb, and the encapsulating process of searching for *Maat* in the closet of the mind as the body is secluded from the community become symbols of the quest for righteousness. The basis for oratory is found in this questing life.

Akhenaton's heresy, after thousands of years of the Egyptian attempt for harmony through *Maat* working internally, was that he sought in Aton the one cosmic generator that gave meaning to life. But this force, this one god heresy was external, outside of the individual, a cosmic weaver weaving from afar. Thus, Akhenaton's heresy was not the elevation of Aton as the only force, nor the de-emphasis of Ptah, Horus, Set, Nut, Osiris, Khnemu, or Thoth, but the replacement of the individual's quest for *Maat* with a giver or chief of *Maat*. The worship of the solar disk, solarism, reached its zenith under Akhenaton (Amenhotep IV) because he prohibited the worship of all gods except the great disk of the sun. He ordered the names of other gods erased from monuments and called Amen-Ra by the name Aton.

One hymn to Amen-Ra goes "Adoration to thee, O Amen-Ra, the bull in Annu, the ruler of all the gods, the beautiful and beloved god who gives life by means of every kind of food and fine cattle." This hymn, itself rhetorical, was meant to serve rhetorical ends.

Furthermore, the priests of Thebes say, "you are chief of all the gods, lord of *Maat,* father of the gods, creator of men and women, maker of beasts and cattle, lord of all that exists. . . ." *Maat* becomes under the heresy a possession of Amen-Ra when before throughout the search for the transcendental state the initiate had relied upon self-consciousness produced by following a knowledge of causes. Initiates were never principal orators. They took their cues from those who possessed innate gnosis, the priests, who evoked consciousness which transcended disharmonies.

The ancient Egyptian quest for *Maat* was not linear and based on acquisition of technology but on the certitude that could only come from an understanding of causes. There again the imperative to the student "know thyself." The uncovering of the inner ear is the first requirement for being a good orator.

Only through knowledge of causes can the person achieve harmony, otherwise disorder and disharmony, which represent evil, dominate. Whenever disorder exists in the individual or between the individual and nature, we have the concept of evil, the equivalent of the existentialist's indecisiveness, the only sin. In African thought, disharmony in the commuity must be quickly corrected. This is why there was often a dependence on the consecration made to the vital function which a particular animal incarnated. We sometimes speak of animal worship which, by the way, occurs nowhere that I know of in Africa. There are medita-

tions, rhythmic meditations, as Robert Lawlor recognizes, that were used to clarify essential functions of nature.[5] This was not a worship of
animals, but a grasping for essentiality.

The scarab, the oval, and a kneeling man with a wave over his head
represents the expression "I shall come into existence." Thus spoke Ra
and therein is the secret to the orator's objective. The inner work of *Maat*
is true life because we are able to self consciously say we shall come
into existence. What we reach for is the source of our harmony with nature,
to be absorbed in the flow of the cosmos, that is the life the ancient Egyptian understood. Throughout the Papyrus of Ani one finds the question,
"What is it then?" The answer to this repeated question is various but
in the end the message of harmony between humans and nature is clear.
"I cackle as a goose, I fly as a hawk." In other words, I am one with nature.
In fact, if the orator's senses are trained by the laws of *Maat*, then he
conforms appearance to function.

The choice of an animal as a symbol was not random. The priests
did not go out and choose the first creature that came along to represent
digestion but they chose the *jackal*. This animal kills its prey, buries it
and returns to eat it when it has begun to decompose. It becomes a
symbol for digestion, physical and metaphysical. We observe life, growth,
death, coagulation, decomposition and transformation. No being can
begin the process of rebirth until its form has disintegrated. All methods
of reaching the mind understand this technically. Rhetoric is no different.
The jackal-headed Anubis always led the soul of the deceased into the
first stage of the *dwat*, world of transformations. When the body of the
deceased was mummified, the organs were removed, dehydrated, and
placed in urns. The urn containing the intestines has a jackal on it, sug-
gesting the connection between the intestines and digestion. The jackal
gives life through that which is poison for others. The destructive process of digestion becomes an element in transformation. As Lawlor points
out the jackal must dig up his buried morsels at the proper time or they
may pass into an indigestible state of chaos.[6]

Maat reveals itself through the spoken word and sculpted images.
A sign is often "hollowed out to signify entering into matter; it is in relief,
when leaving it is signified."[7] In certain ways the tombs show this, the
entry being the placing of the body into the earth; the exit being the resurrection, the rise and fall of the Nile, the ebb and flow of our existence.

Rhetoric becomes a counterweight that evaluates the heart of the living
as *Maat* evaluates the dead. *Maat* is symbolized by a feather, and is present in the weighing process. A heart on a plate of balance is
counterweighted by a feather representing *Maat*. The plummet or weight
attached to a line represents the emotional life of a person. *Maat* has
two dimensions, one is divine and the other is the individual *Maat* whom
the dead should have realized in him or herself. *Maat* is cosmic consciousness, universal ideation, essential wisdom, proceeding ceaselessly
from divine Ra, whose nourishment she is. A teacher is most successful
when the student has a unifying vision. An orator is effective when he

creates a union with his audience.

Our knowledge of the symbol is always limited. We can never know all aspects of the symbol, it is unlimited, infinite. There is no person who could know all the possiblities of a symbol. It would mean innate knowledge of the entire universe. *Maat* does not mean that, it does not imply that, but rather it suggests knowledge of self as the absolute path to knowlege of symbols. This knowledge is constructive, liberating, knowlege of synthesis as opposed to a rational, analytical knowledge which dismantles and destroys. *Maat* becomes a way to a new state of thought, a transpersonal opening of our intelligence. But this takes simplicity of heart-mind as opposed to complexity; synthesis as opposed to analysis.

Ogotemmeli, the Dogon priest, reveals to Marcel Griaule during a thirty-day interview that the Dogon people of Mali know that the time has come when secret things must be said. The Dogon knew that intuitive sensations held the mysterious call to knowledge. Spirit-energy, soul dominates matter and matter may be a temporary phenomenon anyway, particularly in its relationship to life. When the body is dead, life is thought to be transcendental to matter and independent of the physical and chemical laws that govern matter. The Egyptians did not put it just that way but they understood that *Maat*, the ultimate cause, did not operate wholly within the framework of material laws. The images, symbols, found in the temples and tombs were only representative of the innate knowledge and absolute truth that existed apart from the material.

There is a verse in the Ifa divination of the Yourba which reads "ologbon kan o ta koko omi seti aso" or "no wise person can tie water into a knot." *Maat* is like this. It is not subject to the whims of out-side forces, it exists within a person. We must find it in ourselves, flowing forward, harmoniously. This is the lesson of the Egyptians.

Interdependence and reciprocity, according to Richards, are seen in ritual sacrifice.[9] As the ultimate philosophic expression, ritual serves to provide symbolic truth to our relationship with *Maat*. We die and are reborn through symbols and the light as a feather symbol of *Maat*, the judge of our heart, revitalizes us. Rhetoric is pre-eminently theory about the use of symbols.

Finally, "this little light of mine" shines because of *Maat*. We are eternally being born in the affirmation of life. As testaments to the abiding influence of the ancient Egyptians we celebrate the affirmation of a judgment rendered in our favor. *Maat* judgment validates our inner work for harmony and humanness.

Let us understand. The cause is seen through the effect. Observation of a concrete symbol of a fact helps to evoke its abstraction. Throughout the Egyptian myth there is a knowledge of the successive appearance of divine properties which have emerged from the original unity where these properties are in a latent state--then there is a knowledge of these properties in the continuous creation where they are made known by nature. It is possible to speak of the neters, gods of Egypt, as a "hierarchy of the neters" much like in the later Hindu or Hebrew Cabbala, but in one important way this hierarchy of the gods is unlike those traditions--it is not "dogmatized." The neters do not have a hierarchy based on their appearance as primary or secondary causes and do not have a hierarchy based on the nature of their function, spiritual, or material. The Egyptians, like other Africans, have scattered the elements of knowledge, and one has to fit them together like a puzzle in order to know the picture.

Maat is the cumulative appearances of the divine properties. I pick a flower and say "wonderful." I am surely at that moment full of wonder. A myriad of experiences, all connected to the latent unity, work the miracle of Maat for us as we either speak or hear spoken the golden words of Thoth.

There is something which transcends myth; Maat is truth in all things, the reason for life, the purpose for speech, and the source of happiness. Nature itself gives us the concrete meanings to abstractions; it reveals symbolic forms and expressions that may be spoken. That is why no access to the "keys" of this knowledge will help us unless we adopt our way of seeing to the simplicity of synthesis. This is why the sage says, "the one who seeks will perceive the causes and will never be able to exhaust the riches of the symbols. But from the pretentious windbag this treasure is hidden."

NOTES

1. Maulana Karenga, The Husia: Sacred Wisdom of Ancient Egypt. Los Angeles: University of Sankore Press, 1984, p.xiv.
2. Henri Frankfort, Ancient Egyptian Religion. New York: Harper and Row, 1961, p.81.
3. Dona Richards, "The Implications of African American Spirituality" in M. Asante and K. Asante, African Culture: The Rhythms of Unity. Westport, Conn.: Greenwood Press, 1985, p.210.
4. Ibid. p.210.
5. Robert Lawlor, "Preface" in R.A. Schwaller de Lubicz, Symbol and the Symbolic. New York: Inner Traditions, 1978, p.17.
6. Ibid., p.15.
7. R.A. Schwaller de Lubicz, Symbol and the Symbolic, New York: Inner Traditions, 1978.
8. Marcel Griaule, Conversations with Ogotemmeli, New York: Oxford University Press, 1978.
9. Richards, op. cit., p.212.

THE CONTRIBUTORS

MAULANA KARENGA

Dr. Karenga is currently visiting professor of Ethnic Studies, University of California, Riverside and executive director of the Institute of Pan-African studies, Los Angeles. He is also the first vice-president of ASCAC. A leading theorist of the Black Movement, he is the creator of Kawaida Theory, the Nguzo Saba and Kwanzaa. His latest published works are *Introduction to Black Studies* and *Selections From The Husia: Sacred Wisdom of Ancient Egypt.*

JACOB H. CARRUTHERS

Dr. Carruthers is currently professor of Inner City Studies and political science at Northeastern Illinois University and the director of the Kemetic Institute, Chicago. He is also president of ASCAC. The author of many scholarly articles on Kemet, his latest works are *The Irritated Genie: Essays on the Haitian Revolution* and *Essays in Ancient Egyptian Studies.*

MOLEFI KETE ASANTE

Dr. Asante is chair and professor of African and African American Studies, Temple University, Philadelphia. Also, he is the editor of the *Journal of Black Studies* and holds editorial positions with eight other journals. He is author or editor of twenty-two books, including *Afro-centricity: The Theory of Social Change* and *African Culture: The Rhythms of Unity.*

CLAUDE L. CLARK

Mr. Clark is an artist who specializes in woodcarving. He is a member of the Association of Africans and African-Americans, Oakland and owner of the House of Vai, an African Import concern. His research interests are in commonalities of themes in media in African art.

DAIMA CLARK

Ms. Clark is founder of the Association of Africans and African-Americans and a former professor of Black Studies at California State University, Hayward and Merritt College, Oakland. She also served on the pastoral staff of Allen Temple Baptist Church, Oakland. She has travelled to Tanzania where she stayed in an Ujamaa Village.

JOHN HENRIK CLARKE

Dr. Clarke is recently retired as professor in the Department of Black and Puerto Rican Studies, Hunter College of the City University of New York. He has also served as the Carter G. Woodson Distinguished Visiting Professor at the Africana Studies and Research Center, Cornell University. An eminent Africanist and historian, he is editor and author of numerous books and articles including *Harlem: A Community in Transition* and *Malcolm X: The Man and His Times.*

EARL WALTER FARUQ

Mr. Faruq has an M.A. in urban planning and is an educator and director of *Thinkers World,* a Los Angeles-based company which produces educational albums for children. He is the author of several articles on physical and social development. His research interests are in urban planning in ancient Kemet.

W. J. HARDIMAN

Ms. Hardiman is an educator and faculty member, Evergreen State College, Tacoma, Washington. She is also currently working on a Ph.D. in literature and education with emphasis on ancient Kemet and its pedagogical value to the adult learner. She is author of seven dramatic works.

ASA G. HILLIARD, III

Dr. Hilliard is the Fuller E. Calloway Professor of Urban Education at Georgia State University, Atlanta, holding a joint appointment in the Department of Educational Foundations and the Department of Counselling and Psychological Services. He also served formerly as Department Chair and Dean of the School of Education at San Francisco State University. A distinguished educator and lecturer, he has lectured nationally and internationally on various subjects in the field of education. His research interest is in the pedagogy of Kemet and he has authored several articles on this subject.

IFE JOGUNOSIMI

Ms. Jogunosimi has a Masters Degree in Inner City Studies and is a teacher of social studies in the Chicago public Schools. She is a member of the Kemetic Institute and is currently doing research in the area of African civilization, with focus on African women in history and culture.

A. JOSEF BEN-LEVI

Mr. ben-Levi has a Masters Degree in Inner City Studies and is a member of the Kemetic Institute. He has lectured widely and written many articles on ancient African civilization. His research interests are in Kemetic history and language.

WADE W. NOBLES

Dr. Nobles is currently professor of Black Studies, San Francisco State University with grounding in experimental social psychology. He is also executive director, Institute for the Advanced Study of Black Family Life and Culture. A leading figure in the development of Black Psychology, he is author of some of its seminal literature and paradigmatic concepts, especially "the African personality".

REKHETY WIMBY

Ms. Wimby is a Masters Degree candidate at the Oriental Institute, University of Chicago, in Egyptology. She is also a linguist and member of the Kemetic Institute. She has published several articles on ancient Kemet and lectured widely in the U.S., Africa and Europe on African civilizations.

APPENDIX I

CONSTITUTION OF THE ASSOCIATION FOR THE STUDY OF CLASSICAL AFRICAN CIVILIZATIONS

ARTICLE I NAME

The name of this organization shall be the Association for the Study of Classical African Civilizations.

ARTICLE II PURPOSE

The Association is established to promote the study and development of African civilization and an African Worldview.

ARTICLE III MEMBERSHIP

A. Individual membership is open to persons who demonstrate a significant interest in the study and promotion of African Civilization and an African Worldview.
In order to qualify for membership such interested persons shall submit such required application form(s) and pay such fees and dues as shall be specified in the By-Laws of the Association. All applicants must be approved by such body as specified in the By-Laws.

B. Institutional membership is open to institutes, study groups, and other organizations with a primary focus on African civilization; such groups must submit the proper application forms and pay the required fees and dues as stipulated in the By-Laws. All institution applications must be approved by such body designated in the By-Laws of the Association.

ARTICLE IV REGIONAL DIVISION

For the purpose of electing the Board of Directors and certain administrative functions as may from time to time be specified in the By-Laws the Association shall be divided into four (4) geographical regions: 1) An Eastern Region which includes members from the following states, Maine, Vermont, New Hampshire, Massachusetts, Rhode Island, Connecticut, New Jersey, Delaware, Pennsylvania, and New York; 2) A Southern Region which includes members from the following states, Maryland, West Virginia, Virginia, Kentucky, North Carolina, Tennessee, South Carolina, Georgia, Florida, Alabama, Mississippi, Arkansas, Louisiana and Texas; 3) A Midwestern Region which includes members from the following states, Ohio, Indiana, Michigan, Wisconsin, Illinois, Minnesota, Iowa, Missouri, North Dakota, South Dakota, Nebraska and Kansas; 4) A Western Region which includes members from the following states, Montana, Wyoming, Colorado, New Mexico, Idaho, Utah, Arizona, Washington, Oregon, California, Nevada, Hawaii and Alaska.

ARTICLE V OFFICERS ORGANIZATION

A. General plenary powers shall reside with the total membership and may be exercised at the annual conference or any meeting called for such purposes.

B. The National officers of the Association shall consist of a Council of Elders, Board of Directors, President, Vice-President, 2nd Vice President, Secretary and a Treasurer.

C. The Council of Elders shall consist of 5 elected members who shall have attained the age of 60. Their role shall be advisement to the Board.

D. The Board of Directors shall consist of the President, Vice-President, 2nd Vice-President, Secretary, Treasurer, three Association members elected from each of the four regions by the members within the relevant region (Article III) and four Association members elected at-large by the members (individual) of the Association at the annual conference of the Association.

E. The Board of Directors shall exercise the general powers of the Association in conformity with decisions of the membership. The Board shall from time to time pass By-Laws in conformity with this Constitution.

F. The President, Vice-President, 2nd Vice-President, Secretary and Treasurer shall be elected by the membership of the Association at the annual conference and shall perform duties usually devolving on such officers with such modification and functions specified by the Board of Directors or the membership of the Association.

ARTICLE VI AMENDMENTS

This Constitution may be amended at any annual conference of the Association or any meeting called for such purpose provided that notice of proposed amendments be presented at least six months before the voting is to take place.

ARTICLE VII

This Constitution shall take effect when ratified by the Charter membership.

APPENDIX II

BY-LAWS FOR THE ASSOCIATION FOR THE
STUDY OF CLASSICAL AFRICAN CIVILIZATIONS

I. NAME
   1. The initials ASCAC shall be the official acronym of the Association for the Study of African Civilizations.
   2. The official logo of ASCAC will be the Two Scribes Logo as used on brochures and souvenirs at the First Annual Egyptian Studies Conference 1984 at Los Angeles and as modified on the brochures and souvenirs of the Second Annual Egyptian Studies Conference 1985 at Chicago.
   3. The logo will be used on the literature, souvenirs and other items of communication concerning The Association and any conferences called by the Association.

II. PURPOSE
   1. The motto of the Association shall be "TO PROMOTE THE STUDY OF AFRICAN CIVILIZATION AND AN AFRICAN WORLD VIEW."

III. MEMBERSHIP
   A. Individual Membership
      1. All charter members of The Association and all individuals admitted subsequently belong to one membership class, although the designation Charter Member will be permanently recorded by the names of all charter members and the membership cards for each charter member will identify that individual as a Charter Member.

      2. The ASCAC Board of Directors will serve as a membership committee for the Association. The Board will design the appropriate application forms which must be submitted before membership is granted.
      3. The general criterion for individual membership shall be: A demonstrated interest in the study and promotion of African Civilization.
      4. Applications for individual membership will include questions concerning the applicants interests, affiliations and

acquaintances related to the pursuit of African Civilization.

5. Applications for individual membership shall be investigated by the regional board members or such local or regional component of ASCAC as may be designated by the Board.

6. The annual dues for individual members shall be $25.00. Full-time students and senior citizens who apply may be granted annual membership for $12.50.

B. Institutional Membership

1. There will be 3 classes of institutional members.
    1) Local categorical groups
    2) Local study groups
    3) Complementary groups

2. Local categorical groups are organizations whose membership is drawn from the local population and which have as a major focus one or any combination of the four categories stipulated in Article IV B. (as Amended)

3. Local study groups are formally organized clubs that have as a major focus the study of African Civilizations through reading, book reviewing, discussion, lectures and museum and field tours and related activities.

4. Complementary groups are international, national, regional or local groups whose purpose are compatible with the interests of the ASCAC and are deemed appropriate for such affiliation by the Board of Directors or the membership of ASCAC.

5. Institutional members shall perform such functions as approved or assigned by the Board of Directors of the ASCAC and such other functions not prohibited by them.

6. Institutional members shall have no vote in the proceedings of the ASCAC.

7. Applications for institutional or group membership shall include questions concerning the history, purpose, activities, publications, officers and members of the group.

8. The criterion for institutional membership shall be the same as for individual members.

9. Each institutional member shall submit an annual report to the Board of Directors during or before the Annual Conference. Such report shall contain a list of officers, the by-laws as amended, and the proceedings of any activities relevant to the Association.

IV. ASCAC DIVISIONS

A. Regional Divisions

1. The individual members of each region shall elect a President, Vice-President, Secretary and such other officers as deemed appropriate by the members.

2. Each region shall hold a minimum of one meeting per year for the purposes of electing regional officers and regional representatives to the Board of Directors of ASCAC and any other purposes designated, approved or not prohibited by the Board of Directors.

3. Each region shall submit to the Board of Directors of ASCAC an annual report containing the names of all elected officers, the regional by-laws as amended, proceedings of all meeings, reports on all Association activities conducted by the region and any information relevant to the interest of the Association.

B. Categorical Divisions

1. The Board of Directors will establish four permanent commissions to study and make recommendations concerning the four categorical foci of the Association.

2. Each commission will submit to the Board of Directors annual reports 2 months before the Annual Conference and such progress reports as deemed appropriate.

V. OFFICERS/ORGANIZATION

1. All officers and members of the Board shall be current members of ASCAC.

2. The Board of Directors shall hold at least one meeting each year.

3. The Board of Directors shall submit an annual report at each Annual Conference.

4. The President, Vice-President, 2nd Vice-President, Secretary and Treasurer shall serve as the Executive Committee of the Board and have general authority to conduct ASCAC business during the interims between Board meetings.

5. All transactions of the Executive Committee are subject to review by the full Board.

6. When the President, Secretary and/or Treasurer shall reside in separate cities and when otherwise expedient an Executive Secretary and or Executive Treasurer will be appointed by the President and Board approval to facilitate the conducting of ASCAC business.

7. Any Executive Treasurer appointed under V. 6 above shall be bonded at the expense of ASCAC.

8. The Board of Directors shall establish a fundraising commission to study and make recommendations concerning the ways and means of financing ASCAC activities with special emphasis on projects designed to implement the Associations four categorical foci.

Prepared April 1985
by
Jake Carruthers

ASCAC PROPOSED CONSTITUTIONAL AMENDMENTS

(1) Article III
   (add)   All members of the Association are members of the regional division of residence as per Article IV. A.

(2) Article IV
   (add)   (Categorical or Functional Divisions)
         For the purpose of accomplishments of the goals of ASCAC, The National and Regional levels of the organization will focus on four project categories: Research, Education, Creative Production, and Spiritual Development. The Board of Directors of ASCAC may create or the membership of ASCAC such commissions, committees, functional divisions, offices and projects as deemed appropriate for the pursuit of functions in these areas.

(3) Article V
   (change) E, 1, 2 (end of the line) of the *individual* membership.

Prepared April 1985
by
Jake Carruthers